the **BEST** by **MILES**

Also by Miles Kington

Le Bumper Book of Franglais
Let's Parler Franglais!
Let's Parler Franglais Again!
Parlez-vous Franglais?
Parlez-vous Franglais One More Temps
Miles and Miles
Moreover
Nature Made Ridiculously Simple
Moreover, Too
Vicarage Allsorts
The Franglais Lieutenant's Woman
Steaming Through Britain
Welcome to Kington
Motorway Madness
Someone Like Me
How Shall I Tell the Dog?

the **BEST** by **MILES**

A selection of Miles Kington's writings, 1964 to 2008

MILES KINGTON

First published in 2009 by Old Street Publishing Ltd

This paperback edition published 2012

www.oldstreetpublishing.co.uk

ISBN 978-1-908699-05-3

Grateful acknowledgement is made to the editors of *The Oldie*, *The Lady*, *The Independent*, *Punch* and *The Times* for permission to reproduce these pieces; also to *Robson Books* and *Headline* for permission to reproduce material from *Let's Parler Franglais! Let's Parler Franglais Again! Parlez-vous Franglais* and *Someone Like Me*.

10 9 8 7 6 5 4 3 2 1

A CIP catalogue record for this title is available from the British Library.

Typeset by Martin Worthington.

Printed and bound in Great Britain

CONTENTS

FOREWORD

BY CAROLINE KINGTON

'From an early age,' Miles once wrote, 'perhaps confused by my shifting geography, I knew I wanted to be a humorous writer and a jazz musician . . . and when I went to Oxford University I spent most of the time playing the double bass in jazz groups and writing undergraduate humour. Thus when I left university I was almost entirely unfitted for life, and consequently went to London to try my luck as a freelance humorous writer, where I nearly starved to death.'

Miles's professional career began at *Punch*, nothing less illustrious would do, and so he bombarded them with articles till they finally relented and allowed him in. (A photograph exists of Miles, a veritable babe, sitting at the famous Punch table surrounded by various veteran writers.)

Whilst at *Punch* he created *Let's Parler Franglais*. These columns, which poked fun at the Brits' determined inability to speak any other language, were later published in book form, which he described as 'probably the most popular bilingual lavatory books of the 1980s.'

By 1980, Miles seemed set to embark on a career in broadcasting. He was a regular on 'Call My Bluff', went with the BBC to make the documentary 'Great Railway Journey' in Peru and was being courted by other programme makers. To everybody's astonishment he eschewed a career on television, turning down 'Around The World in Eighty Days' and Barry Norman's seat on 'Film Night' because, he said, it got in the way of his writing, about which he was single minded.

When Miles parted company with *Punch* he set his sights on having a daily column in *The Times*. Harry Evans, the editor, wasn't sure but when Miles sent him a humorous column every day for ten days, he succumbed. A space was found on the Obituaries page. *Over My Dead Body* was Miles's suggested title, quickly rejected on the grounds of bad taste. They settled on *Moreover* and he soon established a following.

In 1987, he switched to the *Independent*, again writing daily. He remained with them until he died in 2008, by which time he had written over 4,500 humorous articles, as well as contributing on a regular basis to other journals, including the *Oldie*, and producing sixteen books.

Miles wrote because he found words endlessly fascinating. He was a humorist because he loved playing with them, making language stand on its head to look at life's experiences in a different, tangential way. His writing provided a different perspective, one that made his readers smile, laugh and see things afresh. And it wasn't just in his writing. One can hear it in his broadcasting; and similarly, in his personal life, everything was subjected to the same quirky, humorous dissection.

Some six years ago, he succumbed to pressure and ostensibly set out to write his autobiography. The book, published as *Someone Like Me* was a piece of humorous fiction from beginning to end. He had just started writing the sequel, *Here We Go Again*, when he was diagnosed with pancreatic cancer. He abandoned the book and started on a series of fictitious letters, ostensibly to Gill Coleridge, his agent, proposing ways in which he could turn his battle with cancer into a bestseller. As he'd intended, these letters were the book and *How Shall I Tell the Dog* became his last project.

Writing the book as a series of letters suited his style of writing. He was not a long-haul writer and the idea of undertaking a conventional novel appalled him. No, he was a brilliant short story writer, and that's what his columns, by and large, are. The Gods, Pub Conversations, Nature Rambles with Uncle Geoffrey, One Minute Detective, to name but a few of his regular favourites, are all stories; characters created within seconds with wonderfully easy dialogue.

His ideas came from everywhere. A vast pile of newspapers and magazines and an equally huge pile of cuttings, some dating back to the early eighties, filled his study. Stacks of books dominated every room, and his recordings of television and radio programmes reflect an almost obsessive anxiety not to miss anything that might be interesting.

'The main challenge for a humorist,' he once wrote, 'is to get humour out of the unlikely. Anyway, a humorist shouldn't often write about something. He should start in an obvious place and shoot off at right angles . . .' So having been diagnosed with cancer, there was no way in which he would not write about it; and, devastating though it was, that it would be given the same treatment as anything else he'd ever written about. Cancer became a scenario, a situation that he could view almost dispassionately, winkle out the quirky elements, find the humour, turn tragedy into comedy, neutralise the fear.

'How do you do it, day after day?' and 'how do you churn it out?' were two questions he was most frequently asked. He strongly objected to the use of the word 'churn' and with justification. Everything he wrote was thought about, worried over, re-read and checked again when in print. His fellow hacks regarded his output with awe. He lived to write, and it was entirely apt that his last column appeared on the day he died.

As well as his humorous writing, Miles wrote wonderful descriptions of his travels, beautifully crafted pieces of nostalgia, witty observational pieces about his life and times. To choose the best of an output of such magnitude and such quality has been daunting. And knowing, inevitably, that many readers will look in vain for a particular favourite, I hope and trust that this selection of Miles's work will impress and delight everybody.

INTRODUCTION

BY JOANNA LUMLEY

We first met as guests on the TV show 'Call My Bluff' in the 1970s. In those days we travelled by train to Manchester with the team leaders, Frank Muir and Patrick Campbell. There was plenty of time to get to know each other over lunch: Miles seemed fairly shy but was very funny, and in comparing notes about our lives, we soon found out that our children attended the same school.

A few years later he wrote to congratulate me on a piece I had written for the *Listener*, and added this irresistible overture of friendship:

> You must have wondered why I suddenly got in touch, and even if you didn't I'm going to tell you. Last October my wife decided to move out and live with someone else, and after the initial shock/stasis/disorientation, not to mention being able to stretch out in bed properly after so many years, I've found myself adjusting to and in some ways almost enjoying my new life. I'm now doing things I've meant to do for years, like leaving the washing up till morning, seeing Casablanca and experimenting with wild recipes, and one of the things I've meant to do for years is take advantage of the fact that you live just down the road and say hello . . . I was going to try to become as pretty and famous as you at first, so that you wouldn't think I was trying something on, but then I

reflected a) you wouldn't be impressed by that sort of thing b) I
AM as pretty and famous as you ...

Over the years I would get letters from him out of the blue, the text always
spinning off into some fantastic trope (a true wordsmith, he would have
pounced on 'trope'); writing was to him like talking aloud or doodling. You
can imagine how enjoyable his letters were to read.

Dear Jo,

I don't know if you spotted the coincidence, but you and I both
had pieces in the *Independent* on the same day, both on the subject
of cruelty to turkeys. Not only that, but both pieces were identical,
word for word. I am therefore instructing my legal team to sue you
for millions of pounds on the grounds of plagiarism, mental cruelty,
and locking me up in a small, desperately untidy room to make me
write my pieces ...

At this point, as with so many of Miles' letters, fantasy takes over. What begins
as a sensible letter (I use the word loosely) disappears up a tangent, in this case
a rather heart-warming skit about the Royal Society for the Prevention of
Cruelty to Writers:

*The door was forced open with some difficulty. Then the
investigators recoiled with a gasp of horror. The conditions
were as bad as anything they had ever seen. The carpet was
entirely hidden by paper; an ashtray gave off the lethal fumes
of smouldering cigarettes while several half-empty mugs testified
to a hideous story of caffeine overload. At the desk the writer
himself seemed unaware of their entrance.*

*'Poor devil,' said one. 'It may be too late. He showed no auditory
or visual reaction to our arrival.'*

'How can he do this to himself?' said the other.

*It was then that the writer looked up and registered their presence.
He stared at them for a moment.*

'If you're from the Inland Revenue, you can piss off.'

'Poor fellow said the first one. 'He's hallucinating ...'

*'Come on,' said the other. 'We've got to get him out of here and
into the fresh air. I wonder if he can walk unaided. Or has he lost
the use of his legs?'*

'I don't usually lose the use of my legs till about ten at night,' said the writer. *'Where were you thinking of taking me?'*

Mmmmm . . . I think we have the makings of a piece. Thank you, Jo. Tricky ground we are on here, of course. Am I allowed to copy a letter I have sent to someone else, or will I be guilty of plagiarising myself?

I wondered if he tried out stuff on his friends – like those stand-up comedians who appear to be talking to you very amusingly and personally, until you watch their act later on and discover it contains the same material, only with the bits you didn't laugh at re-worked or discarded. But then I threw the thought away at once: to begin with, it was a slow and impractical way of trying out material for a writer with daily deadlines. And anyway, writing was as easy to him as breathing; his ideas seemed to flow like some strange electric current, as though he was hooked up to a grid of creative lunacy.

I backed the Grand National winner today! It took me two minutes to decide which horse was going to win and half an hour to work out how you lay bets. Betting offices are peculiarly joyless places, like a surgery for incurables or a brothel that can't afford any girls . . . Very odd. I never go in there except when my voices tell me the name of a winner. They really do. Sometimes they tell me the names of losers too. Sometimes they get them mixed up.

Miles wrote every day for years and years. His columns were a small slice of humour in an occasionally black world. Devotees of his writing, of whom I count myself one, always saved reading his piece till last, or grabbed it first, like seizing a slice of cake before sitting down to work. Beneath the entertainment value of his pieces, he wore his considerable abilities lightly; his *Franglais* books became classics, their humour masking his complete mastery of the French language. More than any others, I miss his pieces on the United Deities, which brought the strange and comforting thought that all really would be well if only the human race could get to grips with behaving properly. I don't think he was a believer, and his funeral was humanist; but despite the odd comment that could be sharp, I found nothing in his writing but extremely funny observations and flights of fancy and, if I'm not being too sentimental, a huge and compassionate indulgence of the frailties and idiocies of life.

Miles was as fun and mischievous in his daily life as he was in his writing. He and Caroline would invite us down to compete in the annual boules match in Bath, with Terry Jones or Jonathan Dimbleby making up the team. 'I have been offered a berth in this year's boules match again,' he wrote, 'and you are my first choice – let me know soon, so that I can put it in my diary. I have had the damn thing all year and haven't written anything in it yet.'

Miles always looked rather rakish and handsome, even towards the end when he was very ill. I still have a photograph in the kitchen – the boules tournament again. We are all standing under a shady tree, trying to look cool and lethal: Dimbleby and I are wearing panama hats while Miles goes bare headed, a devil-may-care smile on his face. We never won or got near the last heats, but la! we were stylish.

Looking through his letters has been bittersweet. I appreciate my good fortune in having had such a friend, yet regret enormously that he is no longer with us. Thankfully, his writing remains, a selection of some of the best saved here in this book. And I will always treasure gems like this, again from one of his letters:

Finally – you are a stylist and will appreciate this – I was in Terminal 2 at Heathrow recently, in the gents' loo, and half-listening to a pair of men who had just come in, English, workers, mates, one black, one white. They both started washing their hands at the same time and both leapt back because the water was boiling. They cursed and flapped their hands, and then the white guy said to his mate: 'I'd have thought you'd have been all right with your skin.'

The black guy looked at him reproachfully and said: 'I'm only a heathen, not a rhino.'

Wasn't that beautiful?

It was, and so were you, Miles. You really were beautiful.

For Peggy, Eve and Errol

In the land of the flip-flop, the shoeshine boy starves.

Albanian Proverb

FAMILY DEBT

My father was a very advanced thinker in the field of educational theory. He had devised a system of student loans long before it was fashionable to talk about them. I found this out, suitably enough, the day before I was due to depart for university and leave my childhood behind me.

It hadn't been a bad childhood, all in all, and there were several moments I could look back on almost with affection. There was the time we had gone for donkey rides on a beach in North Wales, and my donkey had suddenly stampeded three miles down the sands. How we all laughed, except me. There was the time we had gone for a cycling holiday in Yorkshire and all our bicycles had been stolen, though I did not know this until my mother forced my father to give them back.

There were treats too, like the time when, aged 16, I was taken to a restaurant for the first time and given smoked salmon. 'This is one of the great dishes of the world, son,' my Dad told me. I thought it was awful: greasy, soapy and very thin. 'The boy's a fool,' said my father, lifting the salmon from my plate to his and tucking in before I could change my mind.

But all this seemed far behind as I filled in the labels for my university luggage and wrote out the placard saying 'OXFORD' with which I hoped to hitchhike the next day. My parents had indeed given me the train fare, but, well trained by then, I had decided to save it.

'Might I have a word with you?' said my father, putting his head round the door.

'I don't have time for poker this evening, father,' I said. 'I am trying to get to university.'

'And before you go it would be as well to start with a clean sheet,' he said. 'I would appreciate prompt settlement of this.'

Whereupon he handed me a bill for £11,650. I looked at it, quite mystified.

'You have heard of student loans?' he asked.

'I don't think so.'

'It is a scheme under which students pay back the cost of their education afterwards.'

'But I have not been to university yet.'

'This is not for university. This is to cover the costs incurred while you grew up at home in the last 18 years.'

I was stunned. I knew my father had a keen business sense, but it had never occurred to me that I was a paying guest in my own home. Still, he had taught me two things about bills; always query them and never pay till you have no alternative.

'I take it you have an itemized account for the whole amount.'

'Of course.'

He handed over a huge dossier. I ran my eye down it. I was being charged for nappies, baby clothes, toys, breakages, books, donkey rides in North Wales . . .

'Hold on,' I said. 'This can't be right. £3.50 for a donkey ride. They only cost 10p even today.'

'If you remember,' said my father, 'it was a very long donkey ride you took. You galloped off three miles down the coast and it was well into overtime before we recovered you. That ride cost your mother and me a lot of heartache and distress for which, I may say, we have not charged you, though we have added a small sum for wear and tear to the donkey.'

'You have charged for bicycles in Yorkshire,' I said. 'Those bicycles cost you nothing. Mother will vouch for that.'

'Foolish boy,' said my father, stung. 'Do you think that transfer of property from one person to another costs less simply because the first owner does not realise what is happening? A burglar has expenses like anyone else — which, I may say, he is not allowed to claim against tax.'

'Smoked salmon,' I said. 'I did not order the smoked salmon and I did not eat it. *You* ate it.'

There was a short silence.

'I am not an inflexible man. I will knock off the smoked salmon and send you a revised bill.'

To cut a long story short, we spent the next six months haggling over the bill and finally settled on a sum of £8,970, an amount which I managed to win comfortably at poker during my first term at Oxford. I took my parents out to dinner to celebrate.

'It wasn't really about the money,' said my father at the end of the meal, 'though that was nice. But in a very real sense you have now paid for your childhood and, unlike anyone else, will never again have feelings of debt or guilt towards your parents.'

'How true,' I said.

I paid the bill for dinner and entered the amount in a new account book freshly marked Parents' Declining Years.

'By the way,' I said, 'do you want this on account or do you wish to settle now?'

Welcome To Kington, 1989

SONG OF THE TEA BAGS

Dancy, dancy, little bags
As I hold you by the tags
Jiggle up and jiggle down
Make the water nice and brown
Cooking such a glorious brew
A cup for me, and one for you.
I am the mighty puppeteer
Pulling strings to bring good cheer!
Nearly there . . . Well, bugger me!
The bags have fallen in the tea!
Now I'll never get them out
And they'll be jammed inside the spout.
Put my fingers in the pot . . .
Damn! The water's bloody hot!
And now the tea is far too dark.
Oh sod this for a sodding lark.
No Earl Grey for me today.
I'll make a mug of Nescafe.

PUNCH REVISITED

When I left Oxford in 1963, I only wanted to do one thing: write humour. In my last university days I met another young man who also wanted to be a comic writer, called Terry Jones, and together we determined to collaborate on some of the most brilliant comedy scripts ever to hit the BBC. By the time we had written together for a year and had nothing accepted, it began to dawn on us that either the BBC was blind to talent or we were doing something wrong.

It was Terry who worked it out first.

One day he took me aside and said: 'Look, Miles, I think to be honest we are going in different directions. I want to write stuff to be performed, preferably stuff that I can perform myself, whereas I think you just want to write for the printed page. I honestly think we would be better off going our separate ways. Together it's not going to work. In any case, there's a friend of mine just leaving Oxford called Michael Palin who I want to write with . . .'

What Terry was saying (apart from the fact that he wanted to write with Michael Palin) was that I was a humorous writer by bent and he was a comedy writer. He wanted to get up on stage. I wanted to see my words in print. He wanted to see his face on TV. I wanted to see my name at the top of articles. How right he was, was proved by the fact that half a dozen years later he was one-sixth of *Monty Python's Circus*, while I was one-sixth of the staff of *Punch* magazine. In other words, he was facing firmly into the future and I was facing fearlessly into the past.

Because the pedestal occupied by the humorous writer, and probably by the cartoonist too, has been forcibly repossessed, and they have both been replaced by the comedy writer, and the strip cartoonist and the animator. There is still a place for a humorous columnist like me, as there is for the travelling rug, the open log-fire and the individually hand-crafted stink bomb, but I have to recognise that history has passed on by another route, into television and film, and that I am in danger of becoming part of a heritage industry.

Nevertheless, there was a time when the humorist and the cartoonist were the most modern comic performing animals it was possible to conceive, and *Punch* was the repository of the best of them, and if we look back to its golden days we will see both at their best. Not only that, but I was incredibly lucky to be able to be a staff member of *Punch* while it was still within hailing distance of its great days.

At any rate, the things that made me laugh out loud were almost all written or drawn within the last fifty years or so. Now, I know this is not conventional wisdom. I know that the golden age of *Punch* cartooning is generally said to centre on Leech and Keene, and later on Phil May and du Maurier, and that the great writers of *Punch* were the A. P. Herberts and E. V. Knoxes and H. F. Ellises from before 1950. Well, yes and no. Yes, they drew and wrote beautifully. No, they don't seem that funny any more.

But then it was always said of *Punch* that it wasn't funny any more. The accepted wisdom in this century is that the dentist's waiting room was the proper place for it, and even in its heyday it was considered normal to laugh about it. Auberon Waugh used to maintain that even very good and funny writers were bad in *Punch*. *Private Eye* used to send out rejection slips marked: 'Why not try *Punch*?' Timothy Shy, in World War II time, used to excuse limp jokes by saying: 'Good enough for *Punch*.' Going back a century, a Victorian editor of *Punch* once said to W. S. Gilbert, 'Do you know, we get hundreds of jokes send in every week!' 'Really? Then why don't you print some of them?' said Gilbert caustically.

In my experience the only people who were ruder about *Punch* than these outsiders were the staff itself. We were so conscious of the great cartoons and good things done by *Punch* in the past that it was rather depressing to bring out a weekly issue and realise that nothing in it was nearly so good. It was also depressing to bring out issues in which there were good things and have nobody notice, just because nobody expected

Punch to do anything new or good. We felt the weight of the millstone of history round our necks. We felt the force of inertia of a somewhat dozy readership. But as much as anything we felt that we had to fight against the editor as well, whoever he might be.

This was especially true of the tenure of William Davis, in the 60s and 70s. Davis felt that he had to drag the magazine kicking and screaming into the twentieth century. He wasn't the first. Malcolm Muggeridge had been hired in the 1950s to get rid of the old readers and attract a new set. His brand of modernism had managed to get rid of the old but not attract the new, which had helped *Punch* on a downward slide in circulation which was never to be halted in the next two or three decades.

In a vain atempt to staunch this, Davis nailed his colours to the cause of being in touch, that is, being topical, being political, being satirical. Nothing wrong with that, except that *Private Eye* and *TW3* were already doing it much better, and *Punch* was the wrong magazine to do it with. There seemed little point in our planting little squibs under the Vietnam War, or Scottish nationalism, or the three-day week, if we were always a week late and didn't add anything to it. Look back through the Punch of the 1979s and 1960s, and you will find a lot of dead humour washing around in the shallows, attached to long-forgotten TUC leaders, and car strikes, and now unrecognisable Cabinet ministers. We all know the sensation of opening an ancient volume of *Punch* and wondering exactly why Gladstone *is* getting cross about Bulgaria (or rather, not caring in the least why he is doing it) but you can get exactly the same effect in recent *Punches*. Who IS Jack Jones? What WAS the Cod War?

(There was one week when I was actually acting editor of *Punch* because both editor and deputy, Davis and Alan Coren, were away. I put into that issue things which I liked because I thought they were good and funny, including one of which I am quite proud, because it was the only portion of his autobiography ever penned by Paul Desmond, the saxophonist with Dave Brubeck. It is a very funny piece, and when Davis came back and saw it in *Punch* he exploded. 'I turn my back for a week, and rubbish like this gets in!'

To get to the *Punch* library you have to go through some ultra-modern offices and then pass back a hundred years into the leather-lined library, where the first time I visited it a Japanese scholar was silently scrutinising the private letters of Tom Taylor, the Victorian editor of *Punch* whose main claim to fame was that he wrote the play at which Lincoln was assassinated . . .

Help! I am sinking back into history already, succumbing to the historical spell of *Punch* again. I don't really want to go back down that road. I escaped from *Punch* fifteen years ago, and have lived a comparatively normal life ever since, despite what Terry Jones forecast.

A pity he and Palin didn't write more. They could have been very good humorous writers, those two, if they hadn't gone off and wasted all their time making films and going round the world . . .

The Best Of Punch, 1998

LA BELLE DAME SANS MERCI

PAR JEAN KEATS

‘Au revoir!’ dit la belle dame.
  ‘Au revoir?’ dit-il. ‘C’est tout, au revoir?’
  ‘Sorry,’ dit la belle dame, blushing. ‘Au revoir, et merci.’

The Franglais Lieutenant’s Woman, 1986

HOW TO GET BY
IN BABY LANGUAGE

When my son was born, I took an oath never to write about him in print. Unless, that is, watching him had helped me formulate a major new theory about children which would be of help to all, or at least get me in line for a Nobel Prize for Child Watching. Well, today is such a day, as I think I may have stumbled across something which will help to explain children's behaviour more accurately than scientists have managed heretofore.

It's to do with the way babies learn to speak. My 16-month-old son has got to the stage where he can understand a lot of things we say – such as, 'Put that cat down!' 'Turn that TV set off!' 'Do not eat that potted plant!' and 'I said, put that cat down!' – but not say them back. This is understandable. A baby going round telling his parents to put the cat down and turn the TV off is clearly being taught the wrong phrases, and will become unpopular very soon. The sort of thing we should be teaching him, really, is, 'Thanks for the meal – it was great,' 'I really like it here at home, you know' and 'Put the cost of all these toys and things on the slate, OK? I'll pay you back when I'm 21.'

But even if he cannot talk, he can speak. He makes a lot of different noises. Some of them are recognizable vowels and consonants such as 'Mumumum', 'Gagagaga' and 'Dudududud'. Others are not recognizable: they are largely spitting, clicking, groaning, wheezing and fizzing noises which give him a lot of pleasure but are not going to be any use when it comes to learning English.

So we fond parents disregard the noises, but leap up and down when he goes: 'Bababab', and say, 'Hey, he's trying to talk!' Actually, this is totally illogical. *He* doesn't know that *Babababa* is going to be useful later on, and that the dribbling noises have no value in English. There are languages in which those noises *would* be useful. Xhosa is full of clicking noises, Afrikaners clear their throats a lot, Scots make noises that the English have lost and Poles makes sounds we never had.

All the noises he makes, in fact, are of possible use in some language. If he were an African baby, his parents might be leaning over him every time he clicked and fizzed, saying: 'Ah, he's saying things already!' But if *Babababa* and *Gagagaga* represented sounds they didn't use in their dialect, they would frown when he came out with them and wonder if he was ever going to learn to talk. There are sounds we all discourage our children from making, and if they need them later on they are going to be in trouble.

We may think, for instance, that the Japanese have trouble with their 'L's and 'R's, but the British struggle with the French 'R'. Quite apart from the fact that the British think it's rather effeminate for a foreigner to talk French with a French accent, we actually find it very hard to wobble the saliva sufficiently in the throat to make the noise at all. We don't think it's a *real* noise, because it's not like any of *our* noises.

And yet children can manage it very easily. My son does it all the time, especially after fruit juice. And yet the odds are that I will get him to unlearn it before very long.

You see, what I think is happening is that the child, happily gifted with all possible noises, is busy listening to his parents to identify which language he has been born into prior to getting rid of the noises which he does not need. At the moment, he is poised to learn an African language or that branch of Chinese where they seem to be sick every other sentence, or even Japanese, but in six months the moment will be gone. Now is the time, or never, to get him talking fluent Yiddish, while he has the sounds for it.

But we shall, rather predictably, continue talking English in the home and his range of noises is about to be drastically pruned, not, as experts say, dramatically expanded. He may, through some freak, preserve a sound he doesn't need, or a consonant from some other language. I often wonder if the 'R' favoured by Roy Jenkins and Frank Muir or Tony Benn's whistling 'S' or that muffled 'S' peculiar to William Deeds, are not really authentic consonants from Ukrainian, or some cheap letter left over from a job-lot clearance of North African sound shifts. This may also explain why some children have trouble with one letter for years and years, getting all the rest perfectly right. The one they get wrong *is one they got rid of by mistake*, thinking it would not be needed in English. Maybe somebody in Africa got it by mistake and hung on to it, liking it.

Well, as I say, it is just a theory, but if the Nobel people are reading this, they know how to get hold of me.

Welcome To Kington, 1989

LET'S PARLER FRANGLAIS!
LE SAILING

Capitaine: Welcome aboard, vieux chap! C'est votre première visite dans un boat?

Ami: Oui. C'est à dire, j'ai pris le ferry de Douvres à Calais...

Capitaine: Mais non, mais non, ce n'est pas le real thing. Boating, c'est le smack de la mer contre les wellies, le sel dans les cheveux, le vent dans les oreilles...

Femme: (*Dans le galley*) ...Le tonic dans le gin?

Capitaine: Oui, merci. (*A l'ami*) C'est Liz, la femme. Elle déteste le sailing. Pauvre Liz. Maintenant, un peu d'explication. C'est très simple. Ici le helm. Le m'ns'l. Le sp'nn'k'r-h'ly'rd. Le j'b-sh't-w'nch. Et voilà! C'est tout.

Ami: Hmm. Et ceci, ils sonts les ropes?

Capitaine: Non, non, ce sont les sheets.

Ami: Je croyais que les sheets étaient les sails?

Capitaine: Non, les sails sont les jibs, les genoas, les m'ns'ls, etc. C'est très simple.

Femme: Du citron dans le gin?

Capitaine: Oui, merci! Maintenant, vieux chap, let's go.

Ami: Bon.

Capitaine: OK, cast off.

Ami: Pardon?

Capitaine: Cast off le warp. Le warp, c'est le sheet qui attache le boat à l'Angleterre. Cast off le warp.

Ami: Bon.

Capitaine: Mais, espèce de flaming idiot, vous avez cast off le wrong end! Vous avez laissé le warp sur terra firma!

Ami: Mais ...

Capitaine: Mais rien, Maintenant hissez le m'ns'l.

Ami: Avec quel rope? Quel sheet? Quel warp?

Capitaine: Avec le halyard, twitface. Non, pas celui-là, celui-là!

Ami: Celui-là?

Capitaine: Non, celui-là. Oh, for God's sake, prenez le helm, pendant que je fais le straightening out.

Femme: De la glace dans le gin et tonic?

Capitaine: Pas maintenant, Liz, fais-nous une faveur! Oui, deux lumps. OK, squire, steady as she goes. Bear away un peu.

Ami: Pardon?

Capitaine: Bear away. Bear away! Jesus wept, on va frapper cette Contessa 32! BEAR AWAY!

Femme: Il veut dire, donnez un push au morceau de bois dans vos mains.

Ami: Ah. Comme ça?

Capitaine: Oui, très bien. Vous voyez, c'est très simple, le sailing. Je suis sûr que vous allez vous amuser beaucoup.

Ami: Je ne suis pas sûr. J'ai un feeling un peu ...

Capitaine: Un peu quoi?

Ami: Un peu queasy.

Capitaine: C'est normal. Liz. donne-lui un gin et tonic et Kwells. Maintenant, on va essayer le spinnaker ...

Let's Parler Franglais Again! 1980

A LIFE ON THE OCEAN BED

When I go sailing, I find it gives me plenty of time to think of answers to all those questions which puzzle me in life. Questions like, did I bring the boots that leak by mistake? Why is it always twenty degrees colder on a boat than on land 500 yards away? And, what the hell am I doing here?

Well, I know the answer to the last one immediately. I am here because my wife is nuts about sailing. As I sit in the cockpit, trying to work out in a rigorously scientific way if one foot really is damper than the other, she is staring round, as keen as Columbus, to see if any ropes need tidying up, if the anchor chain is secured, whether the wind is changing its mind or if a boat a mile ahead will collide with us if we don't do something about it now. Legend has it that many a sailing man puts to sea with a not unwilling wife in tow. I am the only husband I know who follows in the wake of a salt-water maniac.

Don't get me wrong, I like sailing. I don't love it, but I like it. It's just that, for me, sailing tends to come into the category of sports which is headed by kite-flying. There are only two interesting moments in kite navigation: one is getting the kite off the ground and the other is getting it back down again. In between there is a long boring stretch which consists of you holding a piece of string in your hand and looking at a dot in the sky, with no apparent connection between the two. Flying kites is very closely followed by rowing. The Varsity Boat Race is without doubt the most boring sporting event invented by man. In fact, it is even more boring than kite-flying because it is only the start of the Boat Race which is interesting; within a few seconds it is obvious who is going to win, so the finish becomes boring as well.

Kite-flyers obviously realise the essentially boring nature of their sport, as they have introduced features to make it more interesting. In the East they have fighting kites with which they try to bring each other's kites down. Here in the West we have stunt kites on two strings which can dive and spiral and make interesting shapes with their long tails. I dare say, too, the Boat Race would be much more attractive if the rules were changed to allow the boats to ram each other and the crews board each other to engage in hand-to-hand grappling. As it is, the only Boat Races ever remembered are those in which one side has gratifyingly sunk.

But I will say this: sailing is much more interesting than rowing. I am not referring now to yacht racing, which is so full of rules and point-chasing that it is more like county cricket than anything. I am talking about sailing – getting in a boat and going somewhere. Anywhere. *Then* things start to happen. You look at the wind. You put up the right sails. The wind changes. You take down those sails and put up other sails. The wind changes back. You put up the first sails again. The wind dies down. You switch on the engine. The engine does not work. You anchor and have lunch. The wind springs up again and the boat tips. The lunch falls on the cockpit floor. There is never a dull moment. Hardly.

Last weekend my wife and I went on a friend's boat to sail up the Suffolk coast from Burnham, for a week. This I looked forward to, as we were going to many places I had never seen. (Would the Boat Race not also be improved, by the way, if the rowers had to get out at every pub they passed and have a quick pint?) And on the very first day we visited a place that none of us had dreamt we would ever visit. The Maplin Sands.

Quite how it happened is still open to dispute, but I am glad to say that it was my wife at the helm and the captain navigating when it happened. I was sitting in the cockpit, busy with my boot problem. What happened was, in landlubber's terms, that we steered a bit to one side, hit the hard shoulder and stayed there. The keel dug a hole for itself in the hidden sands and stuck. We tried everything we knew. We switched on the engine. The battery was flat. We went to look for the starting handle. It wasn't there. We found it somewhere else. It was too late to try the engine by then. We cursed. We swore. That didn't work either.

After a quarter of an hour we suddenly became resigned to the fact that we were going to be there for twelve hours (six for the tide to go down, six for it to come up and take us off) and from that moment the whole thing became immensely enjoyable. As the boat settled further and further on its side we discovered the delights of walking round the walls of a room (remember Fred Astaire dancing on the ceiling?) The water suddenly became only an inch deep and we could get off and walk around in it. Equally suddenly we were on miles and miles of wet but firm sand and could go for long walks away out to sea. Sea birds, the only inhabitants, came to study this new kind of protected wild life. The two children on board discovered stranded jelly fish and set up impromptu biology classes. The captain announced that it was customary on these occasions to drink more red wine than was good for you, so we climbed into the tiny dinghy towed behind and had the most enormous lunch followed by the most enormous siesta. At about tea-time we even had a caller; a boat anchored nearby and the crew came over in a dinghy to see if we were all right. We gave him a biscuit and he went away.

And soon but gradually the sun went down over this vast expanse of whispering sand and tip-toeing waves, and the moon, a great big orange boiled sweet, floated up out of the distant land. The water began to return. It floated the dinghy. Then it started to right the boat so that, having only just learnt to ignore the floors and walk on the sticking out edges of seats or on the bookshelf, we had to remember all over again about the right-way-up world. Came ten o'clock, and under the bright moonlight we started the engine sweetly first time and smoothly slid back into the right channels.

The rest of the week was fine. We sailed up and down rivers, tackled choppy weather off Harwich and caught the right tides entering the Deben, avoiding skilfully much more tricky sands than Maplin. I enjoyed it. I really did. Especially as by then I had discovered that my boots were the watertight ones. But the funny thing is that, when I look back, the day that stands out for me is the day we spent on the Maplin Sands, the day we didn't do any sailing at all, when a whole new world opened up.

I'm not sure what the moral is. Except, perhaps, that apart from all the other improvements I've mentioned, the Boat Race would be much more exciting if staged at the lowest point of the tide on a part of the Thames where there was only room for one boat to get through without going aground.

Miles and Miles, 1982

THE BIRTH OF MILLS & BANG

*M*en prefer facts while women prefer feelings, Rachel Billington *once wrote; that is why the former read books about war and the latter read fiction, romantic or otherwise. And in her book* Animals In War, *Jilly Cooper confessed that, although married to a publisher of 400 military histories, she had read fewer than half a dozen of them. 'In the same way that men spurn novels, particularly romantic fiction, women tend to avoid war books, as being an exclusively guts-and-glory male province.'*

When two of our leading woman writers combine to express the same thought, I tend to treat it as received truth. And then my mind wanders to the question beyond, which is: if it is really true that there is a sharp divide between men's war books and women's romance, is there not some way in which I can make vast sums of money out of this discovery?

From there it is but a short step to the formation of a new publishing house which will issue novels for men and women – romantic military fiction! The new imprint, which is to be called Mills & Bomb, or perhaps Mills & Bang, will shortly be flooding bookstalls with the initial titles, of which details now follow.

To Call Him Sir, by Angela Distaff

When Robin joined the platoon, he had already heard the stories about Sergeant Withers. Tough, cynical, sadistic, they said. And yet there was some soft pool of hurt concealed in the sergeant's eyes, which told Robin that there was an altogether more complex person tucked behind those sergeant's stripes than the world knew of. 'So you're bleeding Robin-bleeding-Darlington-Smythe, are you?' the sergeant said at their first meeting. 'Well, we'll have those bleeding hyphens knocked out of you before you can say hunt ball.'

The tears clustered hot on Robin's eyelashes beneath the whiplash of these cruel words. How I hate him, he thought. Yet before the war was very much older, the two men would find themselves mixed up in a circle of passion, carnage and ammunition shortage which would change both of them ineradicably.

Jungle Johnny, by Elena Samson

Major-General Bridget Yates, of the Women's Royal Air Corps, was used to interrogating prisoners. But there was something unusual about the man they brought in one day – his crinkly laugh-lines, perhaps; the proud, untameable look in his eyes, or even the way he refused to speak no matter how hard she lashed him with her handbag. When he turned out to be Johnny Kapok, the famous roving American reporter, she had an uneasy feeling that their paths were to cross more than once in this hell without food or good cosmetics that women call war.

The Mountain Flower, by Iris Forage

A recce in war-torn Afghanistan was just another job to ace TV cameraman Max Winton, or so he thought. But he had not reckoned on a meeting with petite, sparkling Ludmilla, a runaway refugee from the occupying Soviet forces.

'You can hang around with us if you like,' said Max gruffly, 'as long as you don't mind carrying the spare camera and the batteries. And don't imagine you'll be getting a slice of our overnight allowances, my little Russian doll.'

'Of course not, Max,' said Ludmilla, playing with his earring. She had not met men with earrings before, especially ones inscribed *BBC News Cameramen Do It Overnight*. 'Tell me, do you think I could get a job with your Central Office of Information when we get back to Britain?'

We? The COI? Back to Britain? Max thought of his boss at Wood Lane. Would he understand if he returned with a Russian crew member? More to the point, would his wife Theresa? Max decided there and then to ditch Ludmilla at the first opportunity. Little did he realise how signally he would fail, or indeed that there was now a tiny bug fixed to his earring.

Moreover, Too, 1985

VIN LITÉRAIRE

All wine articles are the same; only the labels are different. I first learnt this when someone unwisely asked me to be among the judges for a wine- and food-writing contest. I knew nothing about wine and food, so I just judged the writing. And one thing I discovered is that when wine writers go to that darling little vineyard tucked away in a place that you and I will never get to, they all write the same piece. I have combined the best elements in one fruity but surprisingly light article. When you have read it, you will never have to read one again. Even better, I will never have to write one again.

The little-known wine-growing area of Vendange lies somewhat south of the main Burgundy district, near the modern town of Beaujolais Nouveau, and it was in the small village of Bouquet-les-deux-Bouchons that I was privileged to meet Maurice Mineur, whose family have produced wine in the same *vignoble* for hundreds of years. Together with his son Patrick, his daughter Isabelle and their goat Rachmaninov, they tend 14 hectares of land (about 60,000 bottles) to produce the delicate white Moncracher wine for which the area is noted – not to be confused with the famous Montrachet.

Spring is particularly beautiful in this part of France, with almond blossom everywhere, especially on the almond trees, and the delicate scent of eglantine in the hedgerows. It was with a sense of anticipation that I drove up the flinty, dusty track that leads to the Mineurs' ancient farmhouse, where I found the family already hard at work eating breakfast. This consisted of warm *brioches* straight from the oven, crusty French farm butter and a huge bottle of wine.

'This wine is my children,' said Maurice, swirling a small amount round his glass and smelling it tenderly. I noticed, fascinated, his technique of dipping his bushy moustache into the wine, sniffing it appreciatively and later wringing it out into a small bucket, for nothing is ever wasted in wine-making. 'To me, each bottle is different. I can tell just from the introduction of my nose where each one is born. This one, for instance, she is from a chalky vineyard facing east. You can tell from the sniff.'

He took a large helping and drank it all down. Patrick took up the tale.

'Our approach to the wine-making is traditional. Not for us the new machinery with the press buttons and the flashing red lights. Still we use the old wine press and the operation by hand and foot. It takes longer but it is worth it. We are still working on last year's harvest, actually, but you must not hurry wine. Wine is like a woman – she is never ready when you want to go out for an evening.'

He too took a large glass of Moncracher and Isabelle continued the tale.

'My brother is a male chauvinist pig. That suits me well, though, for as his sister I shall never have to marry him. A little wine?'

She handed me the bottle. Not seeing a spare glass, I raised the bottle to my lips and took a large draught. They clapped their hands and laughed.

'I see you English know how to treat a good wine,' twinkled Maurice. 'Now it is time to show you my little estate.'

The Mineurs' farmhouse, hundreds of years old, is a large, shady building covered with tangled ivy, creeper, nasturtiums, roses and, on the south wall, a huge poster for St Raphael. Beneath the farmhouse are large cellars which have housed bottles for hundreds of years, except during the War when they housed up to five hundred fleeing RAF officers at a time.

'*Mon Dieu*, they could drink,' reminisced Maurice. 'During the day they would work for me in the fields and at night they would open the bottles and teach me their traditional drinking songs. *Gringo the Russians Oh!* is the one I liked best.'

'And in 1945 they all went home, I suppose,' I hazarded.

'Not so,' said Maurice. 'They had drunk so much that they owed me wages and many of them had to stay till 1947 or 1948 to work off the backlog. They were good days.'

The Mineurs' vines grow on chalky soil, which gives to the resulting wine what can only be described as a chalky taste, which is not unpleasant but comes as a surprise if you are used to a grapey taste.

'This is what I would call a not successful bottle,' said Maurice. 'Look at the overseas bodies.'

Looking closely, I could see that the bottle contained large quantities of chalk, a few flints and what looked like a twig. Maurice knocked it angrily against a tree and it broke.

'My wines are my children and from time to time I must spank them. Now here is a *good* bottle. A little sampling?'

I tasted it over and over again until I could begin to appreciate its truly noble, flinty, redolent character. Patrick meanwhile was explaining to me the technical nature of wine production with many figures and statistics, while I took notes as best as I could, considering I was also wrestling with a large bottle, a stick of warm French *pain* and some *paté* fresh from the pig. Referring to my notes now, I see I have written: 'It is odd to see someone like Patrick with a handlebar moustache and a neat blue blazer. I wonder if his father was a passing squadron leader?'

The French laws of inheritance demand that each plot of land is parcelled out between the children, so that vineyards tend to grow smaller and smaller. Within a mile or two, Maurice told me, there are no less than 800 different *viniculteurs*, all cousins, which means that there are considerable traffic jams on market day. On the other hand, you are never short of a fourth for bridge. When Maurice dies, the land will have to be divided between Patrick, Isabelle and a certain Wing Commander Bentley of Farnham in Surrey, about whom they never talk. But what will Isabelle do with her share of the property?

'I will continue to grow wine as we have for hundreds of years,' she confided. 'Maybe I will marry, I do not know. We are so remote here that I do not meet many men. In fact, you are the first man I have seen for a good long time. Will you write often when you go back to dear old England?'

I must confess I had not paid much attention to Isabelle hitherto, but whether it was the effect of the wine or the warm spring weather, I found myself suddenly attracted to her grave, chalky eyes and flint-brown moustache, which glowed softly in the French sunshine. Over lunch, which was an impromptu affair of beef casserole, roast pheasant, fresh salmon and home-grown vegetables, with another bottle each, I could not help reflecting that the life of this simple French family was nearly ideal.

'Must you be going off so soon?' said Maurice after we had wiped the last remnants of gravy from our plates with crusty French napkins straight from the laundry.

'Alas, yes,' I said. 'I now have enough material to churn out a 1,500-word article and I must rush back to enter it for a food- and wine-writing contest.'

'Ah, you English,' said Patrick. 'Why is it that you are always writing about food and wine and never enjoying it?'

It was a question which burned in my mind as I got unsteadily into my little hired car, drove down the dusty farm track and steered accidentally into an unsuspected ditch which had lain covered by undergrowth for hundreds of years. The family found me there later in the day, fast asleep. They hospitably invited me to stay until I was able to move on. Now, three years later, I am still here, for Isabelle and I have developed a, how shall I say, certain understanding, as indeed the French have done for hundreds of years, and I look forward now to the day when our little son Rupert will in turn inherit his three and a half hectares, though at present he is obsessed only with the idea of joining the RAF about which his grandfather tells him so many stories.

Miles and Miles, 1982

REAGAN THE POET

There was a widespread feeling at the time of the American election that President Reagan was a much misunderstood man.

Especially by those who voted for him.

I now join myself with those who say that he is misunderstood.

By everyone.

We are told that Mr Reagan, a few days ago, said that a war in Europe was on the cards, or words to that effect. But has anyone studied his actual words?

I have.

Thanks to the *International Herald Tribune*, which had the courage to print the answers he gave at that press conference, I can tell you today that *nobody* could understand what he had said.

Here, when asked if a nuclear war could ever be limited, is what he actually said:

'I don't honestly know. I think, again, until someplace – all over the world this is being, research going on, to try and find the defensive weapon. There has never been a weapon that someone hasn't, come up with a defence. But it could – and the only defence is, well, you shoot yours and we'll shoot ours.'

That passage is short of logic. But it has a certain strange beauty, the far-off elusive quality that we associate with poetry. And there is the clue. Reagan is a poet. And not just any old poet; he is the reincarnation of e. e. cummings. It only has to be set out properly for the true magic of the passage to come through.

i don't honestly know

i think, again, until

someplace

all over the world

(this is being

research going on

to try and find

the defensive weapon)

there never has been a

weapon

that someone hasn't come

defence.

a

with

up

(but it could)

and the only defence is

well,

you shoot yours

and

we'll shoot ours.

Ladies and gentlemen, the man who wrote that could never declare war. He is a poet, not a fighter.

This writer would like to acknowledge gratefully the generous artistic support of the CIA.

Moreover, 1982

WARNING: NEW
CONSTRUCTION AHEAD

It always gives me a thrill when I spot a new usage creep into the language, like coypus infiltrating the hitherto uncoypued landscape of Norfolk, and I would like everyone to give a big hand to the hyphenated noun-plus-participle masquerading as an adjective.

If that sounds ugly, and it's meant to, let me give you an example. 'Index-linked pension'. A noun, a hyphen, a participle. We all know what it means. It means inflation-proof. Only to make it sound slightly grander, we say that it is linked to the cost-of-living index. It doesn't sound too bad, but then one coypu in the landscape is quite acceptable.

Another now common example is the description of diseases like cancer as 'smoking-related'. This is an adjective used by scientists who are perfectly certain that smoking causes cancer but haven't finally proved it, so are reduced to saying that it is linked to smoking. Quite unobjectionable, but two coypus in the countryside should cause no alarm.

When a third appears, I do begin to hear alarm bells. It appeared in the *Herald Tribune*, about a month ago. In the run-up to the elections in the Philippines, nearly a dozen people had been shot or otherwise done to death for their political beliefs, or ambitions, and the *Tribune* had referred to these incidents as 'election-related deaths'. These linguistic coypus are obviously beginning to mate and have strange offspring.

The fourth coypu was duly sighted last week, again in the *Herald Tribune*. (Let nobody think I am criticizing this excellent paper, which is the first one I turn to every morning.) They printed a photograph of a man riding on horseback with water up to his knees, down the main street of a small American town. The presence of so much water, the caption explained, was due to 'rain-caused floods'.

Now, this is where we must start to call a halt, or to go out and shoot these pesky coypus before they take a hold. This little construction will become a bad habit, a reflex-linked action, before we know where we are. I suspect that we are dealing with an American-derived fad, which is why it is a *Tribune*-associated phenomenon, that Paris-domiciled newspaper being an expatriate-orientated publication though it is also a European-angled daily. That, if you didn't notice, was an example-stuffed sentence. I find the whole thing a nausea-operated topic.

The unwieldiness of it comes out best if we apply it to a well-known piece of writing. Here is a Wordsworth-derived stanza:

> *I wandered like a care-linked cloud*
> *That floats on high o'er height-caused hills*
> *When all at once I saw a crowd*
> *Of bulb-connected daffodils*
> *Dancing 'neath the branch-formed trees*
> *In time with the waltz-tempoed breeze.*

If the scientists and medics still think that there is a place for this construction in scientific language, I offer another version:

> *I roamed in cloud-related gloom*
> *Through lake-associated hills*
> *When all at once I caught a rheum,*
> *A nasty go of damp-linked chills,*
> *Beside the acorn-started trees*
> *I shivered in the wind-caused breeze.*

Ladies and gentlemen, my case rests. I adopt a coypu-opposed position.

Moreover, Too, 1985

THE BRILLIG SLEEP

RAYMOND CHANDLER'S
VERSION OF 'JABBERWOCKY'

'Twas brillig. It had been that way all day, and it wasn't getting any cooler. I had loosened my neck-tie so many times that the knot had worked its way down to my navel. Outside in the street the first lights had come on and the slithy toves were doing whatever they do in the wabe. Some days they gyre, some days they gimble. It's no skin off my nose, but I wish they'd make their minds up, then we could all rest easy.

Five o'clock, and I still had no customers. The paper cup on my desk looked dry, so I eased some Bourbon into it. I heard a screech of brakes outside; some mome rath had decided to outgrabe and was paying for it. The pot of borogoves on my window-sill looked a little mimsy, so I poured half the Bourbon down my throat and the other half into the pot, figuring that it would be nice to share a drink with someone, even if only a borogove.

Then there was a knock at the door. I emerged from uffish thought and told the owner of the knock to come and join me. The door opened and there stood a young man with money written all over his face, the sort of nervous young man who has grown up in the shadow of a millionaire father and dreads the moment when Daddy tells him to take over.

'Mr Marlowe?'

I owned up. There was no law against being Mr Marlowe.

'I need your help. My father has asked me to deal with the Jabberwock, and I simply don't know how to go about it. You know the Jabberwock?'

Everyone knew the Jabberwock. It was a club on Ocean Parade, the sort where you went in rich and came out poor. They had a singer there called Jubjub who was reputed to eat men for breakfast and if being eaten for breakfast is your idea of a good time, then she was the girl to get in touch with. Personally, I prefer wrestling with anacondas.

'I'm engaged to be married to a girl called Jubjub. My father disapproves and . . . do you know what this is?'

He put down a large gold coin on my desk. I looked at it. It was a large gold coin.

'It's a bandersnatch,' I said. 'Only a hundred are known to exist. They're very valuable, except when they're frumious, and then they're very valuable indeed. This one is frumious. What's it got to do with the Jabberwock?'

To cut a long story short, I went out to the Jabberwock that night, killed the owner, warned off Jubjub, did some burbling and went galumphing back. The young man wasn't best pleased by my solution, but his father seemed to like the way things had turned out. Frabjous, he called it. He even embraced his beamish boy, and you could tell from the latter's expression that this hadn't happened in a long while.

'I don't know how to thank you, Marlowe,' he said, chortling slightly.

'Don't bother,' I said. 'Just leave me the bandersnatch.'

He did, and they both left, hand in hand. It's always nice to reunite father and son, even if it means leaving old Marlowe alone with a pot of borogoves. I poured myself a measure of Bourbon and listened to the toves gyring outside. Maybe they were gimbling. It's hard to tell, especially when you don't give a damn either way. I ran a finger round my collar. 'Twas brillig. The borogoves looked mimsy on the window-sill. I gave them the ice and took all the Bourbon myself.

Moreover, Too, 1985

STEAMDAZE

I was once brought to a standstill in the late 1960s by an *Evening Standard* placard headline: NUDE POLICE SWOOP. In order to deal with the vision of unclothed policemen wheeling and soaring out of the sky, and swooping on some poor innocent (until proved guilty) victim, I had to come to a physical halt in the street. It was then I noticed the missing colon – NUDE: POLICE SWOOP – and could pass on peacefully once more, since which time I have not been brought to a stop by any *Standard* headline. Not, that is, until last Monday, when I read the message: LONDON STATION FOR SALE.

It wasn't until that moment that I realised deep down, that I had always wanted to own a station. This is probably because for four years, between the ages of about six and ten, I lived in a station. I went home to sleep and for meals, and I must have gone to school, but the rest of the time I lived in the station, simply because it seemed the best possible place in the world.

It was called Gresford; it was a country station and it had everything. It had a level crossing, it had a bridge, it had a signal box and it had buckets hanging up marked FIRE. Behind the station there was a steep hillside with woods which sprouted bluebells in spring and bracken in summer. The other side there were water meadows which specialized in lady's smock and cowslips and through which the River Alyn flowed, though I never found out where to. It had a notice asking passengers to shew their tickets at the barrier, and I often wondered why they had to shew them and not show them. It wasn't till I was grown-up that I realised railways like using words that nobody else uses, such as 'alight', 'commence' and 'terminate'.

Gresford also had trains. I leave mention of them till last because, although at the time I thought I was there to see the trains, I realise looking back that it was the station I loved. I didn't want to be an engine driver when I grew up; I wanted to be a stationmaster.

The line it was on was the main Great Western from London to Birkenhead, and Gresford is just beyond Wrexham, on the last bit of Welsh foothill before the rich Cheshire plains are reached. Why my English father wanted to live in Wales I never found out, but the result is that, although I had a Welsh childhood, I shall never be able to write about it like a real Welshman, not being one of the tribe, and not being called Gwyn or Thomas or both. The next village over the hill had the real Welsh name of Llay, and the Gresford lads had a long-standing rivalry with the Llay lads, but I never felt really involved.

Someone at Gresford station, one of the porters, I think, liked gardening and the main platform had lovely flower beds which one year entitled them to sport a plaque saying: 'Best Kept Station of the Year in . . .' Denbighshire? Britain? The world? It was also a base for pigeon racing. Now and again the stationmaster would lug a big basket full of pigeons off a train and leave it lying on the platform. You could hear them making soft noises inside. Where have they sent us this time? Gresford? Never heard of it. *Wales?* How the hell do we get home from Wales?

Then the stationmaster would re-emerge, checking his big turnip watch, and at the very dot of the very hour would open the basket. The pigeons would launch forth as if inaugurating the Olympic Games, circle above the station once or twice, feel the cold air coming down from the Welsh hills and shoot off in the direction of wherever they lived, apparently unworried by the thought that as soon as they got there they would be put in another basket and sent off again. Occasionally the stationmaster would find one rebellious pigeon skulking in the bottom of the basket and kick him out, then leave the station to me and the flowers. And the trains. The Castles, the Manors, the Halls, the 0-6-0s, the pannier tanks – ah, what engines they were in those days.

The curious thing is that for 99 per cent of the time there were no trains at all. One was always waiting for the next one. And why not? The whole point about being in a station is just being in a station. The one that has just come on the market, Marylebone, is a little big for my needs but now that I know that's what I want, I can wait.

Moreover, Too, 1985

THE UNITED DEITIES

THE FIRST RECORD

*N*ever mind all the bishops milling around at Lambeth – there has been a much more important religious conference going on this year, and that is the gathering of the main Gods of the world which takes place every ten years. Yes, the Hindu, Christian and Muslim deities, and every other one that matters.

I have never attended this divine conference, owing to my non-divine nature, but I do have a press release covering the proceedings of the last conference (May 1998) and I think you will agree that it sounds a lot more interesting than the Lambeth get-together.

Here are a few salient paragraphs from the report of the meeting, just to give you the flavour.

1. The Jewish God and the Christian God had had several more meetings to discuss a possible merger but nothing had been decided. The Jewish God had maintained that he still wanted nothing to do with the Millennium, and the Christian God had said, *All right, be that way*. The next meeting will take place after 2000.

2. There was general agreement among Gods that the 1990s had been a hopeful decade. There had been no major war on earth, which was a source of satisfaction to all concerned, except Thor, Norse God of war and thunder, who asked it to be placed on record that he regretted the stifling spread of peace.

3. A Hindu God said that he (or she, it not being clear) opposed the involvement of Thor in these sessions. The Norse Gods, he/she said, had not had any followers on Earth for at least 1,000 years and were not entitled to representation in these matters. He/she moved that the Norse Gods in future not be asked to these inter-deity conferences.

4. Thor said that normally he wouldn't pay any attention to what some six-armed creep who couldn't throw a hammer with any of them said about life in general, but in this case he was prepared to make an exception and would the lady or gentleman in question come outside and say it again.

5. The Chairgod called for order, and moved on to the next item on the agenda, the Salman Rushdie fatwa. Did Allah have anything new to report on this? Allah said he personally was glad that Mr Rushdie was still in hiding, as this showed that Mr Rushdie took the fatwa seriously, even if nobody else did. He himself, added Allah, had not read *The Satanic Verses*, as he was forbidden by his own religion from doing so. There was laughter.

6. Talking about Satan, said the same Hindu God/Goddess as had spoken previously, had there been any change of mind about inviting devils and kings of the underworld to this conference? The Chairgod said that they had discussed this long and hard and were still of the opinion that inviting devils and demons to a high-level all-deity conference would be taking creeping liberalism too far. 'Which ever way you slice him,' said the Chairgod, 'an Anti-Christ is still against Christ, and the last thing we want is terrorism at the God level.'

7. Thoth, an Egyptian delegate, said he did not normally side with Thor, but really he could not put up with mockery from Gods who were still believed in directed at Gods no longer worshipped. Just because belief in a God has died out, he said, did not mean that God is any the less worthy of respect. There were some Gods still believed in today who could not have gone three rounds with some ancient Gods he could mention. Besides, the ancient Gods had much better stories, and he would back the best of Egyptian mythology against the yarns of the New Testament any day . . .

8. The motion was seconded by a block of Aztec and Mayan Gods.

9. The Chairgod said they could second the motion as much as they liked but a sub-committee of Gods had gone over and over this one till they were blue in the face, and they had never come to a conclusion. In his view, the whole subject was bedevilled by the fact that there were lots of

Gods in the old days and very few new ones, so the old Gods tended to have more votes. Perhaps there was a case for divine PR.

10. The Chairgod asked the Catholic God to report on any noteworthy visions in the Catholic world in the previous decade. The Catholic God said that divine visions were being provided at the usual frequency, but that the failure rate was increasing. This was because children were increasingly being told to be wary of strange grown-ups, and on at least five occasions recently the Virgin Mary, having appeared to a child in a vision, had been told by the child to stop pestering them or they would get their parents to give her a good hiding. On one occasion two years ago St Joseph had appeared in a vision in Guatemala to a group of peasants and had been taken hostage.

11. The God of Ian Paisley at this point stood up and demanded furiously to be give a chance to speak. He would not make a fuss, he said, but the Catholic God was being given far too much airtime.

12. The Chairgod ruled the God of Ian Paisley out of order, saying that there was still not enough proof that the God of Ian Paisley was a genuine God.

Independent, 1998

THE BALLAD OF
THE MIDDLE LANER

When I was but a little lad,
   I asked this question of my Dad:
'Oh, Dad, one thing can you explain –
Why do we drive in the middle lane?

'Would it be a great mistake
If we pulled out to overtake?
Or would it really be so bad
If we were in the slow lane, Dad?'

My father said to me, 'I'm sorry,
I *will* not imitate a lorry,
Nor will I drive like a railway train –
The place for us is the middle lane.'

Oh, I'm a middle laner,
I love the middle lane,
I drive down it to Dover
And drive right back again.

You can flash your blooming headlights
And hoot till you go insane,
But you'll never get me moving
From out the middle lane.

And now that I'm a full grown man
I think I understand God's plan;
That some are naturally fast or slow,
But most down the middle lane should go.

And even when no car's in sight,
And I could pull to left or right,
I hear the little voice of Fate:
'You stay right in the middle, mate!'

And now, when my son, whose name is Wayne,
Says it's boring in the middle lane,
And asks me to go up to eighty,
I turn to him and say, 'Look, matey,

You're a middle laner,
You were born to the middle lane,
And every time you doubt it,
Just sing the old refrain . . .'

Oh, I'm a middle laner,
I love the middle lane!
I simply won't move over
In sunshine or in rain.

I go right down the middle
From Edinburgh to Staines
And refuse to even contemplate
The other two empty lanes.

So you may flash your headlights
Or audibly complain.
But I will never move over –
It goes against the grain.

Oh, I'm a middle laner,
I'll stay there till I die
And when they take me away in a hearse
Down the middle lane I'll fly!

Motorway Madness, 1998

NEW YORK STORIES

NEW YORK, THE TRUTH

'Try to avoid the mistake all journalists make when in New York for the first time. Don't go on about the bigness of everything, from buildings to beefsteaks' – advice given by experienced newspaperman.

I think that what has struck me most about New York as a newcomer is the smallness of everything. The buildings, for a start, are very small. There are of course, as in every city, some taller buildings, which have cleverly been grouped together so as to look good in photographs, but the buildings situated next to the tall buildings are invariably very low, presumably to make the tall buildings look even taller.

In many places there are no buildings at all, just empty gaps. That is known as the construction industry. Still, those gaps do have the effect of making the small buildings look larger, but not much.

I have also been struck by the smallness of the drinks served in New York. Everyone knows that it is impossible to get a pint of beer here, this being a measure larger than anything the Americans know, but the much vaunted generous helpings of spirits and cocktails are also illusory. Once you have removed the chunks of ice, the small plastic sticks, the artificial straws and the twisted remains of fruit, there is very little left in the glass.

I have been struck even more by the small-mindedness of American barmen in their attitude to investigative journalists, especially those like myself who order a drink and then spoon out the ice, sticks, straws and fruit into the ashtrays. We receive little sympathy – short shrift, even.

Manhattan itself is not large; one can walk to almost any point on the Island within minutes, at least any point worth visiting. The illusion of largeness is maintained only by travelling by subway or taxi, or by asking a policeman for directions.

New York policemen, by the way, are all small and often bow-legged as well. They may have started off by being tall, but have been reduced in height over the years by carrying such a weight round their waist: guns, knives, radios, handcuffs, tear gas, extra-strong belts, baseball bats stained black and overnight bags.

Even on the supposedly large Hudson River there is nothing big to be seen. I have sat by the water's edge for hours and seen no larger craft than a small rowing boat which came across from Brooklyn and landed at my feet.

'Are you in training to beat the record for the smallest boat to cross the Atlantic?' I asked the besuited rower.

'No, sir,' he told me. 'I am merely aiming to beat the morning rush hour. Small hope.'

Even the bicycles in New York, of all things, are smaller than elsewhere. Inspect any bike chained to the lamp-post and you will see that they are mostly lacking front wheel, back wheel, saddle and handlebars, leaving only a small frame. This is, no doubt, why their owners seem forced to run to work, for which purpose they wear very little and take very small steps. It is becoming harder and harder for me to believe in the myth of New York bigness.

One morning I passed Woody Allen in the street. He seemed very small. In the evening I had a small gun pressed into my chest by a man who wished to relieve me of what little I had. When I looked closely at him, I realised it was the man I had met rowing across the river from Brooklyn.

'Well, well,' he said, recognizing me. 'It's a small world.'

THE BUSINESS WORLD

It is not uncommon in New York for someone to shuffle up to you on the sidewalk and ask for thirty cents for a cup of coffee. But I must admit I was surprised yesterday evening when a man looked me straight in the face and said: 'Buddy, can you spare $30,000 to help rebuild my loan stock flotation company?'

Although his suit was threadbare and his single earring only two-carat gold, if that, there was something about his frank, honest look that appealed to me. I really believe that if I had not left my money back at my hotel I might have granted his request.

As it was, I took him into a restaurant near-by to listen to his story over a cup of coffee and a tuna-fish salad sandwich.

He had arrived in New York only that morning with a new idea for loan stock flotation and $20 in his pocket. But with that unquenchable dynamism for which the American businessman is famous, he had started work at 7:15 selling his idea to banks and brokers to such good effect that by midday he had his own suite of offices in the Wall Street area and an hourly turnover of $50,000.

'It was a classic rags-to-riches story,' he told me. 'When I got off the bus in New York this morning I was a workless college kid with a business degree and nothing else. By midday I was a member of the top local golf club, had a charge account in ten big stores and had even met someone who claimed to know Woody Allen quite well.

'Best of all, I had moved my wife and two children, Debby, five, and Charlie, three, into a lovely home on Long Island, where we had started to raise bees and make our own imported yogurt. I think this was my proudest achievement of all, especially as at breakfast time I had been unmarried.'

It was at lunchtime that his troubles had started. Torn between the options of training for the New York marathon and working through his lunch hour, he had chosen instead to pop out for a Martini. By 2:15 he was on his third Martini and had a heavy drinking problem.

'I suppose the stress of working non-stop since before breakfast without eating anything had gotten to me. There was also the factor that I wasn't getting any younger, and that other, keener, leaner young men had arrived in New York mid-morning with brighter, better ideas for loan stock flotation.

'When I got back to the office in the afternoon, things were already on the slide, and when I got a phone call from a prominent banker cancelling our jogging session for Friday I knew it was all over.

'We had to sell our lovely home in Long Island at teatime, I sent the children back to my mother at 4:30, and at 5:00 I got a divorce from my wife, who unbeknown had been having an affair with the local tennis pro since lunch.

'Now I have to start all over again. But at least I've managed to kick my drinking problem, and I've learnt one terrifically invaluable lesson from my business career.'

And what is that?

'Aim high. If you ask someone for thirty cents for a coffee, you won't get a penny. Ask him for $30,000 and I guarantee you'll get a cup of coffee with a sandwich thrown in. You wouldn't care to make it a slice of pie as well, would you?'

If I have learnt anything from this experience, it is, quite simply, not to listen to people on sidewalks.

The Times, 1982

OEDIPUS AND HIS MUM:
A CAUTIONARY TALE

Oedipus was an Ancient Greek
Whose future seemed to be quite bleak
For as the baby looked so weedy
His mum and dad took little Oedy
To ask the Oracle if he knew
What lay in store for baby blue . . .
'Oh woe!' the Oracle did intone,
As if through mournful megaphone,
'This lad will have a cursed life
For he will take his Mum as wife!'
'How can that be?' his Father cried.
'He cannot do that till I've died!'
'I have another bit of news,'
He heard the Oracle enthuse,
(For nothing gives an Oracle joy
Like bringing doom to a little boy)
'Your lad won't just take Mum as bride,
But also indulge in patricide.'
Now Father was an ancient Greek
Whose grasp of Latin was quite weak.
'Patricide?' he said. 'What's that?'
When told, he said: 'I'LL KILL THE BRAT!'
'No, don't!' said mother. 'Darling, see –
 He's making googoo eyes at me . . .'
'Oh, IS he?' said his father. 'No!
The little blighter's got to go!'
And so they came to a compromise.
The next day, as the sun did rise,

They left the baby high and dry,
In the desert, doomed to die.
But as is normal in this part,
Some interfering bleeding heart
Found the baby lying there
And took it home and into care ...
To cut a rambling story short
The lad was fed and up was brought,
Until at eighteen off he sped
To pass his gap year round the Med.
And in a road rage incident
He killed a passing aged gent
Which wouldn't have been half so bad
If it hadn't been his Dad.
And later, which was worse by far,
He unwittingly wed his Ma.
He had a baby by his Mother
Then two more, then another.
Reader, imagine if you can,
Children calling their mother 'Gran' ...
When Oedipus found what he had done,
He put his eyes out one by one,
And sat beside the River Nile,
In a state of complete denial.
Because he loved his Mum, you see,
Not wisely, but too passionately.
Moral:
If an oracle offers you news
Of the future, just refuse.
To know the future of your child
Will only help to drive you wild.
Just give him lots of love and hugs
And hope he doesn't take to drugs.

Radio 4, 2000

THE G-WORD

My brother came home from school one day and said to my mother, 'Miss Withers used the g-word in class today!'

'Good Lord!' said my mother. 'How terrible!'

'Yes,' said my brother. 'We were all shocked.'

I felt mildly shocked too, though I didn't know what the g-word was. I felt very encouraged, though, that Ralph knew. As he was my elder brother, I expected him to know everything and this was further evidence that he was omniscient. The only difficult bit, I usually found, was getting him to share his omniscience with me.

'What *is* the g-word?' I asked him later.

'G-word?' said Ralph. 'I don't think there is one.'

'Then how could Miss Withers use it?'

'I don't think she did.'

'Then how . . . ?'

'Look,' said Ralph. 'Grown-ups are always referring to swear words by their initial letters, aren't they? The f-word and the b-word and the c-word, and so on. To begin with, I used to think that every letter in the alphabet had a swear word attached, but in fact it seems to be just F and C and B. So I thought I might make up for all that by inventing one.'

'So what *is* the g-word you've invented?'

'That's the point, you dolt,' said Ralph. 'There doesn't have to be one. All I have to do is say that there is one. And grown-ups will never admit that they don't know what it is, especially to a child.'

When my father came home, my mother told him that Ralph had told her that Miss Withers had said the g-word in class and everyone had been very shocked.

'I see,' said my father. 'I see. I see . . . '

You could see his mind racing through all the English obscenities and swear words. My father was quite good at crosswords and it only took him ten seconds or less to establish that there was, in fact, no gross word in English beginning with G.

'Remind me,' said Father. 'What does Miss Withers teach?'

'Geography,' said Ralph. 'That's not the g-word,' he added.

'Mmmmm,' said my father. 'So what is it?'

'What is what?'

'The g-word.'

I realise now I was very lucky in having the kind of father who would admit to not knowing the g-word.

'I couldn't possibly say it,' said Ralph, looking shyly at the floor.

'I respect you for that,' said my father, gazing at Ralph dreamily. 'I respect you for finding yourself unable to tell me what this terrible word beginning with G is. I admire your delicacy and demureness, your sensitivity and sweet nature. On the other hand, if you don't tell me immediately what the g-word is, I shall tear your arm off and beat you to death with it.'

He often said this. He never did it. But he usually got his way.

'Oh, God,' said Ralph under his breath, realising he had no back-up plan.

'God, eh?' said my father. 'So that's the g-word, is it?'

'Yes,' said Ralph, grasping at the back-up plan which had suddenly been handed him on a plate.

'So,' said my father. 'Miss Withers has been blaspheming in a geography lesson, has she?'

'Yes,' said Ralph. 'She certainly has.'

'Good for her,' said my father. 'If I taught geography, I'd have to let off steam now and again.'

'But that's not all!' said Ralph, desperate not to lose the tactical high ground which he had occupied not a moment before. 'She also said the n-word!'

'Do you mean "knickers"?' said my father.

'Yes!' said Ralph.

'Your spelling is dreadful,' said my father. 'Knickers is not the n-word. It's the k-word.'

'Oh, bugger,' said Ralph, without thinking.

'Ralph!' said my mother.

'Did you say the b-word?' said my father strictly.

'Y-E-S,' said Ralph.

'Well, D-O-N-apostrophe-T,' said my father.

'W-H-Y-N-O-T?' spelled Ralph.

I left the room at this point.

When a family starts spelling out a conversation to themselves, life is being lived at half speed.

Little did I know it, but they had invented text-messaging fifty years before anyone else did it.

Somone Like Me, 2005

LET'S PARLER FRANGLAIS!

DANS LE RECORD SHOP

Client: Bonjour. Avez-vous *Heavy Dreams*?

Shopgirl: C'est none of your business, monsieur.

Client: Non, c'est un disque.

Shopgirl: Ah. Dans Le Top Quarante?

Client: Non.

Shopgirl: Oh. C'est un chart-climber? Un chart-faller? Un disco-miss? Un Mouldy Oldy?

Client: Ni l'un, ni l'autre. C'est un album, par Plastic Stucco Facade avec le New Brunswick Symphony.

Shopgirl: C'est Rock, Pop, Mid-Route, Folk, Jazz, Shows, C & W, Cockney-Rock, Crossover, Soundtrack, Hard Shoulder, Cheapjack, One-Hit, Vox Pop, Greatest Hits ou Remainder Bin?

Client: Je ne sais pas. Plastic Stucco Facade sont un East End group.

Shopgirl: Ah, c'est Dock-Rock.

Client: Mais le New Brunswick est un orchestre.

Shopgirl: Ah, c'est Schlock-Dock-Rock.

Client: Vous avez un Schlock-Dock-Rock rack?

Shopgirl: Non.

Client: Dommage. Alors, je cherche aussi *Can't Start Lovin' You* par les Disco Brakes.

Shopgirl: C'est dans le Black-Bloc-Tick-Tock-Shock-Rock Bin.

Client: Je n'aime pas l'onomatopoie. Avez-vous tout simplement Symphonie No. 38 de Mozart?

Shopgirl: Par qui?

Client: Par Mozart.

Shopgirl: C'est un groupe?

Client: Non, le groupe, c'est le BBC Symphony Orchestra.

Shopgirl: Radio 1 ou Radio 2?

Client: Radio 3.

Shopgirl: Ah. C'est dans le Bach-Brecht-Rock rack.

Client: Où c'est?

Shopgirl: Dans notre branche à Ealing.

Client: Bon Dieu. Avez-vous *Lullaby of 'ammersmith Broadway*?

Shopgirl: Par qui?

Client: Ian Dury, of course.

Shopgirl: Ian Dury est old-time. Il est Nostalgia-Rock. Il est Last-Year's-Layabout. Il est dan le Discontinued Bin.

Client: Et où est le Discontinued Bin?

Shopgirl: Avec les dustmen, of course.

Client: OK. Donnez-moi No. 1 dans le Top Quarante.

Shopgirl: Voilà.

Client: Merci.

Let's Parler Franglais Again! 1980

BASIC GEOLOGY

Geology is that branch of natural history which claims that everything beneath our feet is either igneous or non-igneous rock. In other words, it is the only science which tries to divide nature into smoking and non-smoking compartments. It does this by using the following two phrases at every possible opportunity:

'These rocks were formed at a time of upheaval in the earth's crust, and under immense pressure were buckled, twisted and turned on end to form the rather complex land formation we have today.'

'These rocks were laid down over millions of years by the deposit of tiny sea creatures at the bottom of lakes on the site of the British Isles, and have since been overlaid by other deposits to form the rather complex land formation we have today.'

Geologists, in other words, get very excited over what happened billions of years ago and seem incredibly bored by the evidence left lying around today, rather like a gardener who says: 'You really should have been here last week when the garden was looking wonderful – I'm afraid it's a mess today.'

To hide this boredom, they have resorted to several tricks to get the outsider interested. For a start, they call everything rocks, even when it's clearly only sand or soggy clay. Then they colour their geological maps in stunning bright poster paints and slash them across the country in wonderful shapes. They give exciting or poetic names to their rocks, such as boulder clay, millstone grit, or lower green-sands. And they print exciting time charts, with cross headings like: 'Cretaceous Era – great lakes form over Britain – millions of sea creatures deposited – invention of the fishing rod – half-closing day in Africa.'

None of this stands up to a moment's inspection. Rocks are not bright, interesting colours at all – they are always arts 'n' craft hues, that is, brown, brown-grey, grey-grey, grey-brown and off-yellow. They never look like their names – heaven help anyone who goes in search of something that looks as if it should be called lower greensands. And, worst of all, stones that look exactly the same are, as usual, from different families, whereas pebbles that you and I can see a mile off are totally unrelated always turn out to be granites with different dyes or preservatives used in their manufacture.

What you and I need is none of this. We need merely to learn what is the main stone in the area we happen to be in. And luckily there is a perfectly good method of finding out which no book on geology, as far as I know, has ever been based on. *Go straight to the nearest church and see what it is made of.*

Churches in the good old days were always built of the local building material, so much so that I have decided to reclassify all geological deposits as 'churchstone'. The advantages are obvious. Churches are all above ground – no messy digging around to find bits of rock. Churchstone has been cut and fitted by practised workmen – no chance of picking up the wrong thing by mistake. Churches are not confusing jigsaw puzzles unlike the ground you are standing on. Churchstone is geology with the heartache taken out of it.

So, if you are interested in the local geology, here's what to do.

1. Find a good solid-looking church or, even better, a tumble-down church.
2. Get out your hammer and chisel.
3. Chip off a decent sample.
4. Take it home with you.
5. Identify it.

A word of warning: cathedrals are useless for this. They have always been built from snobby imported stone, brought in large barges from across the Channel for the purpose. Chipping away at cathedrals, especially in the south of England, will tell you a great deal about geology in Normandy but that is not why you and I go nature-spotting – not me, at least.

And cathedrals are usually too well guarded, whereas little country churches are visited only by the occasional brass-rubber and flower-arranger. If however you should be challenged by the vicar, show him this certificate. It should work like a shot.

> **From the Society for Entry Into Rural Churches**
> *To the Rev whomsoever it may concern,*
> *Hi! Today I, the undersigned, attempted to visit your charming little church but found it firmly locked. I am now attempting to make a new entrance. I hope this meets with your approval.*
> *Love and peace.*

If you agree not to make a large hole in the East Wall, the vicar will generally let you keep a small piece of churchstone, relieved that nothing worse has happened.

Nature Made Ridiculously Simple, 1983

THE HISTORY OF KING TONY

or *Labour's Lost, Love*

PROLOGUE

The time is 1994, shortly after the death of army leader Lord John Smith.
The scene is a restaurant in London called Granita. At a table sit two men,
Prince Tony and Duke Gordon Brown.

Gordon: Thou summonedst me to speak with thee alone,
And yet this is no kind of private place.
Would we not be better off sequestered
In some sheltered, secret rendezvous?
Tony: Fear not, old friend! Who would suspect
That two great princes such as you and I
Would venture into such a lowly bistro?
We are safer here than skulking in the dark,
Made invisible by our very brashness!

A waitress appears with notepad.

Waitress: The time has come, fair gents, to make your choice,
Or shall I leave you eke five minutes more,
To scan the menu, and withal the specials . . . ?
Good Lord! Do now mine eyes deceive me?
Or is it young Prince Tony here in person,
Sitting at our humble, scrubbed-pine table top?

Tony: I am he indeed, but here on secret mission.

Pray do not give me any recognition.

Waitress: Of course, my Lord. But first just sign my pad.

Thou art the first big autograph I've had!

Tony: With pleasure. *(Signs.)* Now give us some more grace

To choose between the hake and bouillabaisse . . .

Gordon: Tony, thou art mad to think we're incognito!

That serving girl did know you straightaway!

Tony: And seemed most pleased to see me, did she not?

Whereas for you she did not spare a glance.

This is the truth thou hast to learn, old friend,

That thou may be the cleverest prince on earth,

But I am he the public love to cheer!

Gordon: When I am leader of our gallant troops . . .

Tony: Whoa, there, brave Gordon, stay a little while!

To be a leader thou hast not the style . . .

I have a deal to put to thee tonight.

When our great army do go out to fight

Against the ranks of reigning King John Major,

The enemy at present seem to wager

That thou as leader cannot hope to win.

Thou hast two beetling eyebrows black as sin.

Thy jaw is loose, thou hast a craggy jowl.

And all the world mistrusts that gloomy scowl.

Gordon: So what dost thou suggest?

Tony: That *I'm* made king

But only till we've settled everything.

When once my dashing charm and winning smile

Have won the day, I'll abdicate in style

And give the throne to thee, for thee to rule,

Like some stern teacher in a naughty school.

Gordon: This could work out. But how shall I ever know

Whether I can trust thy word or no?

Tony: Oh, Gordon, Gordon! Thou shouldst know long since

That I'm a pretty regular sort of prince . . .

At a nearby table, Sir Peter Mandelson is eavesdropping.
Mandelson (sotto voce): I like the way that young Prince Tony schemes.
Once I loved Gordon. Now, I'm swapping teams.

As the two men make their way home, they encounter three old hags.

1st Hag: Hail, Tony, that shall be a mighty warrior!
2nd Hag: Hail, Tony, that shall be king hereafter!
3rd Hag: Hail, Tony, that shall be a leader of the world!
Tony (aside): These girls do echo but my secret thoughts . . .
(Aloud) Say, who are ye, and wherefrom are ye sent?
1st Hag: Old Fleet Street hacks are we, who know the score.
2nd Hag: By Murdoch, our grim master, are we sent.
3rd Hag: Who promises to back ye in the *Sun*
As long as ye do offer certain favours . . .

The hags whisper in Prince Tony's ear. He nods.

Gordon: But what of me? Ye offer Tony all!
Have ye no promises for me besides?
1st Hag: Ah, Gordon, ye must wait a little while.
2nd Hag: Ye shall be chancellor for many years.
3rd Hag: And then at last! – Oh no, the glass grows dim!
I cannot see what fate's in store for him.
1st Hag: Come, sisters, come – our deadline waits for us.
2nd Hag: I see the headline now: 'It's Tony – No Fuss!'
3rd Hag: And under that: 'Has Gordon Missed the Bus?'

Cackling, they vanish. Tony and Gordon move on thoughtfully. Mandelson emerges from the shadows.

Mandelson: Warrior, king, world leader – everything!
Thus I can soon be steward to the king . . .

GRANDER THAN BOOKER, WILDER THAN WHITBREAD

STARTING today, the biggest blockbusting novel for years – Book Prize! Book Prize tells of the powder keg created when four men and women are locked away to choose the novel of the year – and discover that the novels they have read do not contain half the passion that explodes among them. Here is the first dynamite instalment of Book Prize.

'I liked Will Artley's novel from Australia enormously,' said Enid. 'The feeling of space created by the outback, the almost universal suffering embodied in the crippled boomerang repairman, was so refreshing after the provincialism of most British novels.'

She hadn't actually been able to finish Artley's endless saga, but she wagered shrewdly that none of the others had either.

'Rubbish,' said Peter Abbey. 'What on earth could be more provincial than the Australian desert? We in Britain always assume that anything set in our country is suburban and anything set in a country without street lighting is noble and universal. I shall use my vote to make sure that nothing from Australia wins.'

'Hear, hear,' said Murray, the literary whizz kid from Auckland.

'Or New Zealand,' said Peter.

'Hear, hear,' said Murray, who hated every writer in New Zealand except himself.

'God, I could kill him,' thought Enid, looking at Peter's handsome features, swollen by years of having, well, just one more drink. Peter, the top literary agent in London, was temporarily without an Australian author to represent, which helped to explain his feelings.

Enid herself was a well-thought-of novelist, that is, one who was hardly thought of at all, either well or badly. She had once had a fleeting affair with Peter which ended abruptly at the Frankfurt Book Fair. It had also started at the Frankfurt Book Fair. It had been very fleeting.

'Look, we haven't even talked about the A. N. Wilson novel yet,' said Sophie Trimbridge. 'I must say, I rather liked it.'

'Can't give a prize to someone with initials,' said Murray promptly. 'Very old-fashioned, very confusing. For years I thought A. S. Byatt was a man.'

'For years I thought A. N. Wilson was a man,' said Peter, and they all laughed except Enid, who said: 'But he is a man.'

'It's a joke, dear,' said Peter, patting her on a hand which was promptly pulled away. Enid looked quickly over to Sophie Trimbridge for unspoken support but Sophie, as usual, was putting her hair in place. Sophie ran a highly regarded television books programme, which meant that it was well thought of but not actually regarded by anyone. To her surprise, Enid got a flashing smile of support, not from Sophie, but from the New Zealander, Murray. She smiled gratefully back. She rather liked the look of Murray who, though only the writer of one novel, was much sought after by the BBC, even if seldom found, as he was usually in the pub.

'I think we have to be sensible about this,' said Murray. 'I think we have to vote for a readable novel, I think we have to vote for a writer who is already respected, and I think we have to vote for a woman, as men have won it for two years running.'

'I think you're talking like a pompous, self-elected chairman,' said Peter. Murray got up. Enid thought for a moment he was going to hit Peter.

'I think it's time for a little drink,' said Murray, ignoring Peter and passing through into the small inner room where the hospitality was kept. Enid went to stand by the window, staring out at the London roof-tops. To her horror, she felt Peter come up behind her.

'I often think of Frankfurt,' said his voice in her ear. Enid, who also thought of Frankfurt but only with disgust, broke away and ran into the inner room to find some sanity. There, to her increasing horror, she saw

Murray deep in an embrace with Sophie Trimbridge, their mouths joined as if both were playing each other like trumpets. They did not notice her. She returned to the main room. Peter grinned.

'I've noticed you making eyes at the little Kiwi. Well, I'm afraid he fancies poor old Sophie, not you. You'll have to make do with me.'

He advanced towards her. Instinctively she picked up the new Iris Murdoch and threw it at him. It was a surprisingly good shot, catching him on the temple and sending him sliding senseless to the floor.

Should she have thrown something lighter, like an Anita Brookner? Has she really killed a fellow judge? And if Peter recovers, will he get his evil way? Don't miss the next exciting instalment of Book Prize!

Welcome To Kington, 1989

A GRAND SLAM

NORTH
♠ A K Q J 10 9 8 7 6 5 4 3 2
WEST
♥ A K Q J 10 9 8 7 6 5 4 3 2
EAST
♦ A K Q J 10 9 8 7 6 5 4 3 2
SOUTH
♣ A K Q J 10 9 8 7 6 5 4 3 2

This unusual hand was recently dealt at a domestic bridge tournament (Mr and Mrs Elkins versus friends) in Slough.

South, who opened the bidding, was tempted to go straight to seven clubs and shout 'Geronimo!' She would certainly have been justified, but after a short strangled silence she decided not to, for two reasons. 1) It would be more fun to work up gradually. 2) She was already prone to overbidding, and this time her partner would think she really had gone round the twist. So she went for the more modest one club.

West for similar reasons went one heart and pinched himself hard. North made a more ambitious asking bid of three spades, which under the Lutomer Convention means: 'Leave this one to me, kid,' and also: 'Is there any more of that excellent white wine?'

When East bid four diamonds, brows were furrowed. West had no diamonds to back East, North could feel his old war wound throbbing dangerously and South did indeed have another bottle of white wine but was loath to admit it. Eventually she went four spades, meaning that there was any amount of cider in the fridge if North could be bothered. West went five hearts and North went to the fridge, where he found the white wine. When he came back he passed, using the Russian Convention to signify that his overall strength was so great he could take out the enemy any time.

East now had a problem. If he made a grand slam in diamonds his partner might overbid on hearts, in which case he would have a coronary. So he went five no-trumps, meaning he was awfully strong in all suits. This was a downright lie, but it seemed a nice idea at the time.

South now went for broke and bid seven clubs, a signal that she really did have a good hand this time, not to mention the corkscrew, and would North *please* not waggle his eyebrows as he normally did when South overbid. West promptly went seven hearts and North, after waggling his eyebrows in an extremely annoying fashion, went seven spades.

This left East with a problem. He had the best hand he was ever likely to have in his life and yet he could not bid his own suit. If he went seven no-trumps, someone else would lead and he would not get a single trick. If he passed, he could only bring North down, and not get a grand slam. In this situation he did the only possible thing: he threw his cards passionately on the floor and started hitting North over the head with a rolled up newspaper.

Play: Everyone showed their one-suit hand. A furious post-mortem ensued, which ended with East and West storming out of the house. North opened the bottle of white wine and got very drunk, while South went to bed in tears.

Moral: Play pontoon with matches for stakes.

Moreover, 1982

WARDROBE ADVENTURES

People are affected in various ways by the Narnia stories. Some people see them as a heart-warming chronicle of the fight of good against evil.

Other people see them simply as a big adventure story.

Lots of people, I have no doubt, see it in the same way that C. S. Lewis himself imagined it, that is, as a Christian allegory of suffering, redemption and triumph.

But my father saw the Narnia saga as something quite different. He saw it as a terrible warning against the things that might happen to you in the back of a wardrobe.

'I've never felt quite the same about wardrobes since reading *The Lion, The Witch and The Wardrobe*,' he admitted to us once when he had just asked one of us to get some tennis shoes from the back of the wardrobe because he would rather not do it himself. 'It was such a terrible shock. One moment you have these not unpleasant children playing around in a strange room, the next moment they are exploring the back of the wardrobe and – bingo! – they find themselves in this dreary world of snow and mock-Christian charade, to which they are condemned for ever to return.'

'I've always quite liked the sound of the place,' said Ralph. 'It may be only mock-Christian, but it's actually more exciting than the Bible.'

'No, I have always hated the sound of Narnia,' said Father stoutly. 'It's always winter there and there's no Christmas. Civilisation is always about to be overturned, and the children always have to become kings and queens to save everything and then wait for a lion to save them, and they always have to go through the back of a wardrobe to get there. It's like a mixture of Norse mythology, the *Just So* stories and the Habitat catalogue. Horrible.'

Well, if you have a phobia and can't get rid of it, you try to come to terms with it, and Father's method of coming to terms with the backs of wardrobes was to limit himself to only taking things out of the front or, if he thought something was at the back, sending someone else in to get it for him.

Mother would always do it for him if she was there, but one day when she was away and he suddenly wanted an old umbrella he seemed to remember having seen in the back of the wardrobe, he sent me in to get it.

'I'll send you in because you're smaller than Ralph. I'll rope you up, of course,' he said.

'Rope me up?'

'Like a mountaineer. I'll tie a rope around your middle and if you get into trouble I'll pull you back.'

I looked at Ralph. He looked at me. It is never too early to start learning to humour older people. Maybe that's what that Commandment about parents should really say. Not 'Honour thy father and mother,' but 'Humour thy father and mother . . .'

So I let him tie some twine round my waist.

'OK,' I said. 'I'll let you know if I'm in trouble.'

'We'll arrange a series of signals,' said my father. 'Pull once for a signal that you've found the umbrella, pull twice to ask to be brought back and pull three times for danger.'

'Hold on a moment!' said Ralph. 'Hold on a moment!'

I thought for a moment that Ralph was going to beg Father not to send me into the wardrobe.

I should have known better.

'Wouldn't it make sense to pull *once* for danger?' said Ralph. 'If he's in danger, he won't have time to pull three times. I mean, if he's being dragged into a frozen world beyond, where rival princes are battling for the rule of their own kingdom against disaffected serfs, or serpents have taken over the normal government and think he looks very tasty, he might only have time to pull once before vanishing, and there we would be, thinking he'd just found the umbrella, whereas in fact he'd been . . .'

Ralph obviously couldn't think of another way of describing my dreadful end.

'That's a good point,' said my father. 'So what shall we do?'

'I've got an idea,' I said. 'I'm only going to be three feet away, behind all these hanging clothes. Why don't I just talk to you?'

'Brilliant!' said my father.

'Let's arrange some signals,' said Ralph. 'If you need help, yell "Help!" If you find more than one umbrella, say "What colour was it?" And if you are dragged away by two men-at-arms who suddenly come through the back of the wardrobe, don't forget to say goodbye.'

'Just get in there and get the umbrella and come out again,' said my father.

So I did go in there and I did for a little while vanish from sight behind the clothes and it was so dark in there that for just a moment I felt scared, but this was quickly replaced by a strong temptation to untie the rope from around my waist and then give a scream and see what Father's reaction was when he pulled quickly at the twine and found nothing at the other end, but I am sorry to say that sense and decency prevailed and I found the umbrella and meekly came out with it.

'See anything?' said Ralph.

'No,' I said.

'No doors opening? No bleak wintry vistas? Nobody asking you to look after their kingdom for five minutes?'

'You may laugh,' said my father, 'but we all have our funny little ways. One day I shall find out what your funny little way is and I shall be sure to make endless fun of you.'

All credit to my father, he did gradually conquer his fear of the backs of wardrobes, though this only extended to the ones he knew well, i.e. the ones in our house. When we stayed with other people or in hotels, I was usually sent for to ferret around in the back of the strange wardrobe, though I only ever once found something out of the ordinary.

This was in a large old-fashioned hotel we spent the night in on the way to Scotland, though which city it was in I have no idea. My parents were in one room, Ralph and I in another (we were still young enough to share, or poor enough to have to share) and before I was even allowed to see our room, I had to go and check the wardrobe in the parental room.

'Do you actually want something out of the back?' I said, 'or is this just to check that it's all right?'

'Just a check,' said my father. 'Just to make sure. You know.'

It was a huge old-fashioned wardrobe, already quite full of pillows and blankets and things, and the back of the wardrobe was so far from the front I couldn't quite see it. While trying to reach it, I stumbled over a pillow and sort of fell against the back of the wardrobe, except that it wasn't the back. It was the wall. The wardrobe seemed to have been built without a back. I felt along the wall and, rather to my amazement, felt a handle in my hand. A door handle.

For a moment the hairs went up on the back of my neck, but then I saw a logical explanation and the hairs all went down again obediently. It was a door. It was the connecting door to the next room, hidden by the wardrobe, which had purposely been placed against it to conceal it. I tried the handle. It worked. The door opened slightly. I peered through the crack. It was another room. There was a person sitting there, looking at me.

'Hello,' said Ralph.

It was our room, next door. I stepped into it, and quietly closed the door behind me.

'Well, well, well, well,' I said. 'Narnia isn't quite what I expected. In fact, it's very like the world I've just come from.'

'Would that be the world of wardrobes?' he inquired.

'It certainly would,' I said. 'A place where cruel fathers send you into dark places to look for they know not what.'

'Talking of fathers,' said Ralph, 'if you've just come through the back of his wardrobe, he'll be coming after you very soon.'

As he said this, we could clearly hear him shout my name. He sounded very worried. He would indeed be coming through any moment.

'Go in the bathroom,' said Ralph. 'Close the door behind you.'

Just as I had obeyed him, I heard my father erupt into the room.

'Where did your brother go?' he shouted.

'I thought he was in your room,' said Ralph. 'Didn't he go in there with you just now?'

'He was there a moment ago, but he came out through the back of the wardrobe through the connecting door into here and . . .'

'Didn't come this way,' said Ralph, 'and I've been here all the time.'

There was an awful pause. My father breathed heavily. Did he believe, just for a moment, that I had been swallowed up into some other space/time/storyboard continuum?

'He must have come through here,' said my father. 'He went into our wardrobe. He didn't come out. I followed him in. This is the only way out.'

'There must be another one,' said Ralph. 'He must have taken another exit, inside the wardrobe.'

My father went silent for a moment, then I could hear him rush back into the wardrobe. The bathroom door opened. Ralph quickly bundled me out, and put me where he had been sitting, then vanished into the bathroom. My father came out again.

'No, there's no . . .' he started and then saw me.

'Hello, Father,' I said. 'Where did you come from?'

'Where's Ralph?' he said, rather wildly.

'I've no idea,' I said. 'I've been here all the time.'

He roared at this and went back into his own room, via the wardrobe.

He never asked me to go into any other piece of furniture after this, nor did he ever refer to the episode again. For my own part, I think this may have been the first time I recognised that Ralph's future really was in the theatre.

Someone Like Me, 2005

OUTSIDE PADDINGTON

As every child knows, space ships can go millions of miles in a few seconds by going into hyperspace; this is done by the captain clenching his knuckles till they are white and then shouting: 'OK – we're going into hyperspace!' A few seconds later everyone is a long way on in the universe and they come out of hyperspace, looking shaken but relieved at the idea of having saved so much fuel.

Something roughly similar happens to trains between Paddington and Bristol. It's on a smaller scale, of course, and rather slower, as the buffet attendant needs time to serve everyone, but nevertheless the general effect is much the same. After Chippenham, the train goes into hyperspace, and people stop looking out of the windows, those slightly smoked Inter-City windows like TVs with bad reception. Just before Old Oak Common after an hour, they come out of hyperspace and realise with a jolt, and a smell of asbestos brake-linings, that they are nearer to Paddington than they thought. Occasionally, but not often, they feel grateful to British Rail.

Henry came out of hyperspace with a jolt and realised they were nearer to Paddington than he had thought. He had spent most of the journey poring over the details of the conference he was attending next day. The man next to him had spent the journey studying a document called 'Draught Cider in Scotland: A Brand Development Market Break-down.' People do funny things in hyperspace. The cider man now jumped to his feet and started getting his coat on, and so did most of the businessmen who took this train, but Henry was too wise an old traveller to fall for that one. Just as the inexperienced air traveller will jump to his feet when the aeroplane comes to a halt and then spend the next ten minutes standing motionless, too proud to sit down again unlike the seasoned traveller who had never got up in the first place, so the novice Inter-City wayfarer will leap to his feet on coming out of hyperspace, unaware that the train always comes to an unexplained halt a mile from the main terminus, and then stays there for ten minutes.

The train had duly come to a stop and stayed there. Henry looked out of the window, through the smokey glass and the greeny-grey dusk. It was one of those odd scenes you sometimes get near the centre of cities, where a large empty space has remained large and empty, apparently unused. If it had been lighter, he could have seen the goal posts spattered across the expanse of Wormwood Scrubs, but now all he could see was the outline of the prison itself. Rather handsome, he thought. It must be nearly a mile away, across the playing fields. The playing fields of Wormwood Scrubs. Wonder what battles were won there?

'I'd sit down, if I were you,' he said to the cider man. 'Could take ages.'

'Yes,' agreed the cider man. He stayed standing.

Henry yawned.

About twenty feet above him, Keith yawned as well.

Henry had no idea that Keith was there.

Keith was standing on a small road bridge crossing the railway. He'd been standing there for about quarter of an hour, waiting for a good train to throw stones at, break the driver's window with any luck. At the age of fourteen, that sometimes seems like a good sort of thing to do, if you don't get caught. Trouble is, all the good trains had been going the wrong way, appearing suddenly from under his feet. The only likely one coming towards him he'd thrown at and missed. It was getting a bit dark, too. And now there was this sodding train stuck still underneath him.

He dropped one stone on the roof of the train, half expecting six policemen to jump out. They didn't. He dropped another. Then another. The next one he threw as hard as he could. Nobody appeared at all.

After the sixth one, Henry said to the cider man: 'Can you hear something?'

The cider man sat down, relieved at the change of subject.

'No,' he said.

'Sort of banging on the roof,' said Henry. 'Listen.'

Up above, Keith started sorting out the bigger stones.

'No,' said the cider man, and opened his report on Scottish draught cider again.

Henry counted eight more bangs, then started having visions of someone on the roof of the train, which was plainly ridiculous. A stowaway from Bristol? Ridiculous. Someone who had got on to the train from the bridge he could just see? Possible, but still ridiculous. Was there perhaps a tiny space between the ceiling and the roof, where a bird had got trapped, a sort of railway attic? Absolutely ridiculous.

'I'm just going to have a look,' said Henry to the cider man. He got up and walked to the nearest automatic door; when it opened, it made the only noise to be heard in the train. He opened the window and stuck his head out.

Keith, ducking down behind the parapet, felt pleased that he had created some effect at last. He went on lobbing stones from out of sight, deriving nearly as much satisfaction from having aroused one man's curiosity as he might have done from derailing a whole express.

However far he stuck his head out, Henry could not even see the roof, let alone anything on it, though he could still hear the strange noise. If only he could stretch out a little further . . . Well, he could. He carefully opened the door and, holding on to the open window quite tightly, gained another couple of feet to narrow the angle of vision. He stretched out in an athletic pose, like Robert Powell in *The Thirty-Nine Steps* or Douglas Fairbanks Jr in . . .

Henry was not expecting the train to start again so suddenly, so when it did, it was hardly surprising that he lost his grip and fell. He braced himself to hit the platform, which was the only thing he had ever landed on from a train. There are no platforms on the Western Region opposite Wormwood Scrubs, so he fell another three or four feet and landed awkwardly on his ankle, then rolled over and lay there helplessly as the train began to accelerate away from him.

The cider man must have seen me, was his first thought. He'll pull the communication cord. Or at least throw a lifebelt.

The cider man did not see me, was his second thought, as the train gathered speed and shrank simultaneously.

My conference notes and clothes are on that blasted train, was his third thought.

His fourth thought, as he got to his feet, was more blasphemous than the previous three. Jesus Christ, my ankle hurts!

He found by experiment that he had not broken it, or even sprained it very badly, just twisted it enough to make sure that he could only put weight on it very fleetingly. He sat down again, to reconsider his position. He was on his way to a conference in London, via Paddington. He had, through no fault of his own, failed to arrive at Paddington by a margin of about a mile. The sensible thing to do, therefore, was to walk on down the tracks to Paddington and run the risk of arriving without a ticket. On the other hand, he reflected with the first smile of the evening, you only need a ticket if you arrive by train. So . . .

A moment later he had sat down again, convinced that it was not after all sensible to walk to Paddington. For one thing, his ankle would not last that far. For another, a train coming out of Paddington had just passed him at such speed and so close, a yellow rattling blur, that he realised walking down the tracks to Paddington was about the most dangerous thing he could do. He had actually been hit by a stone as the train passed, no doubt kicked up by the wheels.

If Henry had thought about it, he would have realised that train wheels do not kick up stones, as they come into contact only with the rails. The stone had in fact been flung by Keith at the driver's cab. He had missed again, and managed only to hit this bloke who for some weird reason had got out of the train. He thought he'd wait for a while and see what the bloke did.

Henry thought he'd sit for a while and think what Robert Powell would do. He could make his way to the edge of the tracks and go across the Scrubs – no, no point, because he'd never walk all that way. So he'd go the other way. He turned round and for the first time studied what lay away from the Scrubs. A wall, as far as he could make out, with trees beyond. That looked all right. Once over the wall, he was bound to be back in civilization. He could cope with things there. Here, he was useless.

For some odd reason, Roy Plomley's voice popped into his mind. What was it he asked his castaways at the end of Desert Island Discs? If you were stranded in the middle of the main line into Paddington, would you try to escape or would you be happy to stay where you were? Well, Roy,

I'd definitely try to escape. I'd walk very carefully over the lines, in case any of them were electrified, and I'd climb the wall over there ...

The lines weren't too hard, despite the local four-coach train that came past when he wasn't ready for it. But the wall was a real bugger. Just too high for him to grab the top of, even if he jumped, which he couldn't do with his ankle. And you're allowed one luxury. What would that be? Well, Roy, I think I'd take a pair of step-ladders. Yes, I think we'll permit that.

Not having a step-ladder, Henry had eventually to make do with a stunted elder bush which British Rail in their wisdom had omitted to root up. Painfully but effectively, Henry clambered up its small branches, and just managed to get his hands on top of the wall. Taking about two minutes to do what Robert Powell would have taken three seconds to do (but I'm doing my own stuntwork, he thought), he hauled himself over and found himself standing on a path which followed the other side of the wall. Between him and the trees lay nothing but a long black road. Sighing with relief, Henry looked both ways – nothing coming – and strode on to the road.

It occurred to him too late that you would never find an unlit road in the middle of London, stretching so straight in either direction. A moment later he was up to his neck in six feet of cold water.

The Grand Union Canal having been in the same position for over a hundred years, you would hardly believe, would you, that there were still some people who were unaware of its existence. Henry was one of those. Having striven so hard to link London to Birmingham with a network of inland waterways, the original engineers would have turned in their grave to realise that their work was still ignored by the public. But Henry's expertise ran chiefly to the effect of refrigeration on dairy products – the subject of next day's debate, as it happened – and canals played little part in the marketing of ice cream.

None of these thoughts ran through Henry's brain as he struck out wildly in the water. He could swim all right, swim quite well in fact, but he had never gone for a bathe in a pin-stripe suit before, and the difference between swimming fully clothed and swimming almost naked is quite appreciable. It now being quite dark, he had thrashed about for a little while before he saw that any progress he was making was along the canal (he recognized the thing he was in for a canal) and, wincing with the pain in his ankle, he changed course for the bank.

The bank he arrived at was not the bank he had set out from. This suited him fine. The further he got from that damned railway, the better. Henry suffered from the peculiarly English habit of blaming British Rail for anything that goes wrong on a train journey, and the fact that British Rail specifically warn travellers not to open windows, let alone doors, on journeys was far from his mind. It even occurred to him fleetingly that he might have here the makings of a fine suit for damages against the said railway company. It would be better, of course, with a witness. He only wished there were a witness.

Keith, crouched motionless on a canal bridge forty feet away, wondered what this crazy bloke would do next.

Henry found that it would be no use walking along the bank he had landed on. In both directions there were huge obstructions of brambles. If he went back across the canal – but he had no intention of doing that. He was already freezing cold from the water. Do you think you would be capable of building some kind of boat or raft? Oh, ha bloody ha, Roy, I'll just stand on my copies of Shakespeare and the Bible, and climb over the next wall.

If you have never explored this particular piece of west London, you will find it hard to believe that Henry could already have suffered these indignities scarcely fitting to the status of a fairly high-up executive in the frozen dairy-product industry. And yet in the midst of life we are in death, or to put it another way, in the midst of a great city we sometimes meet areas which seem as deserted as Newbury Racecourse on a non-racing day, a phenomenon which Henry could have observed some ninety minutes earlier had he not been deep in statistics on ice-cream movement.

But the greatest surprise was yet to come. On the far side of this wall, which Henry managed to negotiate with greater aplomb, perhaps because he was getting practice at his urban assault course, lay the final great obstacle between him and civilization. Kensal Green Cemetery. A vast acreage of tombs and trees, mausolea and mouldering avenues, laid out in the early nineteenth century at a time when a need was felt for a fashionable burial ground which would relieve pressure on London's churchyards and which proved so successful that even one of Queen Victoria's uncles was interred there. Whether the canal or cemetery came first is immaterial to this story (it was, in fact, the canal) but the waterway has always proved an effective southern barrier to this resting place; invasion on other sides has had to be resisted by high walls, higher than the one Henry had just crossed. They are designed on the whole to keep people out. In Henry's case, they were equally effective at keeping him in.

None of this was known to Henry. He did not even know that he was in a cemetery. All he knew was that he seemed to be struggling across some vast orchard (the trees) at about 6.17 on a winter's evening (his waterproof watch) with the distant hum of traffic ahead of him (the Harrow Road). He also knew that he was soaking, freezing, scared, wounded and extremely fed up. Occasionally he stumbled across low objects which he took to be boxes of some kind, but which you and I would call graves.

What struck him most forcibly from time to time was the sheer helplessness of his position. Being disabled and disoriented is bad enough in the country. In the city it robs you of any sense of normality. It cannot happen and yet it has happened. Therefore you feel a kind of underlying panic. Henry felt this rising and told himself sharply that he ought to do something about it.

He realised that his immersion in the canal had put paid to any matches he might have in his pockets, but he suddenly realised that he also had (and for once he was glad he smoked) a lighter, which was unlikely to be affected by the wet. So when he saw a larger than usual shape loom out of the dark, he took out the lighter and lit it.

The mausoleum he had reached had an inscription carved on the side. By the wavering light of his French throwaway machine he made out a few words at a time. 'An officer in the Indian army . . . very gallant . . . his life was tragically cut short . . . on leave in London . . . a wall fell on him in Paddington . . .'

Jesus, thought Henry. Jesus wept. Where am I? Jesus. Jesus wept. He struck the light again.

His life was tragically cut short. A wall. In Paddington. Fell on him.

Henry took a step and his ankle at last gave way. He fell over and lay, sobbing a little. Oh, Jesus. Surely this was all a bad dream? In a moment he would wake up. He'd wake up in his nice Inter-City coach, studying his conference notes. This wasn't happening to him, was it? Come on, one big effort, and you'll wake up from your dream. Come on!

He gradually became aware that there was a banging noise on the outside of the train. He must have dropped off. As he came back to consciousness, he heard the banging noise going on. He shook his head and tried to work out where he was.

There was a porter knocking at the window. He must be in the station. Yes, he recognized it. It was Paddington. He must have fallen asleep on the final run-in.

'Come on, mate – we need this train!' shouted the porter. 'You arrived twenty minutes ago, and we're shunting out now. Off with you!'

He stood up, still dizzy with sleep, and collected his conference brochure. 'Draught Cider in Scotland: A Brand Development Market Breakdown.' He looked, puzzled, at the other well-bound dossier still lying on the table. He turned it round towards him. It was called: 'Long-Distance Dairy Products Movement: A Feasibility Study.' Not his. It must have belonged to that other bloke. Funny that he should have left it behind like that.

'Hey, mister!' said Keith. 'Mister? Mister! Wake up, mister! Mister? Are you all right, mister? Oh, Jesus . . .'

London Tales, 1983

THE THIRTY BEST
EXCUSES FOR NOT
ATTENDING A DINNER PARTY

I am/we are not able to accept your invitation:

1. Due to fear of flooding
2. Because of a terracotta-soldier-related injury
3. Due to a difference of opinion with the Northern Rock Mortgage Society
4. After a crucial revelation made by my recently rediscovered birth mother
5. Because of the unfortunate recent outcome of a Nigel Slater-related recipe
6. As our astrologer has advised us not to make any outings after dusk while Saturn is in conjunction with another planet whose name we did not quite catch
7. After having decided to place a great deal of money on a horse tipped to win by the 'Today Programme' on Radio 4, unfortunately ignoring the sardonic laughter with which John Humphrys greeted this particular recommendation
8. Due to injuries received during a heated Trivial Pursuits post-mortem
9. Having failed to listen in detail to all the instructions given by the pilot during a recent hot air balloon flight
10. Due to a stomach ailment picked up from licking over a hundred postage stamps while sending off invitations to next month's local garden fete held in aid of the Scilly Isles Olympic Games team fund-raising drive

11. As we have meanwhile had a better dinner party offer

12. Because we have recently discovered that our two children have been so much in the company of our Polish nanny, Anna, that they can now speak perfect Polish but barely any English and consequently need emergency remedial action

13. Due to widespread fears of a malaria outbreak in our part of the world following an article in a Sunday paper

14. Because of next week's announcement by Gordon Brown

15. Due to an unexpected legal condition imposed on us as part of a bequest to us in Anita Roddick's will

16. Due to an unfortunate result in one of the recent Rugby World Cup matches

17. Because of stringent dietary requirements following a recent sex change operation which did not go quite according to plan

18. Having not been able full to understand some ethnic jargon during a recent mugging

19. After getting embroiled in disputes over the publication rights of our forthcoming Christmas round robin letter

20. Due to a rescheduled divorce

21. Following a desperate phone call for help from Menzies Campbell which we do not think it would be right to ignore

22. Because of the eclipse in Indonesia

23. Because of Act of Richard Dawkins

24. Due to kidney turbigo failure

25. Due to death of family pet

26. Due to misdiagnosis in hospital

27. Due to our postcode being broken into by hackers

28. Due to the sudden arrival of those people we met on holiday in the Auvergne

29. Due to emergency road works

30. Deutoronomy

Independent, 2007

NATIONAL POETRY DAY

What is National Poetry Day?
Well, it's a fairly crafty way
Of getting poetry to sell
So those who write it can live well.

Is there a National Poetry Night?
Oh, yes, when poets all get tight
Drinking away the profits they
Have made on National Poetry Day.

Don't poets scrimp and save as well?
Of this they are incapable.
A poet has no earthly intention
Of saving for an old age pension.
He'd rather go out to the bar
And spend it on another jar.

But what is National Poetry Day FOR?
Who thought of it? And was he sure
That anyone would willingly
Rally round for poetry?
If it's National Poetry Day
Why don't people block our way
Shaking tins and begging alms,
Saying: 'Give freely for poetry's charm!'
Why not have a PROPER day,

With flags and stickers given away
To put upon our outer clothes
Saying: 'Poetry – not Prose!'?
Well, poets do not work like that.
They're always thin and never fat.
They never make a savings plan,
Except perhaps John Betjeman,
And if they get a Nobel Prize
Just see the horror in their eyes.
Poets never plan ahead.
Sometimes they don't get out of bed.

But why a day for Poetry?
Why not for Biography?
Why not a National day for novels,
When novelists creep from out their hovels
And crave a general benediction
On the art of writing fiction?
Because, my child, a novelist knows
That maturity comes with writing prose
But poets are wet behind the ears
And young at heart, if not in years.
If a poet reached maturity
He wouldn't be writing poetry . . .
And so he likes the jollity
Of having a day for poetry.
It's party time for poets, you see,
Balloons on the gate and jelly for tea!

But what is Poetry anyway?
Well, poetry is a special way
Of saying very special thoughts,
Of love and death, and other sorts,
Which writers often like to use
When prose is not quite right to choose.

They like to wrap their thoughts in verse
To make them snug and tight and terse.
And if they write their poetry well
Their little booklets start to sell,
And then it's poetry recitals
- Where they can sell their latest titles -
Because doing poetry on the stage
Pays more than the printed page.
They then turn into household names
Like Cope, McGough and P.D.James ...

Does P.D.James write poetry?
No, but at least she rhymes, you see.

Does poetry always have to rhyme?
Not always, but there comes a time
When they are tired of liberty
And they would really like to see
If they can still do rhyming stuff ...

OK, OK. That's quite enough.
So now it's National Poetry Day,
How can I help in my own way?
Shall I go out and write some verse?
Dear God! No, that would make things worse.
There's far too much of the stuff around,
Even stuck up in the Underground.
For Poetry Day I want you to say:
'I won't write any poetry today ...'

Independent, 2000

HISTORY OF KING TONY

or *Labour's Lost, Love*

ACT I

*Scene: a battlefield in a marginal part of the Midlands. Enter King Tony
with his victorious forces, attended by Dukes Prescott, Cook, Mandelson etc.
Lord Livingstone stands off to one side, plotting.*

Prescott: See how the Tories flee the field in panic!
This once proud army has become a rabble.
Their shattered troops now barely have the strength
To undertake five years of opposition!
King Tony: Nay, say not five! Say ten! Say fifteen years!
For who can stop our royal progress now?
Will it be William, Duke of Hague, whose cheeks
Do not yet know the razor's manly touch?
Lord Banks: Nay, for he is but an unborn babe in shape.
And they are led by nothing but a foetus!

All laugh, save King Tony.

King Tony: Lord Banks, Lord Banks, this is no way to speak.
The rough and rugged talk of barrack room
May well suit men upon the battlefield,
But now that we have won this famous day,
We are the leaders! We have come to reign!
And therefore must be seen and heard by all
To be right statesmanlike and noble.

Lord Banks: So, no more gaffes?
King Tony: No, none. And no more going
Upon the 'News Quiz' as you were wont to do.
Lord Banks: Alas, for that gave useful pocket money,
Even if I was not always very funny.

Enter the Earl of Ashdown, with his band of men.

Ashdown: King Tony! All hail! A famous victory
That you and I have won this day against the Tories!
See them run to London's crowded City,
To take up safe directorships in town,
Till your new windfall tax shall bring them down!
King Tony: What say you, Ashdown? OUR victory?
We did not fight together on the field!
My men, unaided, beat the enemy,
Under New Labour's flag of change and trust!
We took no help from you, nor have done yet.
Ashdown: So, no seat for me in your new cabinet?
King Tony: I have not seats enough for my own gallant men
Who stuck by me through all the fallow years
When New Labour languished in the wilderness!
Brave Cook! Stout Prescott! Straw and Mandelson!
These are the men I have about me now!
Gone are the years of foul and Tory sleaze!
God give me honest comrades such as these!

Enter a man dressed all in a white suit.

Martin Bell: Beware, your Majesty, of boasts of virtue,
Wherein you paint yourself as better far
Than those poor nullities who came before.
Beware the day when such as your friend Straw
Shall have a son whose smoking finds him out.
Beware the day when e'en the Duke of Cook

Shall try to fix his friend, the lovely Gaynor,
With jobs that look most strangely like a favour.
Beware, beware, the pride that comes with power!
Be humble in your most exalted hour!

Exit the man in white.

King Tony: Who was that man, who looked me in the eye
And did not bend the knee in reverence?
Mandelson: They call him Martin Bell, good sir. He walks alone.
Much foreign fighting has he seen and, so they say,
It hath made him mad. But worry not,
For I shall find some defect in his legal costs
To make him seem as venal as the rest.
King Tony: Good Mandelson, go spin the truth for me,
And tell the world about our victory.
Now, gentles all, let's to the victory feast
And drink the toast: Old Labour, Now Deceased!

Independent, 1998

THE UNITED DEITIES

Time for a visit to the United Deities, that ecumenical gathering of gods past and present, to see what they are thinking about us up in Heaven. Here are some of the minutes from their current session . . .

1 The Chairgod called the meeting to order and asked Thor to put down his hammer. He said that the first item on the agenda was a request from an unnamed Japanese God to clarify the meaning of fundamentalism.

2. The Chairgod said that if words had any meaning at all, fundamentalism meant getting back to the basics. Humanity seemed to think that all beliefs were pure and good in their early days, and got choked up with sophistication and clutter as time went on, and that now and then it was good to clear away the undergrowth and get back to the original patterns.

3. This often took the form of getting back to the original holy writings of a religion.

4. The Catholic God said that if this was applied to any other branch of human study, there would be uproar. Did scientists ever go back to the original writings of Isaac Newton for enlightenment? Would farmers benefit from going back to Virgil's *Georgics*? Would a fundamentalist historian prefer Herodotus?

5. Why was everything old in religion thought to be better than everything new?

6. The Jewish God said that this was not in fact so. The Christians thought that the New Testament was better than the Old Testament. In his opinion, they were wrong, but that was what they thought.

7. As a matter of interest, said the Chairgod, what did the Jews think of the New Testament?

8. They didn't think about it at all, said the Jewish God. It was irrelevant to them. It was like an unnecessary sequel to *Gone With the Wind* or something. The Old Testament was good enough for them.

9. And the Jews didn't even call it the Old Testament. They called it the Torah. And it was so difficult to understand that they had a whole other book called the Talmud which Jews said explained the Torah to them.

10. Well, it was a bit the same with Islam, said Allah. The Koran was the holy book, but it was too hard to get into for most Muslims, so there were a whole host of commentaries on the Koran which people consulted instead.

11. Zeus said he could not understand this fixation with holy books. He said that one of the great things about the Greek religion had been that there were no sacred writings at all. There were lots of great stories which people told each other, but none of this stifling mountain of scholarship and critical footnotes.

12. The Jewish God said that Zeus should not knock holy books till he had tried them, and that if there had been holy Greek books, maybe people would still believe in the Greek Gods.

13. Zeus said maybe, but at least it meant there weren't people charging round slaughtering each other in the name of ancient Greek fundamentalism. You could publish a cartoon of Zeus doing the most awful things, and nobody would burn down the Greek embassy anywhere.

14. The Chairgod asked if Zeus was saying that the only good religion was a dead religion. That seemed a bit defeatist.

15. Zeus said that maybe monotheism was to blame. If you only had Jesus as a figurehead, or the prophet Mohammed, or Jehovah, and you had therefore put all your eggs in one basket, you would naturally get upset if people attacked your figurehead. But if you had a spread portfolio of Gods, as the Greeks had, and as Hinduism still had, it would be harder to upset anyone by attacking one out of many Gods.

16. He could not imagine a cartoon of Ganesh leading to riots in India.

17. The Jewish God said that, with respect, an elephant-headed God did look a bit like a cartoon already.

18. Ganesh himself said that he resented that, but that he forgave him.

19. The Jewish God said he was welcome.

20. The Chairgod asked the Japanese God if he was any closer to understanding fundamentalism.

21. The Japanese God said he was not, and that listening to the discussion he had lost the will to find out.

22. The Chairgod said that they should move on to the next item, which was a proposal to throw a special party for Gaia, the Greek earth Goddess.

Independent, 2006

FATHER GIVES A SEX TALK

'There are four steps in sex education,' said my father suddenly to me one day as we were trying to design a new, improved bicycle saddle together. 'First, you discard all the gooseberry bush and stork nonsense and learn all about where babies really come from. Second, you realise one day that if that is where babies come from then your parents must at some remote time in the past have had sex together. And third, that means that at some remote time in the past your parents must, incredible as it may seem, have found each other attractive enough to have sex with.'

I had already passed through these three stages in sex education, though not entirely thanks to my father.

'What is the fourth stage?' I asked.

'The fourth stage is coming to the dreadful realisation that maybe those times are not so remote and maybe it is just possible that your parents still find each other attractive enough to occasionally have sex together.'

My father had always taught me to be honest about these things.

'And do you still?'

'I think so,' said my father, with the hint of a blush. 'You had better ask your mother. She has a better memory about these things than I have.'

I made a mental note to do this, when I felt strong enough.

'What is the fifth stage in sex education?'

'Did I say there was a fifth stage in sex education?'

'No, but you once taught me that in every sequence of events, there is always one more event than the experts suspect. It was your missing planet theory.'

'Was it?'

'Yes. You said that however well we explain the motion of the planets, there is always some discrepancy in the calculations and it is always easier to account for this by putting it down to the effect of a missing planet than to do the calculations all over again.'

'Did I?'

'Yes. And you also observed that, more often than not, a missing planet did eventually turn up.'

'How extremely clever of me. I must make a note of that.'

There was a pause.

'So, what is the fifth stage in sex education?'

'The fifth stage in sex education,' said my father, 'is for parents to realise that their children realise that their parents still find each other attractive enough to have a sex life and to send the child off to the other parent if he wants any further information.'

That seemed to be that, so we went back to the job of redesigning the bicycle saddle. This was the result of one of my father's theories, namely that while it was quite possible to invent things which had never existed before, such as the stapler to replace the paper clip, it was equally possible to reinvent things which already existed but in a much better form.

'Look at chairs,' said my father. 'People are constantly coming up with new kinds of chairs which are better for you to sit on. But that's mainly because the ordinary kind is so bad. Chairs in the past have been made almost entirely for the convenience of the maker, not the sitter, resulting in thousands of bent spines and generations of bad postures. I predict that in the future chairs will undergo revolutionary change as we find that we have been sitting wrong all these years. Same thing with cooking. All cookery books are about how to make food taste nice. They are never about whether the food is good for you or not. I wouldn't be surprised if one day cooks don't start making a fortune out of recipes, and new foods, that taste dull, horrible even, but are terribly good for you.'

'Where do bicycle saddles come into all this?'

'Ah. Now, the bicycle has always been a very simple design. Once they figured out that the penny-farthing was a terrible mistake and that it was much more sensible to have two wheels the same size, they got the basic bicycle design worked out in Victorian days – gears, brakes, etc – and it has never really changed much since. And one of the things that has never changed very much is the saddle, which, as we all know from experience, is a lot harder to sit on than the average chair.'

It was true. I hadn't really thought about it before. A bike saddle is a hard bit of leather, about the size and shape of an upside-down steam iron, though slightly contoured. The area-to-weight ratio is truly grim. Every square inch of saddle bears nearly a stone. The same goes for each square inch of your bum in contact with the saddle. If it's not much fun for the saddle, how much less so is it for the rider? No wonder it chafes and rubs and numbs and anaesthetises...

(I didn't think of any of this at the time. It was my father who said all this. But when it's you who are writing the story, you can often seem much wiser than you really are by repeating other people's words as if they were your own.)

'The one great achievement of the bicycle saddle was to introduce equality of the sexes,' continued my father. 'It had never really happened with horse riding. It apparently seemed not right and proper for a woman to spread her legs across a horse because it suggested that they might spread their legs at other times, so women were made to keep their legs together and ride side-saddle. What a palaver! How can you ride side-saddle efficiently? You can't grip properly, you can't balance properly, you can't get any decent speed without falling off. No wonder horse-riding accident and death statistics were twice as bad for women as men in Victorian times!'

'Were they really?'

'I'd be surprised if they weren't,' he said, which meant he didn't know.

'Anyway, Victorian women were incredibly lucky that they weren't made to ride bicycles side-saddle as well, but I suppose the earliest manufacturers realised that even if they wanted to there was no way they could design a bike to be ridden sideways on. You can get away with sitting sideways on a horse, but a bicycle *has* to be ridden with central weight distribution. So far, so good.

'The amazing thing to me is that, even when they had decided against bicycling side-saddle, still nobody designed a different saddle for women. After all, men and women are shaped quite differently at that point where saddle meets body, aren't we? Know what I mean?'

'Well . . .'

I hesitated. I hadn't been aware that women's bottoms were shaped differently from men's.

'Here's a book that explains it very well. Take it away and have a good look at it. Afterwards you can ask me any questions you may have.'

And he put a book in my hand and ushered me out of his workroom. Later, I looked at the book. It was called *The Basis of a Happy Marriage*. The basis of a happy marriage? Was this something to do with bicycling expeditions in the country? I opened it. It was full of diagrams of human genitalia. Some were male, some were unfamiliar to me and therefore presumably female. Generally, they were pictured singly, but sometimes they seemed to be deep inside each other.

I closed it, swallowing hard. I had expected some kind of discussion of bicycle design. What I hadn't expected was a no-holds-barred demonstration of sexual techniques, which is what I had got. It was a fearful gear change for a young lad to experience.

I did read the book, of course, and it was actually quite a good book. It was the sort of book that might have been written by a visitor from Mars. It explained all the physiological reactions of our bodies during sex. It explained some things which I had never understood and put me right over other things which I thought I had understood. It also said there was no harm in masturbation, which was a great relief as I could see that that was something I was probably going to be stuck with for a long time, though the book did not give any particular advice or hints on how to masturbate with style, which was a shame.

The main achievement of the book, though, was to devote 200 pages to the act of sex without once making you anxious to try it. Perhaps that was what my father had intended. To put me off the whole idea.

The next time I was in his workroom he asked me, without looking at me, if I had looked at the book. I said I had.

'Good!' he said. 'Then you will now appreciate even more than before the problems of trying to design a unisex bike saddle. Men have external genitalia to accommodate. Women do not. You would think that they would have to have different saddles. But they do not. Our saddles are always the same thin triangle, sometimes so thin that they are hardly a triangle, pretty uncomfortable for both sexes, and I firmly believe that the reason for this design is the reluctance of the first Victorian saddle builders to face up to the differences between the sexes. Poor chaps! What could they do about it? They were probably mechanics in workshops in the Midlands, good at making things and yet totally ignorant of the female form, which in those days was swathed under acres of clothes. The only way a bike mechanic could have done research into the female body was by going to an art gallery, finding a nude female statue and taking measurements, and then getting arrested. I suspect that, rather than take that risk, they decided to just make a common saddle for everyone. If the bike saddle is thin and Spartan for both sexes it seems to have solved the problem. But it has not! It has merely shelved it.'

'Father,' I said, 'when you lent me that book, was that designed to replace our sex talk? Is that the nearest I get to learning about sex from you?'

'And so,' said my father, 'we must think of a revolutionary solution to the saddle problem. We must start again from scratch. We must rethink from the ground up.'

It was useless trying to get my father to discuss something if he wanted to talk about something else. I knew he would return to the subject sooner or later, as soon as he had formulated a reply.

'So, come on!' he said. 'Let's go and pay a visit to Farmer Dutton!'

'Why Farmer Dutton?'

'Because any farmer will do but he is the nearest.'

'The one thing that unites all farms, big or small,' said my father as we drove there in our car, 'is that a farmer can never bear to throw anything away. When something goes wrong with a bit of machinery he buys a new one and keeps the old one, intending to mend it, though he never does. When something gets clapped out he keeps it for spare parts. Tools, bags, implements, rolls of piping . . . Somewhere in every farm you will find a graveyard of old things stashed away, unmended and forgotten. A treasure trove. That's why rural museums are overflowing with ancient things. They've got them that very morning fresh from the farm.'

And sure enough, when we got to the farm, my father muttered something to Mr Dutton who nodded and took us round to a yard at the back which not only had all the items mentioned above but also a caravan that nobody used any more, an ancient plough and a rusting sports car. It wasn't any of these that they headed for, however, but an old tractor which Mr Dutton immediately got to work on, unbolting the tractor seat and handing it over to my father.

'If ever you decide to get the tractor going again, you can have the seat back at once,' said my father.

'Not much fear of that,' said Mr Dutton.

'That's what I thought,' said my father.

On the way back I asked him why he wanted a tractor seat.

'Well, it's only an experiment,' he said, 'but I thought we might try the world's first comfortable bicycle seat and see what happens.'

Enlightenment struck. He was going to try screwing a tractor seat on to a bike! After enlightenment there swiftly came feelings of scorn and then embarrassment.

'Father! You can't put a tractor seat on a bike! It would look ridiculous!'

'Only because we are used to the present ridiculous object called a bike saddle.'

'But . . .'

'Don't be blinkered by your prejudices, child,' he said. 'We have already established in principle that, when bicycling, the human body rests on far too narrow a shelf or cliff ledge. In principle, it makes sense to widen that cliff ledge. Or shelf. You have agreed with that principle. Now, when I am turning the principle into fact, you are growing nervous. But you can only find out if something works by trying it! Benjamin Franklin must have looked ridiculous flying a kite in a thunderstorm, but did that deter him from inventing the lightning conductor?'

Well, we did fix the tractor seat to a bicycle and it was indeed incredibly comfortable and suitable for lady or gent alike and nobody laughed at us in the street when we rode past on it, for the simple reason that when you sit on a tractor seat you more or less cover it and very few people realise you are sitting on one. No, on comfort grounds it was fine. Where it failed was on mechanical grounds. In order to absorb the shock of passing over bumps and rocks, a tractor seat is made springy and bendy.

When you're riding a bike, you need something absolutely firm to push against so that you can drive the pedals round. If a tractor driver had to pedal his tractor he wouldn't have a soft seat. So the tractor seat turned out to be fine for tractors, not so fine for bicycles. And because your legs were moving up and down they rubbed against the front of the seat, which then had to be cut away.

I once rode down to the local shop on our tractor-bike. I locked it up and left it outside. When I came out ten minutes later, there was a crowd of at least a dozen people staring silently at the bicycle-with-a-tractor-seat. I unlocked it and rode away, still surrounded by that unsettling silence.

I am sure you don't want to hear any more about a failed bicycle seat design. I certainly don't. What you want to know more about is my sex education. That's what I would want to know more about if I were you.

Someone Like Me, 2005

LET'S PARLER FRANGLAIS!

AU TEST MATCH

1er Monsieur: Sorry que je suis late. Vous avez vu un riveting morning's play?

2ème Monsieur: Non. Il y a eu le delay pour rain. Puis la pitch inspection. Puis le conferring des umpires. Puis la visite de la Queen, et le départ de la Queen. Puis le tossing du vieux half crown. Puis le picking up du half crown.

1er Monsieur: Puis un sensational opening stand?

2ème Monsieur: Non. Puis lunch taken early. Maintenant on fait le to-and-fro avec le heavy roller. Mais je vois les teams qui sortent du pavilion, dans un petit drizzle qui fait splish-splash sur leurs safety helmets.

1er Monsieur: Ah! Et les fielders, est-ce qu'ils courent, crient, chantent, célèbrent, cartwheelent et calypsonnent!?

2ème Monsieur: Pas exactement. Ils frottent leurs mains pour encourager la circulation.

1er Monsieur: Et qui va ouvrir le batting? Hadlee, peut-être? Ou Radley?

2ème Monsieur: Non, c'est Madleigh, le jeune Derby opener et Sadly, le Somerset tout-rondeur, avec Tradly à numéro trois. Je prévois deux heures de careful stone-walling, suivi par un swift collapse.

2ème Monsieur: Mais vous êtes pessimiste. Le cricket, c'est une gripping bataille intellectuelle! C'est un five-day chess match! C'est un enthralling, blow-by-blow, supremacy-type situation!

2ème Monsieur: Vous ne seriez pas un Radio 3 commentateur, par hasard?

1er Monsieur: Ah, Badlee va ouvrir le bowling.

2ème Monsieur: Avec un troisième homme profond . . .

1er Monsieur: Un mid-off stupide . . .

2ème Monsieur: Treize slips . . .

1er Monsieur: Et un floppy white sweater. Il s'approche, avec ce long loping stride . . . il accélère . . . ses pieds battent la terre comme un mad drummer . . . il passe l'umpire à 180 mph!

2ème Monsieur: Il bowle à 230 mph!

1er Monsieur: La balle hurtle à 460 mph! C'est un blur de rouge!

2ème Monsieur: C'est comme un shooting star!

1er Monsieur: Ou le bullet d'un assassin!!

2ème Monsieur: Mais Madleigh la pousse défensivement à mid-off . . .

1er Monsieur: Fadley fait le pick-up . . .

2ème Monsieur: Et la retourne au bowler.

1er Monsieur: Maintenant la pluie commence à tomber en earnest et tous les players laissent le field comme l'armée italienne. Still, c'était terrific stuff pendant que ça durait, n'est-ce pas?

2ème Monsieur: Non. Moi, je vais au cinéma.

1er Monsieur: Moi aussi.

Let's Parler Franglais, 1979

THE BURMA ROAD

Every capital in the Third World seems to have one hotel that is pointed out proudly as a relic of former grandeur, which is to say colonial days. I have never been to Singapore or Cairo, but the names of Raffles and Shepheards Hotels are well known to me. In Rangoon, capital of Burma, the equivalent is the Strand Hotel and a lovable old place it is too, but I hope for their sake that Raffles and Shepheards are in better nick than the Strand.

My bath was palatial, but there was only two hours of hot water a day. The bedroom was so long that the three lamps in the ceiling cast pools of yellow light which did not join up; walking down the room at night was a bit like going along a badly lit main road. When I asked a girl at reception if I could phone up to one of the second-floor rooms, she confessed: 'It is much quicker if you walk up and knock on your friend's door.'

The effect was that of a stately home whose family have fallen on bad times. There just wasn't enough money. The bar was spacious but the drinks you wanted were not always available. And yet the whole thread-bare service was maintained with great charm and a complete lack of guilt. The Burmese hate saying 'No'. They hate it so much that they do not have a word for 'No', which means that when you ask a barman for a beer he does not say, 'I have no beer'; he says, 'The beer is not here yet,' or, 'What I would suggest instead of beer is . . .' and you take it without feeling deprived or disappointed.

And there are unexpected bonuses. Every evening at 6 o'clock a man came to play the piano in the large hall, and what he played was Burmese music. Now, the piano is not a Burmese instrument and it is totally unsuited to Burmese music, which has no harmony to speak of – only melody and rhythm. If you play two notes at the same time on a piano, you have harmony. This pianist did *not* play two notes at the same time; he played long streams of notes very fast to give a shimmering, impressionistic effect, like Debussy at speed, or perhaps on speed.

I saw him as a kind of symbol of Burma. In any other country I know, that man would have been playing more or less debased cocktail music, but the Burmese don't make many concessions to the West. They are among the last people to resist trousers – it is still very rare to find a Burmese male wearing anything but the loose sarong called the *longyi* – and a man wearing a longyi and playing Burmese music in the foyer of the Strand Hotel seemed to me to represent a country which was not too bothered about jeans and rock 'n' roll.

Don't stay longer than you have to in Rangoon, they told me. Get your black market money and off you go. There are some staggering pagodas in Rangoon, but it's a depressing place when you think what it used to be like. Used to be the Harrods of the East, they say, a shopping centre like Bangkok or Singapore today. Now, there's nothing worth buying at all.

So you seek out the black market to get your 36 kyats to the US dollar instead of the official 6 (actually, the black market seeks *you* out as you leave the Strand Hotel and says, 'Hey, mister – got any dollars?') and then you go to the station to start the journey northwards.

The train for Prome leaves two hours late. Nobody seems surprised. We travel through hour after hour of countryside which manages to be lush and arid at the same time – the train raises dust going through villages bright with flowers and loud with dogs, at that respectable speed which allows you to put your head out of the window without being deafened, blown away or hit by a bridge. Water buffalo lumber about, young rice grows piercingly green, and on almost every rise there is the curve of a *stupa*, that licked vanilla-ice-cream shape peculiar to Buddhism. For an hour it is enchanting, but after three hours it becomes boring, so I retreat to my seat with my book because this train has something I've never seen in my life before: a travelling librarian. He hands out books for a small fee and collects them before the end of the journey. But they are all in Burmese except for a stray copy of *Wuthering Heights*.

'Do you have any other English books?' I ask.

'Yes.'

'What are they?'

'*Wuthering Heights*.'

'They are all *Wuthering Heights*?'

'Yes. It is very popular.'

That is not quite the whole story, I learn later. In fact, *Wuthering Heights* is the prescribed book for English students that year, and the Burmese book industry has risen to the occasion by producing several different editions, all annotated and all with the text considerably pruned. The cover artists do not seem to be familiar with the look of Victorian Yorkshire, as they all feature thatched cottages, smiling landscapes and girls in jeans with blonde hair and ponies. The copy I buy has also a few poems by Alexander Pope, including the one starting, 'Happy the man, who free from care . . .' The editor explains that Pope is lauding the simple English farmer content with his small herd of water buffaloes.

Apart from their Brontë production, the Burmese book trade seems to have no interest in foreign titles. I looked vainly for George Orwell's *Burmese Days*, his first novel based on his three years in the Burma Police. I gave up when a Burmese writer quietly took me aside and explained that, as Orwell had made it quite plain in the book that he liked neither the British nor the Burmese, they had preferred to return the compliment. The book was not actually banned, more forgotten.

So apart from Orwell's unread first novel, Burma has nothing except Kipling's poem 'Mandalay', and that, as befits a poem written after a couple of days in Rangoon, is riddled with mistakes.

On the road to Mandalay,
Where the flyin' fishes play,
An' the dawn comes up like thunder
Outer China 'crost the bay!

China is hundreds of miles away, the dawn doesn't come up over the bay, there are no flying fishes . . . But one thing Kipling got right: the road to Mandalay is the River Irrawaddy. I was going to Prome to get to the Irrawaddy.

[. . .]

The days, seven of them, came and went. There was not much sailing at night, unless we were hurrying for a destination – then the captain would switch on a huge searchlight, the beam of which he swivelled from one bank to the other while it attracted huge crowds of insects. In the morning, most of them lay in a sad, grey pyramid below the light, burnt to death. If it is possible to get an idea of timelessness in seven days, then a boat on the Irrawaddy is the ideal place to get it. Not only does the clock seem suspended, not only is there nothing to do, not only are you surrounded by people staring into space, but you are cut off from the riverbank world, the real world, the world of clocks, calendars and timetables.

You also pass the most timeless place I have ever seen: Pagan. I have been lucky enough to visit a few of the world's great temple sites – Petra, Machu Picchu, Stonehenge, St Peter's – but this is the one. What makes it unique is that this plain was once the site of a great city studded with temples, five miles across. The capital, for once, did not move for over two hundred years and in that time they built huge temples out of glittering white stone and deep glowing brown brick, rising out of what must have been the Rome of the East. But when in our Middle Ages there was an invasion by Kubla Khan, the Burmese king simply turned tail and fled. The city was abandoned, and slowly all the houses, shops and palaces – made of wood – disappeared.

But all the stone and brick temples survived, and most of them still stand, like precious stones on a necklace from which the string has rotted.

[...]

As the boat goes up-river again from Pagan the pagoda count seems to increase, and it rises to a great frenzy a mile or two before Mandalay; the establishment of one of the great holy places there has covered the hills on the left-hand bank with domes like a prize-winning display of meringues. The first sight of Mandalay itself is quite different: a waterfront full of dilapidated jetties and decrepit-looking boats, dusty and down-at-heel.

But once past the shabby waterfront Mandalay emerges as a city of green and leafy charm, a huge garden suburb awash with bicycles. As a farewell present, U Thein San (my guide) introduced me to his cousin and arranged for me to borrow his bike to get around Mandalay. Cousin Jimmy was a sad-faced man who, like many Burmese, had a factory in his house. It was a cigar factory – in other words a small summerhouse in which three very old ladies rolled large cigars very slowly and patiently out of tobacco leaf that looked like thin and not very clean dishcloths. Jimmy presented me with one of these cigars, and from the wrapping I learnt that they had carried off a silver medal at a tobacco contest in Hyderabad in the 1930s. I fear they have not won many prizes since. Mrs Jimmy, a jolly, laughing woman, also had a factory, or rather a schoolroom for teaching English to tiny tots, and in my honour she got them to sing 'London's Burning'.

'You know that cricket is banned in Burma?' said a professor at the university, apparently totally irrelevantly.

'I didn't know it was played here, let alone banned,' I said.

'Only the Indians play it here. That's why the Old Man banned it,' he said, twinkling.

The Old Man is General Ne Win. In 1987 there was no sign yet of the popular unrest which would sweep Burma in 1988 and then recede, leaving things apparently much as before. Still in power behind the scenes is the remote figure whose twenty years of patient stewardship had brought the country from comparative prosperity and optimism to near-bankruptcy. People talked about him with the hopelessness and familiarity with which Russians discuss shortages or the British discuss the weather. They never referred to him as Ne Win, only by circumlocutions like the Old Man, but many stories circulated of the things he had banned in a fit of pique. Gambling, horse-racing, social dancing, cricket, any restaurant staying open after 9 p.m., the teaching of English in schools . . .

'About dancing,' said the professor, 'the story is that one New Year's Eve the Old Man was kept awake by the noise of a party at a nearby hotel. About 1 a.m. he suddenly interrupted into the party, told the band to stop, ordered everyone to go home and decreed, almost as an afterthought, that there should be no more dancing in Burma. The teaching of English he banned, I think, because he wanted to keep Burma purer. It did the country great harm.'

'Why did he restore it?'

'Oh, that was a personal whim as well. His daughter wanted to go abroad to study, but she was not accepted at the colleges of her choice because she could not speak English, due to her father's own policy. So he rescinded it. Bit late in the day for her, though.'

Great Journeys, BBC, 1989

ADVERTISEMENT

When did you last think about rain?

Yes, that's right. Rain. The wet stuff that falls from the sky and later clears from the west. The liquid that comes in under doors or on dogs and cats. The magic stuff that makes taxis impossible to find. The only thing that can make cricketers run.

Rain.

Odds are you haven't thought about it for years, if ever. And even if you did, you thought to yourself: 'Oh God, it's raining again.'

We don't blame you. We'd like you to take rain for granted. Because that means we at the British Rain Bureau are doing our job properly.

What worries us (and we would be less than human if it didn't) is people who seem to think that one kind of rain is much like another. You couldn't be wronger! Drop for drop, British rain is the best in the world.

All right, so it isn't the most sensational in the world. There's nothing in Britain to rival the monsoons of India or the dramatic hurricanes of America. We can't rival those places in the world where the heavens majestically open and a sheet of water falls, until high streets are 6 ft deep in it and people go upstairs just to avoid drowning. There are no rain forests here and no raging torrents. Not even much in the way of rapids.

But would we really want things to be that way?

We at the British Rain Bureau think people would rather have rain that was dependable, regular and reliable. Rain that was soft and friendly. Rain you didn't feel threatened by.

British rain.

And don't go thinking that British rain is all the same. We are proud of our great regional varieties. The soft hanging rain that drifts across the

Cotswolds. The tough, hard-wearing rain that swings in across Dartmoor. The lovely April showers that can arrive in any month, freshen up the landscape and be replaced by sun in ten minutes, as if Britain was going through some gigantic car wash. There are even people who think plain old drizzle has its charms!

Up in Scotland they have invented a special rain of their own called Scotch mist, which is so thin that it doesn't seem to be falling at all, but hovering.

Do you remember that old *Punch* cartoon in which the English lady is saying to the Scotsman: 'The rain seems to be clearing off at last, Sandy'? He says: 'Aye, I doot it's threatening to be dry.'

So next time you hear people singing the praises of foreign rain, give them the facts. Tell them that British rain is still the best in the world. That 100 per cent of the rain that falls in Britain is British-made, and that we import none of it. And that the British Rain Bureau is looking after your rain, night and day, so that grass may grow and rivers may run.

Don't accept any substitute for British rain.

This completely pointless advertisement was placed by the British Rain Bureau, and was paid for entirely out of your money. If you want to know more about the stuff that falls on the just and unjust alike, send off to the British Rain Bureau, the quango they forgot to kill off. We are here to serve you, also to spend our budget like mad before the end of the year so we can get even more money next year.

Write to us at Precipitation House, Whitehall, London. We'd love to hear from you. We'd love to hear from anybody.

Moreover, Too, 1985

MOTHER GIVES A SEX TALK

'Now that we have finished experimenting with bicycle seats,' I asked my father, 'do you want that book back?'

'What book?'

'*The Basis of a Happy Marriage*.'

'That depends. Do you think you know enough about bicycle design now?'

'Yes.'

'Do you think you know enough about sex now?'

'No.'

'Then keep the book and go and ask your mother for some advice.'

'But, Father, you haven't told me anything yet!'

My father looked at me gravely.

'It is a well-known fact that when fathers teach their sons to drive, they become bad drivers. When fathers teach their sons to play golf, they always become bad golfers.'

'That's not true!' I said. 'Most of the best sportsmen started out being encouraged by their fathers!'

'Encouraged, yes,' he said. 'Not taught. Only encouraged. And I am encouraging you to go and talk to your mother. Now go!'

I went and found my mother.

'Father has been trying to give me a talk about sex,' I told her.

'Not before time,' she said. 'I've been asking him to do it for two years. Did he show you that book?'

'Yes.'

'Lord save us. I've looked at that book myself and I didn't understand much of it. Anyway, it's written by a man for men.'

'Yes, but I'm going to be a man,' I said.

'That's true,' she said, 'but you won't be having sex with men. Will you?'

'No.'

'So you've got to understand how women work, sexually.'

'Right,' I said.

I don't think I had ever been so embarrassed in all my life. Talking to my mother about sex! Even worse, her talking to me about it!

'I can't remember much about the book, but I don't think he says much about the way women feel, does he?' she said.

'No,' I said. 'I think he's much more interested in temperature changes and pulses and heartbeats and, um, what happens at the moment of, um . . .'

'That's right!' she said. 'I remember now! He approaches sex as if it were some kind of engine performance, to be monitored, oiled and watered. You can sort of imagine the author appearing beside your bed with an oily rag, looking down at both of you as you get on with it and saying, "Well, that seems to be ticking over nicely. I'll leave you to it. Give me a ring if you overheat"'.

Never in all my born days did I expect to hear my mother talking about such things in such a way. I must have gone puce because she smiled and leant over and pinched my cheek.

'This isn't helping you much,' she said. 'Actually, assuming you know what happens when people make love, there are only a few helpful things that I can tell you. One is not to make it like an Olympic event. Men think that in sex the longer they last and the more often they do it, the more successful they are. I am afraid that's not true. And all those myths about how wonderful it would be to have both your climaxes at the same time, not true. It doesn't work like that. The only real secret is to try to give pleasure to the other person. Then you'll get it back.'

I waited, scarlet with embarrassment and interest.

'Yes?' I said.

'That's it,' she said. 'That's all I know. Well, all that's worth knowing. But it's all wrapped up in there.'

'That's all you learnt from my father?'

'Oh, I didn't learn it from him. I got it from the *Reader's Digest*. But it seemed to work pretty well.'

'Oh.'

'But all this sex business is not so very important. It's only a prelude to much better things.'

God, this was better. What things?

'What things?'

'Oh, love, and getting married, and having children, and settling down . . .'

She must have seen the expression on my face because she burst into laughter.

'I'm not going to do any of those things,' I said, with dignity. 'I'm just going to . . .'

'Make love to the girls?' she said.

'Yes,' I said, going what I later knew to be poinsettia-red.

'Oh, there's something else about sex I forgot to tell you,' she said. 'The girls know.'

'Know what?'

'That that's what you want.'

'Do they?'

'Oh, yes. Girls know that boys want to go to bed with them.'

'Oh. So . . . do they?'

'No. Not usually.'

'Why don't they?'

'Why should they?'

'Wouldn't they enjoy it?'

'They might, but not with a boy who didn't know how to do it properly.'

'With who then?'

'Someone older.'

'Oh.'

'But probably not at all. If they went to bed with someone, they'd only get the reputation of being the sort of girl who would go to bed with someone.'

'Oh.'

Suddenly it all seemed terribly confusing. I looked at my watch. There was plenty of time to wait before I did anything.

'I think I'll go and play table tennis with Ralph.'

'All right, dear.'

Someone Like Me , 2005

THE DANGEROUS WORLD
OF RELATIONSHIPS

Having survived innumerable liaisons, many a tragic affair, several lifelong romances, five marriages and a very long evening with a female Romanian architect, I think I may be said to have an average experience of relationships. And the golden truth I have learnt about relationships, whether they are with the opposite sex, the same sex, a pet or even a house plant, is that they do not come to grief on the big things like love, money, ambition and sex so often as on the small things like personal habits, attitudes, prejudices and sex.

This is because people rush blindly into relationships without doing adequate research. Oh yes, they establish that they're in love; that they enjoy each other's company; that they have the same attitude to life, television and Woody Allen; that they think this is a wonderful relationship which is going to last for ever and ever. Well, that's the basic requirement, the very least you need. What they *haven't* found out is what the other person thinks about party games, puddings, bending paperbacks back as you read them and throwing old newspapers away. The really crucial things, in fact.

Many a wonderful relationship has been ruined because two otherwise well-suited people were totally incompatible in the little matter of, say, temperature. I know one couple whose marriage, has, against all the odds, survived the fact that he likes a sheet and a blanket at night and she likes four blankets, a duvet and socks. It has survived long enough for their children to be now starting university. At last they can break loose and do some travelling. The only trouble is – and it looks likely to wreck the marriage – he can only go north and she has to go to the tropics.

So if you are thinking of combining with someone in the near future and expect them to say those magic words: 'Would you care to initiate a relationship with me?' for heaven's sake make sure you are compatible first. Make them fill in a questionnaire; hold an informal audition; talk to their parents; *but find out first.*

To help you, I have mapped out the areas in which most relationships are later found floating upside down, without a crew and with all the lifeboats gone.

1. Listening to music. Most people don't listen to music completely without reaction, except music critics. They tap feet, click fingers or nod in time with the music. Or, of course, very nearly but not quite in time with the music. Some people hum along, just audibly. A few people sit motionless for up to fifteen minutes, then say loudly: 'Ye-eah!' I myself have an appalling habit of clicking my teeth in complicated rhythms. It's quite inaudible when there's music playing, but when I'm remembering a favourite record, all people can hear is tuneless grinding of molars, unaware that I'm really bashing out the most exotic rhythmic patterns. I'm thinking of making the big switch to electric dentures.

Anyway, remember that where you now watch your loved one enthralled by a record and think how wonderful it is to see someone so enraptured, you will one day say to yourself: 'If he doesn't stop swaying backwards and forwards with his eyes shut, I shall scream till the neighbours come.' Ask him to stop *now*.

2. Party Games. The world is divided into people who like party games, and those who would rather die than get involved. One from the first camp should not live with one from the second camp. The same is roughly true of community singing, wearing fancy dress and putting your hand up when volunteers from the audience are asked for.

3. Money. The world is also divided into people who feel sick if they get into debt, and people who don't know what it's like to be without an overdraft. If you are one of each, you could still make it, but for God's sake have separate bank accounts.

4. Nightwear. Some people always put it on, some never. I don't think it's anything to do with sensuality; it's another facet of the hot vs cold problem. But you've both got to decide to do the same thing. If one person sleeps with nothing on, the other person is going to feel perpetually overdressed, which is something we shouldn't have to worry about after we've got undressed. A friend of mine once had a brief liaison with a girl with very poor circulation who wore a dressing gown in bed. 'Nothing wrong with that,' he said, 'except that every time she turned over things fell out of her pockets. I hurt myself badly on a hairbrush one night.' I personally think girls in pyjamas are rather attractive, but that's my problem.

5. Throwing things away. Some do, some don't. If the two types live together, you sooner or later find one partner routinely going through the waste paper baskets and dustbins to find what the other is trying to get rid of. If you feel now a flash of irritation when your partner says: 'You never know when it might come in useful,' your relationship is already doomed.

6. Arguments. An argument should ideally take place in order to get at the truth, but unfortunately a lot of people (mostly men, I'm afraid) argue to win, and will go on backing a half-baked idea until the other person bursts into tears or throws something. Unfortunately, in the early stages of relationships, when the sun is shining, there aren't any arguments and it's hard to know how things will turn out. Better provoke an argument early on, just to see how it goes.

7. The Countryside. Does he like it? Do you hate it? Or vice versa? Then call it off now.

8. Food. Some people skip starters in order to leave room for the pudding. Others order every course except the pudding. Put one of each kind together, and most of your meals will be spent with one partner staring into space. Unless, of course, you compromise by both having every course, in which case laying the foundations for a very overweight middle-aged couple.

9. Sex. Not as important as eating, but still quite important. A New Yorker once told me: 'A good sex life takes up less than five percent of your time; a rotten sex life takes up all your time.' I can't better that. She then added reflectively: 'My mother told me that.'

10. Funny stories. Why is it that so many partnerships sort themselves out sooner or later into a double act, consisting of one person telling stories badly and the other correcting them the whole time? Because they didn't get it sorted out right at the beginning. It's one of the facts of life that we find ourselves telling stories more often than we have a stock of stories for; therefore we start telling the same anecdotes over and over again. The other person must understand this, and at least hope that the anecdotes improve with age. *Don't interrupt.* Realise humbly that you don't do it any better either.

There is one exception to all this; the person who believes that stories are funnier if you say everything three times, like this: 'It was a lovely day, blue sky, not a cloud to be seen. And this man, just an ordinary bloke, some fellow or other, was strolling along, just walking down the street, minding his own business when suddenly, out of the blue, from nowhere . . . ' Or, if it's personal reminiscence: 'I remember one time we were staying in this hotel in Brussels, ordinary Belgian hotel, usual continental pension . . . '

People like that should not have a relationship with anyone.

Miles and Miles, 1982

THE UNITED DEITIES

1. The Chairgod said that under Any Other Business someone had asked if they could discuss the subject of cartoons.

2. The Jewish God said that one of his favourite cartoons showed two Martians landing from a space ship, and one of them goes into an amusement arcade . . .

3. The Chairgod said he thought the discussion should be more specifically about the anti-Islamic cartoons, which had appeared in a Danish newspaper and had led to widespread rioting throughout the world.

4. The Catholic God said that he thought there was something rather refreshingly old-fashioned about the whole episode. At a time when the death of newspapers was widely forecast, and all publicity focussed on the Internet, it was encouraging that a newspaper could still arouse passions. And a black and white drawing at that.

5. He asked if anyone could anyone imagine a website arousing similar fury.

6. The Anglican God said the Catholic God should be careful about what he called 'refreshingly old-fashioned'. It was not so long ago that the Catholic Church was torturing and burning people for expressing uncomfortable opinions. Would he call that 'refreshingly old-fashioned'?

7. Allah said that while he took no responsibility for what Muslims did on Earth, he was glad that some people still took their religion seriously enough to get enraged about it.

8. The Catholic God said that Allah was in an odd situation. He was the Muslim God. But he, Allah, never seemed to take the direct flak. It was his prophet, Mohammed, who was always in the firing line. Would there have been an equivalent fuss if someone had depicted Allah?

9. Allah said that nobody had ever agreed what he looked like, so he was safe, whereas there was a consensus about Mohammed's image.

10. The Catholic God said that if it was forbidden to depict the image of Mohammed, where did this consensus about what he looked like come from? How did you know what someone who could not be pictured actually looked like?

11. The Chairgod said that cartoonists did not care what people looked like. They just drew a bearded person in Arab clothes and wrote 'Mohammed' on the headgear.

12. The Catholic God said that cartoonists had been drawing him for years as a white-bearded old bloke standing on a cloud, and nobody had ever protested.

13. The Jewish God said that, anyway, this Martian goes into the amusement arcade and pulls the lever of a fruit machine.

14. Zeus said that he had always enjoyed being depicted by painters. He was proud to say that some of the greatest painters in history had gone on portraying the Greek gods long after people had stopped believing in them. His encounter with Leda had been immortalised by not only Leonardo da Vinci but also Michelangelo.

15. The Catholic God said that there must be more to immortality than being painted as a swan. (Laughter)

16. Zeus said it was good enough for him. In any case, he thought that painters had made a poor job of portraying the Christian Son of God. There were millions of paintings of Jesus the baby, and millions of Jesus being crucified, but not many of anything in between. Had Jesus done nothing of interest meanwhile?

17. The Chairgod asked Zeus not to stir up religious hatred (laughter) and said he would make one last effort to get the discussion back to Danish cartoons. He wanted to know if anyone had actually seen the offending cartoons.

18. There being no affirmative answer to this, the Jewish God said that the Martian who had pulled the lever of the fruit machine had hit the jackpot and coins were cascading out of the slot. So the Martian (who is portrayed as a metal robot not unlike the fruit machine) turns to his companion and says: 'I just shook his hand and he was sick all over me!'

19. Zeus said he didn't get it and would someone explain it to him.

Independent, 2006

COCKTAILS

'If you ever want to get drunk really quick, boys,' said Ian 'Froggy' Hunter to us, 'you should try a gin and sherry. Half gin, half sherry. Never fails.'

Ian Hunter was, as 'Froggy' suggests, our French teacher. I can't quite remember now why he was giving us sixteen-year-olds advice on alcohol, but I remembered his advice years later at a time when I had no desire to get drunk but when I did have a bottle of gin and a bottle of sherry standing together on the shelf and his words suddenly came floating back to me. I tried it. He was right. It was very alcoholic. It also tasted terrible. There are certain combinations of spirits which never turn up in the same cocktail recipe, and with good reason.

Yet you cannot stop cocktail mixers from experimenting. After all, when a new cocktail book comes out, it must include a few new recipes, if only to look slightly different from all other cocktail recipe books. I remember once being stranded in a house in the West Indies at the age of eighteen when my hosts had gone out to dinner and had told me to take any food or drink in the house I fancied. As soon as they had gone, I hauled down an old cocktail book and tried to find a recipe whose ingredients corresponded to the rather meagre contents of the drink cupboard. The only one I could find was an Earthquake, which as I recall consisted of one third gin, one third whisky and one third absinthe. Using Pernod instead of absinthe I created an Earthquake, and drank it very slowly for the rest of the evening. It was as horrible as a gin and sherry but curiously addictive and did get me pleasantly merry.

From small scattered beginnings like this came an interest in cocktails which to this day is still small and scattered. From time to time I buy a second-hand cocktail recipe book and experiment wildly for a few days, then lose interest for a long while, which is why every time I pick up a book from my cocktail collection I find in my own shaky handwriting notes such as 'far too sweet' or 'try again with more lemon juice' written against certain recipes which I cannot remember ever having tried.

The odd thing is that after so many years of trying my hand at odd and out-of-the-way cocktails, most of the potions I have experimented with have failed to delight me and there are only two that I ever liked enough to repeat and enjoy on a regular basis. One is a Petite Fleur and the other is a Boardsailer. The Petite Fleur has the almost simpled-minded three-part harmony which so many cocktails share (something alcoholic, something sweet, something sour), consisting as it does of one third white rum, one third Cointreau and one third grapefruit. Shake with ice and pour.

That recipe came from a thick book which purports to be the *International Barman's Handbook*, containing not only all the familiar ones like Sidecar and Manhattan, but rare cocktails which won second price in cocktail competitions in Denmark in 1936 . . .

The Boardsailer, on the other hand, came from an advertisement in a glossy magazine some years ago for Johnny Walker whisky, and was presumably dreamt up specially for the ad, along with the disgusting name – I have certainly never met it in any book. It involves among other things whisky, orange juice, passion fruit juice and Blue Orange Curacao. Sounds revolting, doesn't it? Well, it's wonderful. The combination of the blue liqueur and orange juice turns the drink the most wonderful turquoise colour, while the combination of whisky and passion fruit juice, unlikely as it sounds, is delicious.

(The French have discovered this. I was once given a present from France of a bottle labelled Whisky Passion, which combined whisky and passion fruit juice and which disappeared very quickly. I never recreated the effect until I went on a visit to Madeira, where passion fruit juice is as common as orange or apple juice is here. I used to order passion fruit juice at the bar, and a whisky to go with it, then in front of the horrified eyes of the barman combine the two . . .)

What slightly depresses me, looking back at my dabbling in cocktails, is the realisation that it is very like my dabbling in cooking in that I try lots of recipes but never invent anything. My theory is that while there are still classic mixtures to be browsed among and discovered, it is a waste of time making up anything. It wasn't very long ago that I rediscovered (from a first edition of the very wonderful *Savoy Cocktail Book*) the recipe for champagne cocktail which involves pouring champagne (or New World bubbly) over a sugar cube soaked in Angostura bitters and is delectable.

My wife, on the other hand, only uses recipes in cooking as a starting point and it is the same with her drink-making. At the very same session where I was last fooling around with the Boardsailer (which everyone hears as The Bored Sailor, a much better name), she created a new drink called African Queen which involved brandy (one part), mango juice (three) and champagne (four). It was sumptuous, and the woman is not even interested in cocktails. Damned demoralising. Give me a gin and sherry, someone.

The Oldie, 2000

THE COMPLEAT ANGLER

PAR IZAAK WALTON

Un rod, ligne, etc.
Un net.
Un stool (folding).
Un grand basket.
Un très grand umbrella, préférablement golfing, préférablement 2-striped, préférablement vert et blanc.
Une paire de boots (longs).
Un ex-army jacket (couleur: spinach green).
Un paquet de sandwiches (un fish paste, un fromage, un tomate).
Une pomme.
Un paquet de crisps.
Un thermos flask (de thé, pre-mixed avec sucre, lait etc).
Une grande bouteille de lemonade.
Une grande bouteille de Scotch.
Une banane.
Un packet de biscuits (fig roll *ou* ginger nut).
Quelques petits bars de chocolaterie anglaise, par exemple, Mars Bar, Bounty, Kit Kat, etc.
Un demi-gâteau, probablement sponge.
Un autre paquet de crisps, d'une flaveur différente.
Un paquet, ou probablement deux, de peanuts (salted, *pas* roast).
Un petit pork pie (10% pork, 80% pie, 10% wrapping).
Une petite tube de Smarties, ou similaire. Polo, peut-être. Peut-être tous les deux.

4 tins de lager.

Un boiled oeuf.

Un twist de salt.

Aussi de pepper.

Un autre paquet de crisps, la même flaveur que le premier.

2 paquets de cigarettes (filtres).

Un paquet de tablets digestifs.

Une carte de membership de BUPA.

Un body donor card.

L'adresse de next de kin.

The Franglais Lieutenant's Woman, 1986

ALBANIAN PROVERBS

If you have not come across Albanian proverbs before, I should warn you that they are quite different from ours. Ours tend to be practical ('You can take a horse to water but you can't make it drink'), or bossy ('Look before you leap'), whereas an Albanian proverb tends to be vaguely poetical, initially attractive and mostly unhelpful.

In the land of the hedgehog the motorist goes on foot.

The tractor driver will never know the small pleasure of overtaking another vehicle, only the huge happiness of stopping other people overtaking him.

An upside-down wheelbarrow is no good to anyone but at least it's dry inside.

You cannot make an omelette without breaking a bird's heart.

We all know that a tomato is classified as a fruit, but none of us would put tomato in a fruit salad; that is the difference between knowledge and wisdom.

There is no such thing as body-building. Your body is already there. The most you can do with it is put on an extension, lag it or add another small eating area.

Lucky the country that can afford to clothe its scarecrows.

Independent, 2001

HOW TO WRITE A
THANK YOU LETTER

One year I couldn't help noticing that my brother Ralph got more Christmas presents than I did.

Only one more than I did, but that was enough.

He got a present from Uncle Henry and I didn't.

I was furious.

Why him and not me?

I was so furious that instead of sulking I had it out with Ralph. They say that in marriage it's better to talk about problems than to keep silent. Of course, nobody is married to someone like Ralph.

'Well, perhaps the reason Uncle Henry sent me a present and not you is that he knows of my existence and not yours,' said Ralph. 'Or, more likely, perhaps he likes me and doesn't like you. Perhaps Uncle Henry thinks you have got enough possessions already and doesn't want you to have too many. Perhaps he thinks you're a spoilt brat . . .'

I leapt on him.

'Why are you two boys fighting again?' said my father, coming in.

'Because Uncle Henry sent him a present and didn't send me one,' I said.

'The secret of getting presents is sending thank you letters,' said my father. 'And the main thing is to write a thank you letter as soon as possible. It doesn't matter what you say. Speed is all. The donor will remember speed of response and give you another present next time. It's an investment for the future.'

'Well,' said my mother doubtfully, 'I'm not sure that speed is the *most* important thing. I'm happy to get a thank you letter at any time. In fact, sometimes children write to me two or three weeks later and I'm never cross that they've waited so long. I'm just happy they've done it. In a way, it's really nice to get one when you're not expecting it.'

'As far as I can gather,' my brother said, 'you and Dad want us to write two thank you letters to each person. One straight after the event and one a lot later.'

'I think that would be excessive,' said my mother.

'Look!' I said. 'This is no good to me! Uncle Henry has never given me a present! So how can I say thank you?'

'The whole trouble with making the effort to write thank you letters,' said my father, as if I hadn't spoken, 'is that once you have got the present, the incentive to write back has gone. It's like being paid in advance. When someone gets the lolly in advance, they feel they don't really have to do the job. Well, getting a present first is the same sort of thing. Ideally, you should write the thank you letter before you get the present.'

'I think that would be excessive,' said my mother.

Later, when Ralph and I were friends again, I asked him what he would do.

'Mum and Dad have given their advice,' I said, 'and pretty rotten it was too, so what's yours?'

'Funnily enough,' said Ralph, 'it's the same as Dad's. Write the thank you letter before you get the present.'

'That's stupid.'

'Well, it's what I did with Uncle Henry.'

'You *what*?'

'Yes, I did. Way before Christmas, when I was feeling very poor, I made a list of people I might get presents from. Uncle Henry was not on the list. I thought it would be nice for him to be on the list. So I wrote him a letter thanking him for a present from the Christmas before. I didn't refer to what the present was, as he hadn't sent me one. I reckoned that he would never remember that he hadn't sent me anything and it would never occur to him that any child would write a thank you letter for something he *hadn't* got and he'd be shaken enough to put me on his gift list and send me something this time.'

'That's stupid,' I said.

'Seems to have worked,' said Ralph.

'Are you going to write a thank you letter for this present?' I said.

'When I get round to it,' he said.

That gave me a chance. I suddenly saw that if I wrote a thank you letter to Uncle Henry *now*, I would be ahead of Ralph next year.

So I wrote a letter to Uncle Henry which went roughly like this:

> *Dear Uncle Henry,*
>
> *Thanks very much for the present, it was very kind of you. We had a wonderful Christmas, except for the mistletoe catching fire. We went to the pantomime in the New Year and it was great, especially the bit where the pumpkin would not change into a stagecoach and the fairy godmother said a very rude word.*
>
> *With love from your nephew.*

Someone had once told me that grown-ups liked it if you put things in letters which had gone wrong, so that's why I mentioned the mistletoe and the pumpkin trick.

A little while later I got a letter from Uncle Henry which said:

> *Dear Nephew,*
>
> *I was very pleased to get your thank you letter, especially as I had never sent you a present, as you well know, you cheeky little bugger. Still, one should always reward enterprise, so I enclose a £10 note to make up for me being mean at Christmas. If you feel like it, give half to your brother Ralph as I never sent him a present either. One day you must tell me how the mistletoe caught fire.*
>
> *Your old Uncle Henry.*

I had never thought of Uncle Henry as anything but a rather quiet and boring old chap before, but this rather changed my view of him. It also rather changed my view of Ralph.

'Ralph,' I said to him one day, 'just supposing, just *supposing*, you had never written to Uncle Henry. I'm just supposing. And supposing he had never sent you a Christmas present. Then who do you suppose that present from Uncle Henry at Christmas time was really from?'

Ralph looked at me closely. I obviously knew more than I was letting on. And I obviously knew there was something fishy about Uncle Henry's present. And he knew when it was time to come clean.

'It wasn't a present from Uncle Henry,' he confessed. 'Well, it was. But I gave it to myself and made pretend it came from Uncle Henry.'

'Why?'

'To make you jealous.'

I took this in for a moment, in silence. It was just the sort of thing that Ralph would like to do. I was surprised that he actually had the energy to do it, though.

'It must have been very disappointing not getting a present from Uncle Henry,' I said. 'So I hope this makes up for it a bit.'

And I gave him £2.

It wasn't quite the £5 that Uncle Henry had suggested.

But it was a lot more than I felt he deserved.

And it was worth it, to see the expression on Ralph's face. Which, I have to say, didn't go away until I told him the full story.

And that wasn't for another four or five weeks.

Someone Like Me, 2005

HISTORY OF KING TONY

or *Labour's Lost, Love*

ACT II

Having defeated the Tory Army in battle, King Tony now has the task of pacifying the kingdom, keeping his own side loyal and spotting any conspiracies which might threaten his throne. We have reached the point where King Tony has entrusted the financial management of his kingdom to the capable but hugely ambitious Duke Gordon Brown.

In the Palace, at Westminster. Duke Gordon Brown is addressing the assembly on his plans for the nation.

Gordon Brown: In former years this land did rise and fall
In constant cycles of unsteadiness,
From boom to bust, from stop to go and back,
Until our minds were dizzy with the motion,
Like a blind ship upon a drunken ocean.
No more of that! Our course shall now be steady,
With mine the hand upon the country's tiller.
Under my enduring stewardship
This land shall grow in strength and dignity,
Till everyone shall have a job at last,
And men in Sheffield not be forced to strip

To earn enough to keep their wife and kids!**
That reference do I make to show you all
That I can keep in touch with common culture . . .

Enter the Earl Hague with the remnants of his army, attended by Gummer, Widdecombe, etc.

Hague: (aside) Hark how this jumped up Scotsman witters on!
Why, every Chancellor since the dawn of time
Has said the same and then been shewn quite wrong.
Gordon Brown: From welfare to work shall be our battle cry!
I shall not rest till every man and woman
Has been untethered from the jobless queue
And given some noble work to match his state.
Hague: (aside) Why, what he says is very true indeed.
Widdecombe: How so, my Lord?
Hague: How so, stout Widdecombe?
Why, see you not that this same Gordon Brown
Will never rest or pause till he himself
Has risen to the job he craves to have,
The Premiership of this country, nothing less.
The endless rise of this Duke Gordon Brown
Will never cease till he's brought Tony down . . .

Earl Hague and his cohorts slip away, followed by spies. Duke Gordon Brown speaks on, unstoppably.

Gordon Brown: Turning now to diesel fuel, and wine . . .
King Tony: More of this anon. It's time to dine.
Gordon Brown: But sire, I have not nearly finished yet.
I have not put up tax on cigarette,
Nor said what I shall do with PEPS and TESSAS,
Nor made my most informed financial guesses.
I have not done my bit for unleaded fuel . . .
King Tony: Listening to you, I feel I'm back at school,

Uncomprehending while the master drones.
Your corporation tax and single parent loans
Have left me feeling dizzy, deaf and dumb.
Gordon Brown: Nay, sire, a simple child from school could come
And understand the hardest thing I say.
King Tony: Oh, would he now? In that case, let's away
And test your theory in a real life school.
'Twixt you and children let there be a duel!'

The scene is a school, where Duke Gordon Brown is endeavouring to explain his policies to the gathered pupils.

Gordon Brown: And so you see, the curve of annual borrowing
Doth intersect with income HERE and HERE ...
King Tony: Come, come, dear Gordon Brown, let not the smell
Of rank statistics fright these innocent minds.
The thing is very simple. We must forge
A golden country for a brand new age!
To you I say, fear not the future but behold
Where youth goes boldly, while fear restrains the old!
Together we shall build, and build we must!
For what is just is fair, and fair is just!
First Journalist: *(aside)* This Tony talks a load of tosh, and yet they love it.
They all believe his smile, not what he says.
Second Journalist: Yon Gordon has a dark and jowelly look.
He knows that all King Tony says is dross
And cannot understand why he is loved,
Nor yet why he himself is frowned upon.
First Journalist: A man who frowns and scowls like Gordon Brown
Shall not by love, but force, secure a crown.
Second Journalist: Well said! That's very deep, or so I think.
First Jounalist: I'm sick of this. Let's go and have a drink ...

Independent, 1998

PUB CONVERSATION: WAR AND PEACE

'You know they always say that newspaper circulation goes up in time of war?' said the resident Welshman.

It was a pub question.

That is, not a question which needs to be answered, but a question which is aimed at attracting people's attention within ten feet of the speaker. Just one person will do.

It succeeded.

'What about it?' said the lady with the green hairdo, as she came through the door.

This is the woman who changes her hair colour according to her current tipple. Last week it had been brown and she had been drinking coffee. This week...

'Yes,' said our Welshman, 'apparently people get anxious to know the war news, so they buy papers more often, and sales go up, which leads one to wonder whether any paper has ever started a war to boost circulation.'

'I think Randolph Hearst used to start wars for that purpose,' I said. 'Though whether any paper has ever sponsored a war is another matter.'

'*Der Sturmer* proudly brings you World War Two!' said the man with the dog, who sometimes fancies himself a bit of a wag. '*Yachting Monthly* is pleased to be associated with the retreat from Dunkirk. The Falklands War, brought to you by *Port Stanley News* in association with Mrs Thatcher...'

'Yes, I think we get the point,' said the Major, who doesn't fancy the man with the dog as a bit of a wag.

'What can I do you for?' said the landlord to the green lady. 'Creme de menthe? Horrible stuff made from mango? Don't think we've got anything else that's green . . .'

'Ginger wine, please,' she said firmly.

'Is that green?'

'It is, if you hold it up to the light.'

'Thing is,' said the resident Welshman, wresting the conversation back, 'I was passing that place in Dorset last week, the Tank Museum at Bovington, and I suddenly wondered if the same held true for war museums. Do they get better attendance figures in times of war? Does talk of war make people more war-conscious? Is war good for war museums?'

'I don't know,' said the man with the dog. 'Is it?'

'I don't know,' said the Welshman. 'I was only asking.'

'Does it work the other way round?' I said. 'In times of peace, do people go to peace museums?'

'What's a peace museum?'

I thought wildly.

'A church?' I said.

'Nothing bloody peaceful about a church,' said the Welshman. 'Most churches I have been in have been full of battle honours, and trophy flags flying on the wall, and war memorials to people fallen in battle . . .'

'And stone effigies of crusaders in full armour,' said the man with the dog.

'Depends how you define war,' said the Major. 'People use all sorts of transport in war. Buses, trains, cars, God knows what. But is a transport museum a war museum? I doubt it.'

'That doesn't make it a peace museum,' said the man with the dog. 'In fact, I don't think there *is* such a thing as a peace museum. People are always more interested in war than peace. Even if they're against it. You don't get peace marches when there's no threat of war.'

'Onward, Christian soldiers, marching as to war,' said the Welshman. 'That's not very peace-loving, is it? No, I don't think the church is a peace museum.'

Sometimes our Welshman gets into a bit of an anti-church tirade.

Something to do with his youth and all those hours spent in the chapel, perhaps. At such moments it's best to ignore him.

'The big question,' said the man with the dog, 'the BIG question, the VERY big question is this: is war the natural state of mankind, with periods of peace occurring as a natural break between, or are we naturally at peace, with occasional wars breaking the monotony?'

'Only a man could ask that question,' said the green lady. 'It's men that start wars and men that fight wars. If it were left to women, there wouldn't be any wars.'

Just then the vicar came in, and out of deference to his presence we stopped talking about war and peace and church and religion, and got on to the weather.

Independent, 2003

LAST MAN IN

A MODERN CRICKET STORY FOR BOYS
(SPONSORED BY THIRD MAN AFTERSHAVE)

'One-day cricket mania is sweeping Australia . . . beer cans flew, drunks fought, and women bared their breasts.' *Sydney Sun*

'Middle and leg, please,' said Jack.

'Find it your flaming self,' said the umpire.

Jack felt sick. Nine wickets down, and he was the last man in for England. There were 624 runs still to get, and only ten minutes in which to get them. Could he do it?

He gave himself guard and looked round the field. The Australian fielders snarled back and continued throwing lager cans to each other; the dying evening sun glinted on the ring pulls which littered the outfield but the light was still good enough to read the advertisements tattooed on their chests. Jack glanced at the enormous electronic scoreboard. It said: 'Miss Australia Lager will commence her streak in five minutes' time.'

'Play!' called the umpire.

The ground trembled slightly as the Australian fast bowler started his run-up. He was a tall man, heavily built but smelling elegantly of Third Man aftershave, with pistol holsters dangling on both sides. As he ran past the umpire something fell from his pocket to the ground. It looked like a bottle of Australian wine. Nuits St Bruce.

'No ball!' shrieked the umpire.

A red blur flew from the bowler's hand, struck the pitch and reared up to hit Jack on his All-Round Vision Plexiglass Space Helmet. Jack sank into unconsciousness, and moments later woke up in his comfy bed in Stevenage New Town, his teddy bear in his hand and his British Home Stores duvet on the floor, where he had kicked it in his sleep. Thank God, it had all been a dream!

'Wake up,' said the umpire, leaning over him. Jack opened his eyes. Oh my God! It was Stevenage that had been the dream. It was the Sydney Cricket Ground that was real.

'623 to get, and eight more minutes, you pommy bastard,' said the umpire, not unkindly.

The fielders were shouting raucous insults at him in a foreign language now, Australian probably, and the first flakes of snow were beginning to fall. Small earth tremors had made cracks in the outfield, which would make boundaries harder to get. This time the fast bowler approached the wicket on a 500cc motor bicycle; amazingly, Jack managed to get an edge and the ball flew past extra cover.

'Run up, you chaps!' called the English captain from the pavilion steps. He was felled by a well-aimed beer barrel. But Jack and his partner were running well between the wickets, for the Australian fielders, hopelessly drunk by now, were unable to focus enough to find the ball. By the time they had run 400 runs, the stumps had been thrown down three times, but only by lager cans.

Ten minutes later, with time added on to complete the ball played, England had run all 623 runs and had won a famous victory. As Jack left the pitch he raised his bat, partly in triumph, partly to fend off the crowd who were closing in on him. Later he was given the Man of the Match title. It had never been awarded posthumously before.

Moreover, 1982

MILLS AND BANG MARCH ON

The success of Mills & Bang, a new imprint which satisfies both male and female fantasies, seems unstoppable. The secret of these tender, thunderous novels is that they are as soft as an eyelash, yet as uncompromising as a kick in the shin with an army boot. Accordingly we present to eager readers a run-down of new titles on our list.

Horizons of Love, by Gwendolen Fastnet

High in the skies over Dorking, the Spitfire and Messerschmidt twisted and turned, each trying to gain ascendancy over the other. 'Hurricane' Kate, at the controls of the Spitfire, had already shot down twenty Huns, yet she knew that this time she had an opponent worthy of her.

'Got you now!' she whispered, as she turned and banked towards the sleek shape of the German plane. But all she found was empty sky. Glancing back over her shoulder, she saw with horror the Messerschmidt coming down at her out of the sun. There was no way she could escape now. With resignation, she patted her hair into shape and closed her eyes.

'We'll meet again, *Weiss nicht where, Weiss nicht wann*,' said her radio softly. She opened her eyes, just in time to see the enemy cockpit flash past and a cheery face wink at her. Johnny von Arnsdorf! The one they called the Handsome Hun. How she hated him. Horribly humiliated, she realised that he had just spared her life.

'I'll get you, Johnny,' she vowed. And so indeed she would, but she never suspected that it would be as Mrs Johnny von Arnsdorf, after twists and turns of fate that would leave history breathless.

The Silken Sands, by Trudi Blessed

'We do not normally take women in the Foreign Legion,' said Major Pierre Danois. He paused, regarding the way her trim figure fitted into the uniform. 'And yet, in your case . . . I presume you are joining to forget a great and tragic love?'

'Not at all,' said Joan briskly. 'I am looking for adventure, a hard life and a bit of a sun-tan.'

Adventure came sooner than she thought. That evening she was pinned in a corridor of the fort by an unshaven Yugoslav recruit called Yukovic, who smelt of cheap wine. His hands started to explore her uniform.

'I have never had a girl from Guildford,' he leered.

'Nor will you, laddie!' sang out a voice. It was Alec, the cheery Glaswegian she had met earlier. But before Alec could move, Joan had kneed Yukovic in the groin, chopped him to the back of the neck and kicked him twice expertly as he sank groaning to the floor.

'This fort needs cleaning up and I aim to see it gets done,' said Joan clearly as she strode past the open-mouthed Alec. Behind a hidden screen Major Danois smiled and twirled his moustache. He would break this little desert beauty before long, he thought, which showed how little he knew about girls from Guildford.

The Hot Summer Campaign, by Wendy Thrumb

On the retreat through Greece in front of the advancing Germans, Captain Leonard Tasker felt strangely protective towards the 3,000 men and 2,000 mules under his command. He also felt strangely protective towards Xenia, the proud Greek peasant girl who had attached herself to the company, even though accommodation was desperately hard to find for her.

'Hope you don't mind me mentioning it to you, sir,' said the old sergeant to him one day, 'but the men are beginning to talk about the way that girl sleeps in your tent at night.'

'Heavens,' said Leonard, flushing. 'Surely they don't think there's anything . . .'

But Leonard's loyalties are sharply divided when Xenia, out foraging for yoghurt, is captured by the Germans. Should he continue the retreat without her, or turn and fight them for possession of the girl whom he finds so inexplicably fascinating despite not being able to understand a word she says? A taut epic of revenge, pursuit and military incompetence, with many riveting details about mule maintenance.

Moreover, Too, 1985

LET'S PARLER FRANGLAIS!

LE CHRISTMAS SHOPPING

Shopman: Bonjour, monsieur.

Monsieur: Bonjour. Avez-vous un perdrix?

Shopman: Dans un pear tree?

Monsieur: Bien sûr.

Shopman: Non. Les perdrix dans le pear tree sont épuisés. Maintenant seulement dans le privet hedge, dans le box tree ou dans le creeper de Virginie.

Monsieur: Hmm. OK, le box tree. Deux turtle doves?

Shopman: Vous voulez des tortues qui volent, ou des oiseaux avec turtle markings?

Monsieur: Le deuxième.

Shopman: Dommage. On n'a que le premier.

Monsieur: OK, ça va. Trois poules françaises? Pour ainsi dire.

Shopman: Deux seulement. Il y a un trés bon line en poules néo-zélandaises.

Monsieur: OK. Deux françaises, une néo-zélandaise. Cinq anneaux d'or?

Shopman: Vous ne voulez pas de calling birds?

Monsieur: Si, si! Silly moi.

Shopman: Calling birds sont discontinued. Les Japonais font un très cheap bird recording device. Et nous faisons le demidouzaine d'anneaux d'or à un discount remarquable.

Monsieur: Parfait. Et les geese a-laying?

Shopman: Ce n'est pas la saison pour les oies pregnantes. Nous avons

133

des deep-frozen goose pieces. Et des table mats très tasteful avec swans a-swimming, en sept attitudes différentes.

Monsieur: Merveilleux. Avez-vous huit demoiselles capables de retirer le lait des vaches, own stool provided?

Shopman: Est-ce que vous accepteriez un milk-float Unigate pour une semaine?

Monsieur: Mmmmm...

Shopman: Unlimited mileage?

Monsieur: OK. Maintenant, les joueurs de flûte et tambour...

Shopman: Pas de problème, squire. Nous avons un contingent moonlighting des Scots Fusiliers, très bons lads.

Monsieur: Alors, il ne reste que les lords et les ladies.

Shopman: Voyons. Lord Lucan n'est pas available, Lord Snowdon tient un low profile... On peut faire un mixed lot de crowned heads, oui. Mais il y a plusieurs ex-kings...

Monsieur: Cheap stuff, eh? Never mind. Vous acceptez Dinars Card?

Shopman: Yugobank? Bien sûr.

Monsieur: Merci. Au revoir.

Let's Parler Franglais, 1979

PEDDLING WHEELS

The gangs of bicycle thieves at present infesting London have become even more daring. Until recently they had contented themselves with stealing bikes left behind by their owners, but now bikes are not even safe when the owner is sitting on them. In Oxford Street, for example, pick-pockets are now operating on bicycles. They come up behind bicyclists at traffic lights and before they turn green, neatly take away all the contents of their back pockets, shopping baskets and side panniers. If they don't have time to take everything, they simply follow their victim to the next red lights.

Mr Peter Archangel of Croydon fared even worse.

'I was out on a tandem with my fiancée Irene,' he reports, 'and we had drawn up at the crossing of Tottenham Court Road and Charing Cross Road. After we started again the pedalling seemed much harder, so I turned round to remonstrate cheerfully with Irene, but she was gone, nowhere to be seen. She'd been stolen in broad daylight. If the thief should read this. I'd like to urge him to return her. She was not of great financial worth, but she had great sentimental value for me.'

Some gangs have become even more daring, and more skilled. Mr Reg Roberts of Esher had his bicycle stolen from him when he was on it. During the fifteen seconds he waited at Oxford Circus, he felt himself being very lightly lifted in the air and lowered again – so softly that he fancied it was the air shifting in his tyre, or the saddle springs easing. But when he came to start again, he found he was standing in the road with no bike. When he tried to pedal off, he fell nastily.

'This is an exceptionally skilful gang,' says Inspector Derailleur of the Bike Squad. 'Most bike thieves are happy just to take the back half of the bike at lights. Over 1,000 back wheels and saddles have disappeared this year alone. May I urge all cyclists who stop at red lights to chain their bike securely to a post or railing till they go green? Better still, go by Tube or bus.'

But what happens to all those stolen half-bicycles? Latest theory is that they are being shipped to Holland to be repainted and turned into unicycles. But who is buying the unicycles?

'Everyone is buying unicycles!' claims Adrian Wardour-Street, head PR man of Friends of the Wheel. 'Roller-skating is old hat now; unicycling is where it's at. All the top people and trend-setters are one-wheeling their way to work!'

It must be a very exclusive trend, as no one has yet been spotted unicycling.

'Put it another way,' says Adrian. 'Although no one as yet is unicycling, if we say that they are loudly and often enough, they'll start, mark my words. This is how trends are born. And my goodness, this *is* a trend. One-wheeling is the safest, funnest, quickest way to travel. I'd do it myself except that I can't get hold of one. But as soon as the country is flooded with cheap unicycles from Holland, nothing will be able to stop the one-wheelers. It's going to be a monster trend, believe me. Probably by this afternoon, I'd say.'

But opposition to the growing unicycle trend is mounting among motorists. Defence of the Road, the motoring lobby determined to safeguard what it sees as a besieged position, has issued a statement blasting the unsafe presence of one-wheelers on the road, which it blames for three-quarters of Britain's road accidents. To check these figures I rang up the movement's head offices in Soho and talked to its head, Adrian Wardour-Street.

'Oh, hello, it's you again,' Adrian told me. 'Yes, this is just another little ploy we're trying to get unicycling on the map. We've always found that a little controversy does more to get things going than anything. Remember how skate-boarding really took off after it was banned from Hyde Park? It took me three months to persuade the GLC to do that.

So I thought, well, it might be worth having a bash at raising the alarms over unicycling, as if it were a dangerous pastime. It is, actually. Only a loony would go out on the roads on one of those. You won't catch me doing it. But I confidently predict that one-wheeling will be a monster trend. Maybe not this afternoon. I have to knock off early. But tomorrow morning, definitely.'

Miles and Miles, 1982

IS THERE LIBEL AFTER DEATH?

LEGAL history is being made by a case in which a living man is being sued for a libel uttered after his death. How is this possible? Let us find out by studying this extract from the start of the trial on Monday.

Counsel: You are Gerald Fang?

Fang: I am.

Counsel: Are you dead?

Fang: No, I am alive.

Judge: Have you ever been dead?

Fang: Not to my knowledge.

Judge: This is an extraordinary line of questioning, Mr Garstang.

Counsel: Libel can only be committed by a living person, my Lord, so I have to establish if the defendant is alive.

Judge: I have presided over many libel cases before, and never as I recall was the defendant a dead person. Though occasionally the defence counsel showed very few signs of life. (*Laughter in court*) There, I have made my little joke, and now you can carry on as you like for a while.

Counsel: Thank you, my Lord. Mr Fang, I presume you have made your will.

Fang: I have.

Counsel: I believe you have made a video to be shown as the will is read.

Fang: Yes, I have. There will also be a short but very funny animated film from Hungary.

Counsel: Quite. Could you briefly describe your video?

Fang: It is a fast-moving, entertaining, slickly edited short film which shows considerable promise for a first production. How sad to learn that it is also this producer's last production.

Counsel: It is not a rave review I am after, Mr Fang, but a bald précis of the film.

Fang: It is a wave from beyond the grave. It is an on-the-spot report from Gerald Fang, River Styx, *News at Ten*.

Counsel: Death is no laughing matter, Mr Fang.

Fang: It is my death we are talking about. I can film myself saying goodbye and good riddance, can I not?

Counsel: Ah! Good riddance! An instructive phrase. Are you suggesting, Mr Fang, that you make some comments in the film about those still alive? Have you taken the opportunity of uttering words of malice and contempt about those of your contemporaries whom you wish to wound from beyond the grave?

Fang: All right, yes, I have made a few barbed comments, but there isn't that much talking in the film. I mean, it's mostly archive film of my early life, sequences of me tap-dancing . . .

Judge: Tap-dancing, Mr Fang?

Fang: Yes, my Lord. I was a bit of a hoofer in my day, and I wanted to get it on film before I lost the knack.

Judge: I hope you do not sing 'My Way' on this video.

Fang: Certainly not, my Lord. Nor 'Send in the Clowns'.

Judge: Good. I come to this court to get away from television shows. Carry on.

Counsel: At any point in the film do you make comments about my client, and your business partner, Mr Victor Musket?

Fang: Yes, I do.

Counsel: Are they of such a nature as to suggest that Mr Musket is incompetent, fraudulent, evil-smelling, unreliable, unable to tap-dance and possessed of the most annoying laugh known to man?

Fang: I really can't remember. I made the film some time ago.

Judge: Mr Garstang, would it not be simpler to produce the film and see for ourselves?

Counsel: I do not have access to the video, my Lord.

Judge: You mean, you haven't seen it?

Counsel: No, my Lord.

Judge: Then how on earth do you or your client know there is any libel in the film?

Counsel: By a strange coincidence, the technician who worked on the film is related to Mr Musket's wife. He happened to mention the rough gist of what Mr Fang has said. It seemed highly libellous.

Judge: Then we must order this video film to be produced at once. Mr Fang, please arrange for this.

Fang: I cannot, my Lord.

Judge: And why not, pray?

Fang: My Lord, this film is designed to be seen after my death. It contains material which, if shown in my lifetime, could involve me in litigation.

Judge: It already has.

Fang: What I say about Victor Musket is quite mild compared to some of the other things I say about relatives and friends. If you order this film to be shown in court, then *you* will become the instigator and accomplice of libellous statements of which the world yet knows nothing.

Judge: You claim that showing the only piece of evidence in this trial would make a criminal of me?

Fang: I certainly do.

Judge: This is quite unprecedented. The case is adjourned while I think about it.

Welcome To Kington, 1989

MINUTES OF
THE UNITED DEITIES

1. The Chairgod said that before they turned to the war in Iraq, he had a serious matter to bring to the attention of the assembled Gods. There had been an outbreak of a hitherto unknown killer disease in China and Hong Kong, which was causing great panic in those areas, and a lot of worry worldwide.

2. Mars, Roman God of war, said he was only a humble God of war, but a new variant of influenza didn't seem to be nearly as interesting as the war in Iraq. People sneezed, then they died. That was life. But if you really wanted to die well, die in battle, that was his motto.

3. Persephone, a Greek goddess, said that she never ceased to be amazed by the enthusiasm of war Gods for dying in battle, especially as it was a thing they would never have to do personally. It was ironic that immortals were so very keen on death. She knew what she was talking about as she was the wife of Hades, God of the Roman underworld, a favourite resort of people who had recently died, and she couldn't help noticing that not many Gods were among them.

4. In fact, she added, war Gods were like commanding generals; they expected all the fighting and dying to be done by someone else.

5. Thor, the Norse God of thunder and hammer-throwing, challenged her to come outside and say that again. He then went outside. Persephone stayed where she was.

6. The Chairgod said that if Mars cared to wait for a minute, he would explain to him the importance of this in a way that even a war God could understand. The thing was that this new disease had all the appearance

of a good old-fashioned plague. The kind of plague sent down in olden days by vengeful Gods.

7. The Jewish God said he had great memories of his plague-sending days, when he was trying to get the Jews out of Egypt. Frogs were great. Boils were great. Flies were great, if you had enough of them. Locusts, too, he could recommend.

8. An Egyptian God said that he had a very good cure for boils, if anyone was interested.

9. The Chairgod said that he had not yet come to the point. The point was that there had been a time when Gods had inflicted lots of plagues on human beings. The Gods had driven men mad. The Gods had sent famine and drought and floods and monsters and dragons and giants. But those days were over. There had been an agreement, the Supreme Powers Non-Proliferation of Plagues Treaty, under which all Gods had agreed to refrain from punishing humanity in this way. Humanity was getting very good at punishing itself, after all.

10. Gods could still send bad weather or natural phenomena like volcanic eruptions, if they had got planning permission from the necessary divine sub-committee. But plagues were out. And he thought that this new China-based illness looked suspiciously like a plague. Had any God, he wanted to know, taken illicit, unauthorised action in this matter?

11. There was a silence.

12. The silence was broken by Thor coming back in and asking if anyone could remember why he had gone outside.

13. The Chairgod asked Thor if he had recently inflicted a plague on the people of China.

14. Thor said not as far as he could remember, and it was the sort of thing you didn't forget easily.

15. The Chairgod said that, well, if nobody was going to own up, he didn't see what more he could do. Perhaps they could take a break for five minutes to see if anyone's memory was refreshed. He had all the time in the world. It was only their own time they were wasting.

Independent, 2003

A STIFF IN TIME

SOMETHING *a little different today, as we bring you a complete science-fiction police thriller . . .*

The East Wessex police force had a dead man they couldn't identify. They had tried everything, including slipping it by dead of night over the border into West Wessex and leaving it there. Next day it was back, with a note from the West Wessex police pinned to it: 'Do your own dirty work, lads.'

'What do you reckon, Bob?' said Inspector Target. 'Slip it into South Wessex?'

'No,' said Sergeant Bob Tremlow reluctantly. 'He's getting a bit shopworn as it is. His tie got pretty crumpled in the last move.'

They looked admiringly at the hideous green, blue and orange fantasy round the late departed's neck. It could only be an old school tie.

'If I had been to a school with ties like that, I'd conceal the fact,' said Target. 'Still, I suppose we'd better run it through the file.'

It isn't commonly known that the police have a file on old school ties, also on regimental insignia, cricket club blazers, livery company markings or anything which might help identify dead people who insist on wearing such things.

'Fat lot of good,' said Bob Tremlow. 'Say we come up with his old school. What do we do then? Check all people who ever went there? Bring the oldest teachers in to look at him and say – "Do you remember teaching this corpse French"?'

'Have you got a better idea?'

They sent the tie away for questioning. Three days later the answer came back: this tie belongs to no known school. The tie had been cleaned

143

and pressed. They went down to the morgue, put it back on the man and stared at him again.

'He's looking better,' said the sergeant. 'Shall we get the rest of his clothes cleaned?'

'Look,' said Target, 'maybe it belongs to an overseas school, or a school that no longer does ties. I've got a friend in the haberdashery business who might recognize it. I'll give him a ring.'

It was a shot in a million, but sometimes shots in a million come off. The friend looked up the tie in his archives and revealed that it belonged to the old boys of Nossex Grammar School.

'Nossex?' said Bob Tremlow. '*Nossex*?'

'You know, I presume, that Wessex is short for West Saxon?' said Target. 'And Essex means East Saxon?'

'And Sussex means . . . ' said Bob, to whom it had never occurred before.

'Precisely. Nossex is the missing kingdom of the North Saxons. My haberdashery friend also told me something else. Nossex Grammar School was closed down in 1923.'

They considered the implications of this. A Nossex Old Grammarian could not be any younger than 90. Their man was 35 at most. Why would a young chap go around claiming membership of a school which hadn't produced an old boy for 65 years?

'I'm going to get a check done on the rest of his clothes,' said Inspector Target, who rather fancied the idea of haberdashery archives by now. When the results came through, he wasn't so happy. The manufacturers of the clothes worn by the dead man had all ceased trading before 1937.

'What we've got here,' said the sergeant, 'is a man who was too poor to buy new clothes.'

'These are very nice clothes. They cost a small fortune.'

'What we've got here . . . ' tried Tremlow again.

'Is a man who died in the 1930s,' said Target.

It was the only theory that fitted the facts. This man had left Nossex in the 1920s and died in, say, 1938. He hadn't been found until 1989, and he was still in perfect condition.

'But *how*?' said Tremlow.

'This may sound crazy,' said Target, 'so don't tell anyone I said so. But what if a 1930s police force had found a better method of getting rid of corpses than just slipping them into West Wessex? What if they could slip them *through a time-warp into another decade?* Pop! The mystery corpse vanishes from 1938. Pop! It reappears in 1989.'

'You've been watching too much telly, old son,' said Bob. 'Give us a bit of evidence at least.'

There was a knock and a constable came in.

'Sorry to interrupt, sir, but we've got something pretty weird out here. They've found a body in the street, dressed in pre-war gear with a newspaper in his hand.'

'So?'

'Well, the main headline in the paper says: Chamberlain Flies to Munich.'

There was a long silence. Then Bob Tremlow said: 'That sounds like evidence to me.'

Welcome To Kington, 1989

A COMPLETE RIP-ROARING, THUNDEROUS NOVEL

Chapter One

'Waal, I ain't one fer admitting defeat,' said old Will Wordsworth, spitting with amazing accuracy at a daffodil near by, 'but this little ol' limerick's got me beat.'

'Blamed if I see how it works,' said Alf Tennyson. 'It ain't like an epic at all. It's so tiny there ain't nothing to it – more of a lady's weapon if you ask me.'

'Talking about my invention?' said a long, cool voice.

They gasped and swung round. There, in the middle of the Last Chance Saloon, Henley-on-Thames, deep in the heart of shootin', rowin' and puntin' country, stood a stranger. They knew him from his long moustaches and the rhyming dictionary poking from one corner of his otherwise well-cut coat. Edward Lear!

'We was just saying, Mr Lear, that your limerick is mighty hard to handle. No offence, but ten dollars says you can't get it to work.'

'*A singer from out of El Paso,*' said Lear instantly, '*Got caught up one day in a lasso. When he finally got loose, From that darn pesky noose, He was no longer profundo basso.* You owe me ten bucks, gentlemen.'

After the stranger had departed, they sat and stared at each other.

'El Paso don't rhyme with lasso,' said Alf.

'Right,' said Will. 'But he still licked us.'

Chapter Two

'They say "King" Lear's in town,' said Kid Swinburne. 'What's more, they say he's found a rhyme for Albuquerque.'

The poets gazed moodily at the bottle of hock and wished to heaven 'King' Lear had never been born. What use were their long drawn-out stanzas and etiolated similes against the quick-fire, rapid repeat limerick? It was plumb unfair. When the saloon door of the Paradise Inn, Stratford-on-Avon (bang in the middle of the Shakespeare ranch) opened, they didn't look round. They knew who it was. 'King' Lear.

'Anyone got anything to say to me?' drawled the King.

'Yes, I have!' declared young Cov Patmore, jumping to his feet. 'Take this, Mr Lear! *There was a young man of Dunstable, Whose morals were wholly unstable . . .* '

'It ain't Dun*stable*, kid. It's *Dun*stable. Get wise.'

Patmore slumped over the table, deeply wounded. Lear grinned wickedly.

'Well, gents, if that's the best you all can do . . . Oh, and by the way, murky, turkey and Circe, if you're looking for a rhyme for Albuquerque. Another thing. I'm working on a new model. The Chinese limerick. Be seein' ya.'

Chapter Three

'Tell me one thing,' said grizzled Matt Arnold. 'How come we're all talking in this pesky accent?'

'To sell the whole story to the Yankees, they say,' muttered Bob Browning. 'By the way, I figure that Circe is no kind of rhyme for Albuquerque.'

'I believe you,' said Matt. 'Now all we need is someone who dares say it to his face.'

Chapter Four

They were all there for the shoot-out at the OK Corral. Bob Browning, with Liz Barrett begging him not to get involved, young Alf Tennyson, now old Alf Tennyson, Bill Thackeray, Ed Fitzgerald, 'Doc' Poe, Gerry Hopkins and Art Clough. All against the one man, 'King' Lear.

Trouble was, Lear hadn't showed up.

'Trouble is, he ain't showed up,' sneered 'Doc' Poe, whose accent did at least sound authentic.

'Oh yes, he did,' said old Alf Tennyson, pointing to the wall behind. There, written in big white paint, was the following message: '*They all came to the OK Corral, Fit to fight and plumb full of morale, But they hadn't the brain, To write a quatrain, Or a bar of an old Bach chorale.'*

Chapter Five

'You cain't rhyme "corral" with "chorale"', said 'Doc' Poe, coughing.

'I can,' said 'King' Lear.

Chapter Six

'All right,' said 'Doc' Poe, 'but I bet your talk about the Chinese limerick was so much hogwash.'

'I like your nerve, Poe,' said 'King' Lear. 'So I'll tell you. You know the Chinese do things back to front? Writin' and readin' and that?'

'Ah've heard so,' said Poe.

'Then listen to this,' said Lear. *'In China, the limerick's wrong, A kind of back-to-front song. And this is the worst, The last line comes first, So there was a young man from Hongkong.'*

Chapter Seven

Edward Lear jumped into his bed, along with a dashing redhead. He had drunk so much whisky, he felt kinda frisky, so he ... (*That will do, thank you. – Ed.*)

Moreover, Too, 1985

NEW ORLEANS

THE FIRST FEW NOTES

When I first fell in love with jazz in the mid-1950s I knew that New Orleans was the place to go to. I also knew that I had left it far too late if jazz history was to be believed, which it sometimes is. Most of the best musicians had left the Crescent City by about 1920 to go on and make their names in Chicago, New York and the world. All that was left in New Orleans was a few old men barely keeping the tradition alive.

And now quite unexpectedly I have got to New Orleans at last, only to find that there is a great deal of jazz here, probably much more than there was in the 1950s. It isn't so much that it has revived here as that it has been brought back, mostly by young white players from America, Britain and Scandinavia, players who have so fallen in love with the music that they are prepared to lug their trumpets and clarinets half-way across the world to set up home here. Even in the traditional marching bands you will spot eager young white faces among the older black ones.

This is about as extraordinary a thing as it would be if London were rediscovered as the home of music hall, with pilgrims coming to London to search out the old singers and comedians, or if young Americans flocked to London to sing traditional music hall songs in East End pubs. What makes it odder still is that jazz is not central to the lives of most people in New Orleans.

It certainly doesn't play a central part in the life of the black community, from whence it came all those years ago. I had lunch yesterday at Buster Holmes, a small eating house on the edge of the French Quarter, which features red beans and rice, the dish beloved of Louis Armstrong. There were one or two jazz relics on the walls along with boxing posters and pictures of black celebrities but among the hundreds of records in the juke box there was only one by a jazz artist, Louis himself. All the rest were a rhythm 'n' blues, soul, modern rock, and even a few singles by British groups.

If you wander at night down Bourbon Street, the tourist strip of the French Quarter, you will hear – just as the guidebook says – music coming out of almost every doorway. A lot of it is young white jazz, but a lot of it is other stuff – country music, rock 'n' roll, strip club backing tracks and, at the 500 Club, some very good all-black rhythm 'n' blues bands. On the corner of St Peter's Street you come at last to a really classy black jazz artist, trumpeter Wallace Davenport. But ironically he isn't elderly and traditional enough to get a good crowd; the spectators are all round the corner at Preservation Hall.

This stark room, looking rather like a National Trust property before renovation has started, has been devoted for the last twenty years to giving the old guys a place to play. Impossible to tell how old some of them are, but over seventy and eighty is not uncommon. You pay a dollar to get in and you may not smoke, drink, eat or even sit – only listen in reverence to the survivors doing their thing, and doing it rather well, especially in the case of clarinettist Willie Humphrey. After forty minutes we give them a standing ovation, no other kind of ovation being possible, and we are ushered out in time for the next shift.

Authenticity is not just a key word, it is now a gimmick. It suddenly occurred to me, as I stood wedged between German students and a group from Wisconsin, that by dispensing with all tourist gimmicks these old guys had packed in more visitors than any of the clip joints on Bourbon Street. Two hundred of us at a dollar a head, a fresh house every sixty minutes. That is a lot of money. I certainly hope that most of it is going to the boys in the band. After a lifetime of being left behind by jazz history they deserve it.

DANS LE QUARTIER

The French Quarter of New Orleans is everything the name suggests; it's about one-quarter French. The rest is Spanish, American and Creole, and it adds up to the sort of place where you can wander through all day long without getting bored or repeating yourself.

I wasn't expecting this. I was expecting a few quaint street corners with a few quaint balconies, the whole scene set to music by a few quaint jazz bands – not an extensive township. The reason for this, I now realise, is that whereas some landmarks, such as the Giants' Causeway, look bigger and better in photographs than in real life, places like the French Quarter which depend on accidental town planning and a quiet scale never look very good in detail, just as it's impossible to photograph the back streets of Venice or Greenwich Village.

The balconies, for instance. They're different from other balconies not just because they're more ornate – although they are – but because they're bigger and therefore can actually be used for doing things on.

Most balconies on old houses in London are not for human occupancy – they're just about big enough for a couple of geraniums holding their breath – but you have to crunch your way around New Orleans for a while until you realise that people have on their balconies tropical plantations, barbecues, restaurant overflows, sun-bathing areas, storage places and reading rooms.

They are also useful for sheltering under during New Orleans rainstorms, which fall by the inch rather than the raindrop. I always used to wonder why the men in New Orleans brass band parades were shown waving umbrellas as they danced crazily down the street. I now realise that lugging my oversize umbrella across the Atlantic, bringing strained smiles to the TWA stewardesses' faces, was the best thing I could have done.

The worst downpour we encountered defeated even the umbrella and we were blown indoors into a small bar called The Clinic, where a nurse was in attendance ready to pour healing liquids out of hundreds of different bottles.

'I'd like to try a typical New Orleans drink which isn't sweet,' I said. They have a fiendishly sweet tooth here. The Hurricane, the local cocktail, is as syrupy as tinned fruit salad, their Beignets are showered in icing sugar and the Ramos gin fizz is like shaving foam in texture and taste.

'Give him a Sazarec,' said a man at the counter.

'Honey,' said the nurse, 'I ain't never made a Sazarec. Whenever I'm asked for one I say I'm fresh out of the ingredients.'

'I'll show you,' said the man. 'Take some crushed ice . . .'

Between them they took ten minutes having fun working up a Sazarec.

Then we all tasted it. Mmm. A bit liquoricey, but not bad. They spent another ten minutes telling us which restaurants to go to, another ten which restaurants not to go to, then the rain stopped and we set off into the steaming streets, crunching onwards. This was way off the beaten track, or, to put it another way, more than five minutes from Bourbon Street. The tourists don't like to venture very far from Bourbon Street, which leaves a lot of French Quarter for discerning people like you and me. There's a lot of Chelsea which isn't on the King's Road.

Today it's as hot and blue as a prize English summer day, and we've been using the balconies to get some shade, as we crunch our way into the deepest, unexplored French Quarter. I say crunch, because the infill they use for the roads here is not gravel or sand, it's seashells; piles of tiny white seashells like the outflow from an enormous fish restaurant. With oysters at 25p each and shrimps as common as dirt, you might be forgiven for thinking that New Orleans was an enormous fish restaurant. When asked to sum up life in New Orleans, one famous novelist and native of the city said she thought it was most like drowning very slowly under water. Well, perhaps it is, but what a way to go.

ALLIGATORS AND ANNIE MILLER

Before I ever left London, I was told to make sure I went on Annie Miller's swamp tour. In New Orleans they said I shouldn't miss Annie Miller's swamp tour. Now, in Houma, I've been on Annie Miller's swamp tour and I'm here to tell you not to miss it. Or, in the words of the man from Oklahoma sitting next to me in the boat: 'I've driven all round the States and this is the best thirty dollars' worth I've had any-where, yes, sir.'

First, though, you have to get it into your head that Terrebonne parish, this last bit of America before you fall into the Gulf of Mexico, is wet, very wet indeed. Twenty-five per cent of the parish (elsewhere it would be called a county) is land. Seventy-five per cent is water: swampland, floating marshes, lakes, bogs. Through it all run the bayous, slow-moving rivers that flow down to the sea and which for a long time provided more reliable local highways than any road. Annie Miller, a veteran trapper, hunter, character, even commercial pilot, has two fast boats moored alongside her bayou home and makes a living showing people the recesses of the swamps that she knows better than anyone. Even the alligators come when they hear her voice, it's said, though this seems unlikely.

What makes Annie special as a guide is that she loves showing people her world, and gets excited each time she goes out. Late afternoon is the best time, when the birds are coming back from their feeding grounds – long-legged snowy egrets, spindly herons, hawks, exotic ibises – but she never knows quite what will turn up. Today she thinks it's just possible we might see a pair of bald eagles, more likely we'll spot a nutria. 'Nutria is a South American animal. A man near here brought seven back as pets, but they broke free during a hurricane and multiplied in the swamps. Everyone said they were a pest as they love eating the roots of sugar cane, but then they found they made good fur and now they're not a pest any more. There's a nest right up here that I know of.'

We glide past the nest. It's empty. But in the first tall trees back of the swamp we see bald eagles, enormous even a hundred yards away, sitting motionless like king and queen of the bayou beside their tree-top nest which looks as big as an exploded raft. You feel they haven't begun to recognize the arrival of man in their land.

'Although it's the national bird of America it's pretty rare now. They have a wingspan of about eight feet. They live about thirty years and once they choose a mate they keep together for life.'

'That makes it a mighty strange bird to choose as an American symbol,' says the cynical cameraman. We have a film crew on board, doing a last day's shooting on a swamp opera called *The Horror from Boogalusa Bayou* or some such. What they're looking for is shots of animals fleeing in terror. They'd like to fire a gun in the air to get the eagles going. Annie puts her foot firmly on that idea. Next, we pass some marsh birds very close to. The producer claps his hands while the camera turns, ready for the flight.

'Never saw those birds fly in my life,' Annie mutters to herself.

We shoot out from under the Spanish moss and past the beautiful lilac water hyacinths ('brought here in 1884 by a kindly Japanese visitor to the New Orleans World Cotton Fair,' says Annie, 'and been multiplying ever since – now their roots *are* a pest'), into an enormous canal about 300 ft across. It's the Intracoastal Waterway, taking ships of any size from Texas to New Jersey if that's where you want to go. We overtake a cortège of rusty barges, and plunge again into a small bayou, but then turn right into a forgotten lake, where to our surprise Annie stands up and starts calling: 'Baby! Baby!'

Several large alligators immediately swim up to the boat and, if they weren't such fierce creatures, you'd swear they were gambolling round it. Annie feeds them bits of raw chicken off a long stick, and they jump for it. The eyes of the film crew shine.

'Hey, Annie, could you get one to land and then have it run off in terror?'

'Sure, why not?'

We land on a soggy island. A six-foot alligator follows us, and the raw chicken, up the shore. It turns and goes in the water, but not terrified enough for the film crew.

The film crew give up and we go off to watch the return of the birds, who sure enough come wheeling in, white and mysterious, over the waste wetlands of the bayou. The sun goes down like a huge pumpkin, and dusk rolls in. You suddenly feel a million miles from anywhere, and a million years from today.

Moreover, Too, 1985

BURNT AT THE STAKE,
OR YOUR MONEY BACK

'IHEAR they're having a medieval weekend over at Short Shrift village,' said Father.

'Oh, good,' said Mother. 'Will they be having archery, and jousting, and falconry?'

'Oh, yes, I jolly well imagine so,' said Father. 'And medieval music, and a bit of banqueting, and a whole ox, and perhaps an all-day mead bar.'

'But what if the children don't want to go?'

'What, Sylvia, Dick, Liz, Petra, Vivien, Wayne, Melvyn and the rest?'

Sylvia, their eldest, had been planned as an only child. All the other nine were accidental afterthoughts. It was not exactly what you might call a planned family, unless of course you were Catholic.

'Yes,' agreed Mother. 'They always seem a bit bored by this sort of traditional activity.'

'Well, children will be children,' said Father. A false idea, when you think about it. Children are children now – what they *will* be is something different and certainly not children.

But this time they were in for a surprise. Sylvia and Dick and all the rest were very keen to go to the medieval weekend. They said they had heard it was going to be good fun. Not one volunteered not to go.

'It certainly looks different,' said Father doubtfully, as they strode through the entrance come Saturday morning. Nowhere to be seen were the usual gay tents and proud flags that one associates with medieval times. Instead, there were a series of sad-looking wooden shacks, a man in the stocks whom people were bombarding with missiles, and what looked very like a gibbet with a body dangling from it. The children scarpered to have a look around.

'I find that in very bad taste,' said Mother, looking up at the dangling carcass.

'The Middle ages *were* in very bad taste,' said the corpse, much to Mother's surprise. 'That's the whole point we're trying to get across through this weekend.'

Father was about to ask who 'we' were when he was bundled out of the way by a couple of lepers rushing past, shouting 'Unclean, unclean!' Then Mother screamed. She was pointing at a full-scale rack, where two torturers were stretching a body on the diabolical instrument. The reason she was screaming was that the body belonged to her son Dick.

'Let him go!' she shouted. 'Let my son go at once!'

'Oh, for heaven's sake, Mother!' said Dick, looking up at her. 'It's only a *game*. I'm supposed to see how long I could have withstood medieval torture. It's really great. Oow!!'

Mother might have said something else except that just then an arrow thwanged into the building next to her, and she fainted.

When she came round, Father was beating off a First Aid helper who was trying to attach leeches to her.

'There's something very strange going on round here,' said Father grimly, 'and I intend to get to the bottom of it. Let's go and talk to the corpse again – he seems to know what's going on.'

'Hello, again. Having a good time?' said the corpse affably as it dangled aimlessly.

'Where,' said Father firmly, 'is the jousting, the archery, the falconry?'

'We don't have any of that sort of rubbish here,' said the corpse. 'Go to a theme park or an English Heritage function if you want a bit of plastic history, some pre-wrapped culture. We give you the real thing here.'

'AND WHO IS WE?' shouted Father.

'We are the Campaign For Real Heritage,' said the corpse. Just then a loudspeaker crackled and spoke.

'Good afternoon, ladies and gentlemen, and thank you for supporting the Campaign for Real Heritage in our fight against the heritage industry. Just to let you know that in a few minutes' time the Sealed Flask will be re-enacting the Black Death in the main arena. Half an hour after that, at 3.30, the Children's Crusade will depart for Jerusalem, and at 4 o'clock we will be ducking some of the mothers to see if they are witches. Meanwhile, look out for footpads, highway-men, pick-pockets and low thieves who have all been trained at our Campaign for Real Heritage school. Thank you.'

Just then Dick and Wayne turned up, pulling excitedly at Mother's hands.

'Mum, Mum, come quick, we've volunteered you to be drowned as a witch. Come on. And Sylvia and Liz are being tried for heresy. Come on!'

Despite himself, Father couldn't help smiling. It was the first time the children had ever displayed any interest in history.

(Would you like to know more about the campaign and help the fight against keg heritage? Write for details.)

Welcome To Kington, 1989

ELEGIE COMPOSÉE DANS UN RURAL CHURCHYARD

PAR THOMAS GRAY

Le curfew sonne le knell du jour partant,
    Un gang de vâches va homewards à la farm,
Le ploughman rentre à high tea, lentement,
    Et laisse le monde à moi, tranquille et calme.

La dernière trace de sunshine disparaît,
    Et maintenant le soir est un peu froid;
Le weather n'est pas excellent pour May;
    Je voudrais avoir un thick jersey avec moi.

Ici, dans le churchyard, tout est dark;
    Et j'ai perdu mon dernier pencil stub.
Je ne peux plus écrire. – Oh, sod ça pour un lark!
    Je vais immédiatement au village pub.

The Franglais Lieutenant's Woman, 1986

NATURE CORNER WITH URBAN NATURALIST 'BIN LINER'

TODAY: THE SUPERMARKET TROLLEY

The supermarket trolley is a comparatively recent newcomer to our shores (writes Bin-Liner). Until about twenty years ago it was unknown, but a large-scale immigration pattern from the USA occurred until quickly it became a familiar sight in our supermarkets and larger groceries, where it was kept in captivity.

What has happened recently to alert naturalists' attention is that the trolley has started to break out of captivity and live in the wild. It is almost impossible these days to go for a walk in our suburbs or inner town areas without coming across one or more of these large creatures browsing quietly on a traffic island or just standing peacefully on the pavement. So far we have been totally baffled by this new behaviour pattern.

The phenomenon is quite common in old-fashioned rural nature studies, of course, where an import such as mink or coypu later escapes from captivity and inhabits vast stretches of East Anglia. But this is the first time it has happened to a purely urban creature. Nor has it happened to such close relations as the British Rail trolley or airport trolley, which very rarely stray far from their home. Only the supermarket trolley seems driven by the urge to escape.

Quite why it should want to do so is not clear, especially as it is totally unadapted to life in the wild. Its daily diet involves a considerable intake of washing powder boxes, packets of flour, frozen fish fingers, etc., and this it simply will not find out on our city streets. Many of them, I'm afraid to say, starve to death after only a few days and meet a tangled and rusty end, unless recaptured by their owners. And yet they persist in escaping.

Some larger stores such as Sainsbury's have tried a programme of keeping the trolleys chained up when not being taken for a walk yet even here they have met failure and have been forced to give up the idea, as if the trolley's drive to freedom is too strong for chains.

Professor Karelius, in *Urban Nature Studies*, Vol. XI, No. 6, puts forward the interesting theory that trolleys somehow develop a strong if temporary affection for visitors to supermarkets and try to follow them home. He even cites cases of families who have adopted a trolley as a pet and let it live in their house with them – in one or two cases the trolley has changed its diet entirely and takes only newspapers or the family laundry.

If this is so, however, it still does not explain why so many trolleys are found in the street, having patently not followed anyone home. He suggests that this may be because families grow tired of their demands or their great size compared with most household pets, and simply throw them out on the street as they might an unwanted dog or cat. If this is so, we certainly need more documented evidence than he provides.

My own personal theory is that the supermarket trolley's burst for freedom is prompted by an urge to inter-breed. If a well-known species such as a Tesco trolley finds itself surrounded entirely by other Tesco trolleys, it may well have an innate compulsion to search out and mate with, say, a Safeways trolley, in order to keep the pedigree well mixed. Having said this, however, I must admit that I have no evidence to support it; I just happen to like the idea.

As a final postscript to these notes I must report a very rare sighting last month: a fully operating, adult in-flight trolley seen in West London. These are normally only ever seen inside airplanes, where they have been trained to carry loads of miniature spirits, small hot lunches, duty-free cigarettes, etc. This trolley, spotted near West Drayton, had, perhaps predictably, lost all its load of drink and cigarettes. None of the hot lunches, however, had been touched.

Moreover, Too, 1985

ALL QUIET ON THE GLORIOUS TWELFTH

'QUIET out there,' said McAllister.

'Too damned quiet for my liking,' said Duncan Wood.

Together they stared out into the gathering gloom. From their positions they could just make out the line of the wood across the two or three hundred yards of moorland which separated them from it. They had built rudimentary defences of wood, and had a couple of rifles between them, but any determined rush would certainly sweep them away. They could not see anything moving in the woods at all, but they knew the woods were full of them.

'How many do you suppose there are?'

'Four or five thousand.'

'What do you think they are up to?'

'Hard to say. You never know what the grouse are thinking. People always say they're a stupid bird, but in my experience they learn fast if given the chance. The old Earl of Inverspey had a tame grouse, you know, which could say seven words.'

'What were they?'

' "Double whisky, please", and "Ich bin ein Berliner." '

'That doesn't prove intelligence.'

'Well, it was four more words than the Earl could say. It was a family joke whether the Earl had a tame grouse or the grouse had a tame earl.'

They fell silent. In the woods a distant murmuring noise could be heard, so soft you weren't even sure there was a noise there at all. It was the sort of noise you get from a distant sea or, alternatively, the moment just before the enemy charges. The two men's nerves were as sharp as raw rhubarb.

'Do you know what worries me?' said McAllister suddenly. 'What worries me is that every 12 August, regular as clockwork, we've gone in and cleaned 'em out. It would be a singularly stupid bird that didn't tumble to this sooner or later and act accordingly.'

'How do you mean, act accordingly?'

'Try and wipe us out on 11 August. In other words, tonight.'

They stared out again through the gloom, though less was now visible than before. The thought that, at any moment, thousands of grouse might bear down on them, whirring madly and beating at them with those savage claws, was unbearable. A single bird suddenly came out of the dark air and Duncan Wood swung up his gun, but McAllister laid a hand on his arm. It was only an owl.

'Steady on, old boy. You've been too long in the butts. It's getting to you. The reinforcements will be here tomorrow.'

Duncan Wood laughed savagely. 'Reinforcements? Japanese financiers, English football managers and Belgian politicians? Dear God, can they not send us any good shots up the line these days? Last year we even had an American who shot himself in the foot.'

'If we can hold on until they get here, we'll be all right.'

Somewhere away on the hills a single cottage light flickered and went out. The country folk would be getting an early night and staying well clear on the morrow. Experience had told them it would be death not to.

'I wonder if it will always go on like this?' said McAllister suddenly. 'Will grouse and man always be at war? Will we always have this carnage? I sometimes dream of the day when man and grouse live at peace and call each other brother bird.'

'Brother bird?' said Duncan Wood, amazed. 'Have ye gone mad? The grouse will not rest until every man has been swept off the earth, or at least from this part of Glen Usk.'

'That is what we have always been told. Yet I remember a tame grouse that used to be with Mrs Robertson of Glen Killin. I was talking to this grouse one day, and he told me that he couldn't understand man's murderous hatred of grouse.'

'Us? Hatred? Murderers? You've been talking to too many tame grouse. It's the grouse who hate us, as well ye ken. You wouldn't be a secret grouse-lover by any chance, McAllister?'

It was the worst insult Duncan Wood could think of. It was the worst McAllister knew as well. He flushed and said nothing.

Out there, in no man's land, nothing moved in the air at all. The two men never thought of looking down at the ground. If they had, they might have seen several hundred handpicked grouse creeping through the heather on a special 11 August daredevil mission.

Duncan Wood and McAllister never knew what hit them, and the reinforcements had not the faintest idea what could have happened when they found them the next morning, dead, neatly plucked and hanging upside down from a branch.

Welcome To Kington, 1989

HISTORY OF KING TONY

or *Labour's Lost, Love*

ACT III

It is midnight in the royal bedchamber. King Tony, awake, is pacing the room, unable to sleep, while his wife Queen Cherie slumbers in their Tuscan Tudor-style four-poster bed.

King Tony: What dreams are these that crowd upon my sleep?
What voices crying, 'Give me power again!' ?
Methinks I hear the sound of erstwhile friends
Who clamour for a chance to regain rank,
Harriet Harman, Frankie Field and others,
And above them all I hear the tones
Of young Duke Mandelson. Oh, I did love him
Before he went and got that cursed loan!
Once he was a helper. Now a problem.
'Tis strange how things, once good, can turn for ill.

Enter the spirit of Baroness Thatcher.

Spirit: Oh, stop this useless show of endless moaning!
Self-pity is a base and useless thing!
Pull yourself together! Be a king!
King Tony: Avaunt, thou witch, thou glaring phantom figure!
Thou hast a look of Thatcher, my old foe!
Spirit: Of course I do. I am her spirit self,

164

Come to visit you and give advice.

King Tony: This cannot be! We are old enemies!

Spirit: On different sides, maybe. But otherwise

We are the same, in lust for power and rank.

Once at the top, we aim to stay for ever.

Unlike your predecessor, John the Major,

Who had no appetite for battle, little wimp!

Admit, King Tony, we are both the same.

Committed to th'eternal power game!

King Tony: There's something in what you say, but I cannot

Allow my people to believe such things.

The folk should always love, not fear, their kings.

Spirit: What tosh! My greatest strength was always this,

That I could never give a damn what people thought.

Love me, hate me, 'twas all the same to me.

Whereas you court your popularity.

One day this love of being loved will cause

Your downfall in some internecine wars!

Enough of this. How can I help you now?

King Tony: Two problems I do have. One's Northern Ireland.

The other, my old friend Duke Mandelson.

Spirit: Then one shall solve the other.

King Tony: Tell me how.

Spirit: Ye gods! Must I spell all this process out?

The trick with two competing problems is

To settle one by feeding it the other.

I had a problem once, called Sir Chris Patten.

Another was the poll tax, of ill fame.

I put them both together and, hey presto!

They gave each other such a nasty smell

That no offending odour stuck to me.

What other problem can I solve for you?

King Tony: How to fight the forces of Lord Hague.

Spirit: Alas, that army that I once did lead?

It wounds my heart to tell you what to do,

But you must part the opposing troops in two
By hiving off the European part
From those opposed to Europe and the mainland.
Say to Duke Heseltine, and Sir Kenneth Clarke,
'Come sit with me upon the selfsame platform
And we shall talk in friendship of the future!'

King Tony: They'd never come.

Spirit: Just try. You'll be surprised.

King Tony: All right, I will. One other thing.
Who shall I make mayor of London Town?

Spirit: YOU make mayor? It lies within your power?

King Tony: No, not at all. The people all can vote
For whom they like – as long as it's for my man!

Spirit: You are a cunning pupil! You have learnt
To meddle without your fingers getting burnt.

Queen Cherie: (sleepily) My Lord, come back to bed!

King Tony: And so I will!
(softly) Good spirit, thanks for this. Some other time.

The king returns to bed. The spirit vanishes. From behind a pillar comes the figure of the Duke of Livingstone.

Red Ken: I fear you not. You'll soon be in my power.
Wait till I'm London's Mayor! Then comes my hour!

Independent, 1999

HOW I KICKED
THE VIDEO HABIT

Today's piece may prove harrowing for some, ugly even. To others it may bring a message of hope. It is the story of how addiction can be fought and conquered, and how a family can come through darkness into the light beyond. It is, in brief, the story of how I finally began to master the video habit.

It all began as a bit of a joke. Someone at work suggested I might want to review a couple of TV programmes. I had to be out that night, so he arranged for me to hire a VCR machine.

The first experience was delicious – no longer was I tied to the whim of the television companies and I could enjoy their offerings any time I liked. So I bought several tapes. I peeled all the adhesive labels off their backing and stuck them on to the tapes and their boxes. I even numbered the cassettes and indexed them in a little book. I displayed all the symptoms of what I now recognize as an addiction, though at the time I told myself I was controlling my TV intake.

My family began to get worried when I started recording *The Jewel in the Crown*. What worried them was that I didn't watch it, just taped it. I had to be out during the first two episodes, and by the time I was in for episode three, I hadn't got round to watching the first two, so there wasn't much point in watching number three. I taped it instead.

I got my son to tape subsequent episodes. I bought more tapes. And finally I had all twelve hours of *The Jewel in the Crown* stored away, with none of it watched.

I was particularly anxious to watch it, as I had missed all of *Brideshead*

Revisited and had thus been a social outcast for several months, unable to take part in conversations except with feeble bleats of: 'Well, I read Evelyn Waugh's novel when I was at school and I didn't think it was one of his funniest.' People would stare acidly at me without replying. I didn't want this to happen with *The Jewel*.

It happened, of course. Everyone started talking about the damned thing, and all I could say was: 'Well, I've got it on cassette and just as soon as I've watched it . . .'

Then Salman Rushdie attacked it and I didn't even know why he was attacking it. He went on TV one night to attack it and I taped his attack, knowing that I could see it after I'd seen the whole series and understand why he was attacking it.

You mustn't think, of course, that I was glued to the TV set during my period of addiction. I think I watched less than usual. It was just that I was taping more, creating a backlog of programmes.

Then last week I had to tape a BBC European football programme because my home team Wrexham, surging from the Fourth Division, were off to play Roma in the seething cauldron of the Roma FC stadium, and the BBC had promised to show the best bits.

But I had no tape available. My cassettes were all jammed with great movies, vintage film and early episodes of *The Young Ones*, some of which I had seen. I sank so low as to ask my son if he had a spare tape I could borrow.

'Dad,' he said, and I realised from the way he said it that I, his father, was being taken aside for a filial lecture; a sobering moment. 'Dad, we think it's time you started taping over *The Jewel in the Crown*.'

I thought about the unthinkable. The more I thought, the more a weight lifted from me. I had assumed that one night I would have to give myself a session of life in India.

I suddenly realised I didn't have to. I knew deep down that I would now never watch *The Jewel in the Crown*. I rushed over to the VCR machine and ordered it to wipe out the first two episodes.

So you see, if your family stands by you, you *can* beat it. I have begun to return to normal life. I have not taped anything since then. I haven't even seen Wrexham go down by 2–0 (but we'll beat you in the second leg, signore). I can even walk past the VCR machine without twitching. Anyway, they're bound to repeat *The Jewel in the Crown* soon enough. I wouldn't mind seeing just ten minutes of it. If I'm out, I can always tape it.

Moreover, Too, 1985

A CLERGYMAN FOR OUR TIME

The Rev. Jack Marsh had a pleasant smile, a small bald spot and three small churches to look after in a part of Hampshire much frequented by trout. He was also an accomplished bank robber, though no one knew this except the Bishop, with whom Jack had occasional confidential chats.

'Stands to reason, Bish,' said Jack the Rev., as he liked to think of himself. 'Out of all the clergyman in the C. of E., there is bound to be at least one into serious crime, right?'

'I suppose so,' said the Bishop, not happily.

'Well, that's me. Saves you worrying, don't you see? Now you don't have to agonize over which one it is – you know it's me. By the way, this is confidential, I take it?'

'Yes,' sighed the Bishop. 'I gave you my word, unfortunately. But look, when you're doing your ... bank raids, you won't hurt anyone, will you?'

'Lord bless you, Bish, not a hair on their head. What is it the Bible says? "Bash not the little sparrows on the head, or you will surely get thumped in the after-life." '

'Something like that,' said the Bishop, wondering fleetingly what Jack Marsh's sermons were like. He need not have worried. They were racy, down-to-earth and very well attended.

'You know,' declaimed Jack Marsh that Sunday, 'I often think that life is a bit like a horse race. It's over before it's hardly started, and you've got no money at the end of it.'

The choir laughed and leant forward, listening for the tip which was to come.

'Take the 2.30 at Uttoxeter next week, for example. Fifteen horses all straining to come first, and yet knowing in their heart of hearts that only one of them can win. But who is to say that the first horse is any better than the last horse? If Dead Gladioli were to win, for example . . . '

'He's tipping Dead Gladioli,' muttered old Woodbridge, the game-keeper, in the front row, and throughout the church there was a rustling of paper as people wrote the name down in their hymn books. After the service, the local rich farmers shook him warmly by the hand and drove off home to phone their bookies. There was quite a contrast between the big fat Volvos they drove and the Rev. Jack Marsh's little car. It was a Lamborghini.

'Darling,' said Mrs Marsh over Sunday lunch, 'there's a bit of talk in the countryside about you and your money. People are saying that . . . well, that you're selling apples from the orchard in defiance of EEC regulations.'

Jack laughed. 'You just tell them that my wife runs the best-organised jumble sales south of Birmingham, and that anyone could make a fortune that way.'

That Tuesday there was a big bank hold-up in Basingstoke and the Bishop felt constrained to summon Jack.

'Your work, I take it, Jack?' said the Bishop, pointing to the local paper.

' "Local Man Crosses Sahara on Unicycle", read out Jack. 'Yes, I did donate a few bottles of communion wine to keep him going.'

'These bank raids have to stop,' said the Bishop, ignoring him. 'For heaven's sake, Jack, anyone would think the Mafia was taking over the Church.'

'No blasted Catholics are muscling in on my racket, Bish,' said Jack angrily.

'All right, all right, I'm sorry, but remember: no more bank raids.'

Instead of answering, the Rev. Jack Marsh leant forward and turned on the Bishop's TV set. A voice said: 'And the result; first, Dead Gladioli . . . '

'No more bank raids,' said Jack. 'I promise you that.'

The Bishop gazed fondly at the clean-cut, devil-may-care features of his favourite rural clergyman and wondered why, for all the heartaches he caused him, there weren't more vicars like him.

'What is it the Bible says, Bish?' said Jack. 'Blessed are the cool in heart, for they shall verily get away with the loot?'

'Something like that,' said the Bishop.

Moreover, Too, 1985

FIGS AND UNCLE WALTER

My Uncle Walter was a brilliant classical scholar. He had also, as a youth, been subject to long and debilitating attacks of some fashionable nervous complaint, which meant that he had missed long periods of his education.

'I used to get these attacks in some vital year like 560 BC,' he told me, 'or at least when our group had got as far as 560 BC, and by the time I was well enough to come back they'd got up to 450 BC or some impossibly modern date and I would have missed a hundred years. Well, you can't study classical history a century here, a century there, so although I was top of the class in the bits I did know, I was bottom of the class in the other bits.'

This had a dire effect on his circle of friends at school. It meant that he literally had to sit at one end of the class when he was top of the class and right at the other end of the class when he wasn't, thus mixing him with two totally different sets of chums.

'The ones at the top of the class were bright as hell and all pretty boring. The ones at the bottom of the class were not necessarily stupid, but they had decided that classical studies were not going to help them much in life and they preferred to do other things, so in the short periods I spent at the bottom of the class, I learnt how to play poker, do crosswords, perform magic tricks and so on.

'And yet, curiously enough, it was from one of those lower-caste friends that I acquired the line of inquiry which has maintained my interest in the classics ever since.'

I kept quiet. I had heard the story before, but never tired of it.

'Humphreys was the boy's name and one day we were looking through a book of dirty Roman paintings – from Pompeii, I expect – when Humphreys said, "How do you suppose they keep their fig leaves on?"

' "Who?" I asked.

' "All those men you see as Roman statues," he said. "Their private parts are covered delicately with fig leaves. All very discreet. But in real life, how did they stop those fig leaves falling off?"

' "Well, I don't think they actually wore fig leaves in real life," I said. "I think that was just something they did on statues."

' "So in real life they were naked, without fig leaves?" he said. "Naked statues had to be covered up with fig leaves, but real-life Greeks and Romans could walk around naked? It's more important for *statues* to be decent?"

'And the more I thought about what Humphreys said, the more I realised that he had stumbled across one of the few areas of research that nobody had ever explored. Fig-leaf culture. People talked about fig leaves and sniggered, but that was it. Yet there were some interesting problems there. Why did Roman men in statues cover their modesty with fig leaves? Why not some other type of leaf? And, more importantly, how did they get their fig leaves to stay on and not fall off? Eh, boy?'

This last was addressed to me or to any nephew within range. I always blushed and said nothing, but my brother once said bravely, 'Perhaps they used elastic bands to fix them to their willies, Uncle Walter.'

Uncle Walter fixed him with his keen eye and said, 'Romans didn't have elastic bands. Don't think they had rubber, even.'

'Well, string, then,' said my brother recklessly. 'Or thread. They had thread, surely.'

'Have you ever tried fixing a fig leaf to your willy with string?' said Uncle Walter strictly. 'Well, have you, eh boy? Damned painful, I can tell you.'

And the thing was, we knew he knew, because it was an open family secret that he had spent a lot of time experimenting on himself to achieve the fig-leaf effect. He used to wander along the corridors of his large house in Shropshire, dressed only in a toga which concealed his latest attempt to reconstruct the fig-leaf effect, looking for his wife, Aunt Maud, to try it out on. Aunt Maud told me once that no matter where she was in the house, she was never quite sure that Uncle Walter might not come round the corner and insist on having her judgement there and then. Once, Uncle Walter had come up behind her in the conservatory, coughed, and said, as he opened his toga, 'What do you think of this then?' Only it hadn't been her at all, but a visitor called Mrs Arbuthnot who had come to look at their orchids and who then fled from the house screaming.

'Stupid woman,' said Uncle Walter. 'Has she never seen a fig leaf before?'

In order to pursue his classical studies, Uncle Walter needed a fairly constant supply of fig leaves and had planted a whole selection of fig trees on any south-facing aspect he could find. They grew well and by the time Uncle Walter died, he had bred a magnificent collection of fig trees. I met Aunt Maud again not so very long ago and asked if she was keeping busy.

'I certainly am,' she said. 'Here, take a jar of this.'

And she handed me a small jar of, according to the label, 'Aunt Maud's Fig Chutney'.

'Fig chutney, fig jam, figgy pudding – you name it, we do it,' she said. 'We shift about £400-worth a week.'

There was a picture of a Greek statue on the label, a warrior with upraised sword. The man wore nothing but a fig leaf. It seemed to be tied on with pink ribbon.

Someone Like Me, 2005

CHEMICAL WARFARE

In the longest trial in pharmaceutical history, Lord Howard de Pilatory, current chairman of Grotty Body Products, is facing 13,450 charges of deceiving the public. He pleads not guilty to all of them. This is an extract from day 43.

Counsel: I have here another of your products, a tin marked Cucumber Skin Conditioner. Would you please tell the court what effect this product has?

Defendant: Certainly. When rubbed on, it makes the skin of a cucumber exceptionally supple and lustrous.

Counsel: What effect does it have on the human skin?

Defendant: It makes it green.

Counsel: Do you not think the public is being deceived?

Defendant: Not at all. It is very fashionable to be green.

Counsel: Hmm. I have here another product, a shampoo called Milkmaid Cream. On the label it says in large letters NEW! IMPROVED! Now, laboratory tests show that it is no way different from your previous shampoo called Milkmaid Cream. Can you tell us what is new and improved?

Defendant: Certainly. The lettering is new and improved. It is twice as large as before. Also, we are using a totally new picture of a milkmaid which is much more attractive than the previous one.

Counsel: Are you suggesting that the change of a label can change the product?

Defendant: I would go further than that. It is the *only* thing that can change a product. We spend hundreds of thousands of pounds on the design of labels and packagings.

Counsel: With what result?

Defendant: We have to increase the price of the product. But that, of course, also improves it.

Counsel: How?

Defendant: It is well-known that you only get what you pay for. Therefore, the more you pay, the better you get.

Counsel: I see. I have here another bottle of shampoo, marked: Greasy Shampoo, for Lemony Hair! Are you seriously suggesting that people suffer from lemony hair?

Defendant: Of course. They use too much lemon shampoo. Greasy Shampoo restores the natural oils. It also makes a good salad dressing.

Counsel: Well, that is as it may be. Now, here I have a jar made by you marked Skin Reconditioner. Could you explain what this means?

Defendant: Glad to. In the ordinary face-care session, a girl will wash her face, apply cleanser, add moisturiser, use pre-conditioner, put on cream and then apply make-up. As a result of this treatment her skin is absolutely exhausted. Hence the need for Skin Reconditioner.

Counsel: What is the result?

Defendant: Her skin falls off, but not for years yet. Meanwhile it makes her look extremely alluring and leads to romantic attachments.

Counsel: How can you be sure?

Defendant: We have tested the product.

Counsel: On young girls?

Defendant: No. On rats.

Counsel: With what result?

Defendant: In every case, we have enabled young, lonely rats to develop strong and enduring relationships. Also, they go out dancing a lot.

Counsel: With other rats?

Defendant: Well, no. With empty bottles of Skin Reconditioner, actually. But the general effect has been good.

Counsel: I would like to put it to you that you are marketing at great expense products which have little or no effect on the customer.

Defendant: Of course. That is what beauty care is all about.

Counsel: What have you to say about Honey and Camomile Tea?

Defendant: That's very kind – I'd love a cup.

Counsel: I really meant, how do you justify your marketing of this product? Your slogans say 'Look good enough for a Royal Wedding – drink Honey 'n' Camomile Tea!' Are you suggesting that this tea will make you like Lady Diana Spencer?

Defendant: No. Like Prince Charles.

Counsel: How?

Defendant: It makes your ears stick out.

Counsel: How exactly?

Defendant: You stick a cube behind each ear.

Counsel: I see. You also market a kind of soap called Orange and Oatmeal. What advantage can there be in mixing orange with oatmeal?

Defendant: It makes your porridge an interesting colour, I suppose.

Counsel: I meant, in a soap?

Defendant: Ah, well. At the moment there is a great vogue for mixing two flavours in everything. Yoghurts, for instance, are all Apricot 'n' Melon; ice creams are Rum 'n' Chocolate . . . we are merely following public taste.

Counsel: That's interesting. So that's the reason, is it?

Defendant: No. The *real* reason is that most girls are trying to slim. So they are always feeling hungry. So the more foods we mention on our beauty products, the more likely they are to buy them. *But they don't actually eat them.* So our shampoos are, really, a slimming aid.

Counsel: Is that why you market a Mushroom 'n' Tomato Shampoo?

Defendant: Not really. It's a failed ketchup we bought cheap and relabelled.

Counsel: And does it work?

Defendant: Well, our rats love it. Also, most of them have developed long, soft, silky hair.

Counsel: What is so good about soft, silky hair?

Defendant: If you had it, you wouldn't ask. But I cannot help noticing that you are bald.

Counsel: There is nothing I can do about that.

Defendant: Not so fast! Have you tried our Oyster 'n' Bacon Hair Restorer?

Counsel: No, but it sounds nice.

Defendant: Of course it does! All our products sound nice to the people they are aimed at. That is why it is foolish to accuse me of deceiving the public. The public *wants* to be deceived. Here – take a sachet of our Smoked Salmon Shampoo. Makes lawyer's wigs look even more distinguished.

Counsel: Gee, thanks.

Miles and Miles, 1982

BERTRAND'S MIND
WINS OVER MATER

BERTRAND RUSSELL AND THE BIG RED DUSTBIN

I AM told that there is an enormous demand for children's stories with intellectual rigour as well as an exciting story, so I have devised a series based on famous thinkers of the past, which I am convinced will make my fortune.

It was a cold, snowy day in 1888, and all Bertrand wanted to do was stay indoors and think about things. But his mother had other ideas.

'Bertie!' she cried. 'Bertie? Oh, where can he have got to? He seems to have vanished.'

'How many times must I tell you, mother,' said Bertie, appearing behind her, 'that there is no such thing as vanishing? A person cannot dematerialize. Matter is indestructible. So is Mater, come to that,' added Bertie, making one of his rare jokes.

'What about your Uncle George?' said Bertie's mother, who liked nothing better than a rousing philosophical debate. 'He vanished five years ago. So did half the family silver.'

'You are using the word "vanish" in a very loose sense, mother,' said young Bertie, loftily. 'Uncle George merely took a passage to Australia, presumably accompanied by the silver.'

'How did you know that?' said his mother, genuinely surprised. 'Even the police could not trace him.'

'I took the precaution of checking the passenger lists on boats bound for Australia. He was listed as Albert Prince. It was an old joke of his.'

'Why didn't you tell us that?'

'Nobody listens to a five-year-old child on police matters,' said Bertie. 'And now if you don't mind, I've got some thinking to do.'

'Oh no, you don't,' said Bertie's mother. 'I've got a job for you. I want you to take the big red dustbin down to the end of the drive ready for collection by the dustmen.'

'Why should I?'

'Just do it and don't answer back,' said his mother, giving him a clip round the ear-hole.

Young Bertie reddened and tears came to his eyes. This was for two reasons, he quickly analysed. One, because it was shameful to have a mother who was so quick to forget modern educational theory as to substitute physical coercion for sweet reason. Two, because it bloody well hurt. Well, he would get his own back, that he would.

No, no, he thought hastily, petty revenge is NOT the answer. That was as illogical a primitive reaction as his mother's box on the ears had been. If he could not rise above the behaviour of his mother and act logically at all times, what chance of progress was there?

'Bertie!' said his mother crossly, coming back into the room. 'Take that dustbin out before the dustmen come, for God's sake!'

'I hardly think that an appeal to a non-existent deity will have much effect,' said Bertie, with dignity. 'I believe in the existence of the dustmen, yes. The big dustbin, yes. But God, no.'

Another box descended on his ear. Right, thought Bertie grimly. Petty revenge it is, then.

He put on scarf and gloves and went outside into the cold. There stood the big red dustbin in the yard, full of rubbish. Take it down to the road, his mother had said. Right, he would take the dustbin to the road. But he would leave the rubbish behind at the house. That would serve his mother right for not issuing a logical order.

As he was emptying the bin on to the ground, he realised a tramp was standing a few yards away, watching him.

'Having a good time, son?'

Bertie explained briefly the reasoning behind his actions. The tramp nodded approvingly.

'Matter of fact, I need an empty bin myself,' he said, 'so this will come in handy. I also need all the stuff that's on the dining-room dresser. Nip in and get it, there's a good boy.'

Bertie went to fetch the rest of the family silver and put it in the big red dustbin.

'How was Australia, Uncle George?' he said

The tramp smiled.

'Still, the clever one, eh, Bertie? Well, Australia's very expensive, hence my reappearance. But I did remember to bring you a present.'

He gave Bertie a boomerang stamped *Australia Centennial – 100 Years Old*, winked and went off down the drive with the bin on his back. 'Did you take the big red dustbin down to the road?' said his mother later.

'Mother, I promised the bin would be taken down the drive, and it was,' said Bertie, phrasing his sentence to avoid lying. Logic, he had already realised, was the most important thing in the world. After getting your own back, of course.

Coming Soon: Wittgenstein Goes to the Supermarket *and* Naughty Little Nietzsche.

Welcome To Kington, 1989

WAR AND PEACE

PAR LEO TOLSTOY

Chapter One

Bang bang bang bang bang bang bang bang bang bang bang bang
bang bang bang bang bang bang bang bang bang bang bang bang bang
bang bang bang bang bang bang bang bang bang bang bang bang bang
bang bang bang bang bang bang bang bang bang bang bang bang bang
bang bang bang bang bang bang bang bang bang bang bang bang bang
bang bang bang KER-SPLAT! bang bang bang bang bang bang bang
bang bang bang bang bang bang bang bang bang bang bang bang bang
bang bang bang bang bang bang bang bang bang bang bang bang bang
bang bang bang bang bang bang bang bang bang bang bang bang bang
bang bang bang bang bang bang bang bang bang bang bang bang bang
bang bang bang bang bang bang bang bang

Chapter Two

'Pierre?'

'Oui?'

'Vous êtes OK?'

'Oui.'

'Tatiana, vous êtes unharmed?'

'Oui.'

'Vladimir, comment vous êtes?'

'Shaken, mais untouched.'

'Boris, vous êtes OK?'

'Oui, oui.'

'Fyodor Mikhail Pyotrvich, vous êtes dans le land des living?'

'Absolument.'

'Anna Verovna, vous n'étiez pas attrappée dans la cross-fire?'

'Non, non.'

'Ludmilla, vous n'avez pas eu des difficultés avec les soldats de Napoleon?'

'Au contraire.'

'Alors, for God's sake, qui a eu le KER-SPLAT?!'

The Franglais Lieutenant's Woman, 1986

DEATH BEGINS AT FORTY

My six-month-old son had a caller the other day. She asked if she could come in, get him undressed and look him over. I didn't know he knew anyone that well. She turned out to be the health visitor, so she came in and gave him a check-up, questioned his diet and investigated his hand-eye co-ordination – that sort of thing.

We asked if it was normal not to be crawling yet, and she said, yes, many babies skipped that stage and went straight to walking. In fact, some children these days skipped the walking and waited till they could get a moped. She then made some marks on a height-weight graph and prepared to leave.

'No bruises on him, anyway,' she said jokingly, 'so you're probably not beating him up.'

'All the bruises are on me!' I said. 'He doesn't know his own strength. He pulls my hair, nearly twists my ear off . . . '

'These are serious allegations,' said the health visitor, taking her coat off again. 'I'd better examine you.'

It sounds ridiculous, but apparently in some local authorities there are no upper age limits on an examination by a health visitor. To her, I was just a large male child in its forties. She weighed me and measured me. She made marks on a graph. She frowned.

'He's not coming on as well as I would like,' she told my wife. 'We don't like to see too much weight increase at this stage in their development, and I'm a little worried by signs of height shrinkage. What are you giving him to eat?'

My wife described my diet.

'Ugh, no wonder. Try him for a while on plain fish dishes and brown bread. Look for the food packages labelled No Salt, No Sugar, No Pesto,

Mayonnaise-Free and No Added Maître d'Hôtel Butter. Is he still taking the bottle?'

'Taking the *bottle*?' I expostulated, but it was as if they could not hear me.

'Yes,' said my wife. 'He gets through quite a lot of a popular red Bulgarian bottle feed.'

'No more of that,' said the health visitor. 'They do a very nice bottled spring water at Fathercare. Try him on that for a couple of months. How's his walking coming along?'

'He's perfectly capable of it, but he doesn't do much. He prefers bicycling.'

'A lazy way of walking. Take his bicycle away from him. Does he have any recreational activity leanings?'

'How do you mean?'

'Well, if you leave him alone, does he cry and grumble, or can he amuse himself?'

'He has his old collection of jazz 78s, which he enjoys. Steam trains he likes. He reads a lot – I think he's getting through his Raymond Chandler again at the moment.'

'Dear, oh dear! Oh dear! Oh dear!' said the health visitor. 'That's painfully retrogressive.'

'And he finds it hard to throw old papers away.'

'Oh dear! Oh dear! OH DEAR! Any signs of competitive sport activity?'

'No.'

'Really? Unexpected sign of maturity there.'

'Look!' I said. Nobody looked.

'How is his mind/hand/eye co-ordination?'

'I don't know. How can you tell?'

'Well, if you ask him to cut the lawn, sort out the bank statements, or fiddle with the car, how well does he do?'

My wife told her.

'Very slow reactions,' she wrote down. 'Abnormally small technical response. Pitifully low motor awareness. Negative financial responsibility.'

'Listen!' I said. Nobody listened.

'Any other hobbies?'

'He likes to switch on things like the BAFTA award ceremonies on television and shout: "Cultural incest! Rubbish! Smug poseurs!" at the screen.'

'Infantile jealousy,' said the health visitor briskly. She turned to me at last.

'What do you think of the Government's performance, little man?' she said.

'To be frank,' I said, 'I think that the amount of interference into people's daily lives it allows, especially from you, is scandalous. If people want to go down the primrose path of old jazz 78s and Bulgarian Cabernet Sauvignon, they should be allowed to. People want to be left alone, not nannied.'

'Hmm, well, his creeping conservatism and loss of socialist reflexes is pretty much to be expected, I'm afraid. All in all, I'd say he was mentally regressing, subject to horizon shrinkage, physically declining, recreationally ossified and suffering occasional bruises through inept child handling.'

'Is that bad?'

'Not at all,' said the health visitor. 'Absolutely normal at his age. I'll be back in six months for another check.'

I think I'll be out that day.

Welcome To Kington, 1989

A CHRISTMAS NOVEL
FROM MILLS & BANG

A FALKLAND PASSION, BY VENETIA BARNSTRAW

Chapter One

Georgia's first thought when she arrived in Port Stanley was that the shops were terribly drab. Oh, she knew that she was 7,000 miles from Bond Street, but really! Did everything have to be so provincial and boring? It was, after all, the week before Christmas and the nearest thing she could see to a Christmas present was an SAS balaclava helmet with holly stuck in it.

Then suddenly she realised it didn't matter. She had no one to buy presents for. She had come out here to the Falklands to start a new life and to forget Terry. For a moment, Terry's familiar crinkled face with its roguish smile swam in front of her, but she fought against the memory. She had to report to Falklands Stores HQ, where she was to act as secretary to one Captain Bolsover. They said that work made you forget . . .

Some soldiers were coming down the street, singing.

'Captain Bolsover?' said one of them, leering. 'Don't bother with him, love. You'll have a much better time with B Company, eh lads?'

Chapter Two

'Don't worry about the men,' said Captain Bolsover. 'They mean no harm. It's just that they haven't seen a pretty girl for years and you mustn't forget that men are brutes below the surface.'

'You too?' said Georgia, daringly. It was only her second day in the office, but already she felt she could trust his straight, Italianate features, so different from Terry's – damn! She mustn't think about Terry.

'I'm not a man,' said Bolsover. 'I'm an officer.' He laughed attractively. 'But seriously, you'd do well to keep away from the soldiers. And the construction workers. And the natives. I'm afraid that just leaves the sheep. But tell me, what *really* brings you here?'

'The end of an affair,' said Georgia, blushing. 'His name was Terry. I thought he loved me, but really he loved his boat more. And when he told me he was going to sail round the world . . .'

Chapter Three

It had been a hard day for Dick Bolsover. As if it wasn't bad enough having Italianate features – his nickname among the men was Luigi, and the officers called him Rococo to his face – he had been out for a stroll among the hills and come across a soldier who had run amuck. Driven crazy by boredom and rain, the man had taken his rifle and started shooting sheep at random. Captain Bolsover had to arrest him, of course, but the big problem was the dead sheep. Could the men face roast mutton again?

'I know a rather good recipe for lamb marinaded in wine and garlic,' said Georgia later.

At supper that night there was a near-mutiny among them over what they called this foreign muck.

'Is this love?' he asked himself.

Chapter Four

I'd rather be living in Argentina
'Than marching around for Sergeant Tina!'

The soldiers' song in the street outside floated up to the window of the room in downtown Port Stanley where Captain Bolsover and Georgia were working on the final details of the Christmas catering.

'Who's Sergeant Tina, Dick?' said Georgia.

'What? Oh, that's Sergeant Duckworth.'

'And why do they call him that?'

'Hard to say, really. Perhaps because the sergeant likes dressing up in frocks on his night off.'

'We're in trouble, Georgie girl,' continued Bolsover briskly. 'The Hercules bringing in our entire shipment of Christmas puddings has come down in the Atlantic. Nobody's hurt, but they've reported a Christmas pudding slick two miles long, looking just like a minefield. Question is: what do we do for dessert now?'

'I've got a super recipe for instant Christmas plum duff,' said Georgia. 'I just need a ton of flour and a couple of lemons.'

'You're on!' said Dick. 'By the way, don't forget that tomorrow night is the officers' Christmas party. You're my guest.'

Chapter Five

Port Stanley was all decked out for Christmas. They had strung one streamer across the main street. Georgia had gone window shopping and was wondering whether Dick Bolsover would like a hand grenade or some barbed-wire cutters in his stocking.

Chapter Six

Dick Bolsover smiled at Georgia. 'Having a good time, Georgia? Forgotten about Terry now?'

Georgia, emboldened by a glass of sparkling Argentine white wine, smiled back, though she couldn't help wondering how far dear Terry had gone on his round-the-world trip.

'Come outside, Georgia,' said Dick thickly. 'There's something I have to ask you.'

Outside, the rain was falling harder than ever. Georgia suddenly realised, horrified, that Dick had put his arms round her.

'I love you,' said Dick hoarsely. 'I want to make my own conquest of Georgia!'

She shrank away, aghast. How could she have felt warm towards this man? Would no one rescue her? Suddenly, out of nowhere, came a form in yellow oilies and green boots. It was, unbelievably, Terry. He dispatched Dick Bolsover with one hook to the jaw and took Georgia in his arms.

'My darling,' he said, 'this is my first landfall on my voyage round the world and I fancy I have come just in time. I stopped for supplies and I found – you! Would you care to fill my extra berth?'

'I certainly would,' said Georgia. 'And while I'm at it, I'd like to rearrange the furniture on your boat and get it painted a nicer colour.'

If Terry had taken the hint, he would have gone on without her, but he didn't and that's another story.

Moreover, Too, 1985

ELIZABETHAN BLUES

Professor Oscar Bullock of Oxford University is very excited. For he believes he has found the very first blues lyric ever written. And the reason that he is so excited is that he is a Professor of Tudor Literature, and he thinks he has unearthed this daddy of all blues lyrics in a collection of Elizabethan poetry, written over four hundred years ago. He now thinks the history of the blues will have to be completely rewritten.

'We always think that the blues started in Victorian times,' he says. 'You know the sort of thing. Those couplets with the first line repeated. "Lord, I woke up this morning and my girl had gone. Yes, I woke up this morning and my girl had gone. And nobody I met knew where she had run." Simple stuff, but effective. Well, we know that the music was African-derived, but the lyrics are another matter. They could not possibly have come from Africa, being in English. So where did they come from? Nobody has ever traced them back to a convincing ancestor. But now I think I have cracked the mystery. The blues came from Elizabethan poetry!

Listen to this.'

He picks up a crackly bit of paper, and reads:

> *I did wake up this morning with an aching head.*
> *Yea, verily, I woke up this morning with an aching head,*
> *And my lady was not to be seen anywhere in my bed.*
>
> *I ran like a madman, and did cry out her name,*
> *Yea I did run like a madman and also cry out her name,*
> *But Echo, for to mock me, cried back the same.*

'You see!' exclaims the Professor. 'It sounds Elizabethan! It has sixteenth-century diction! But it is the very form of the blues! And the subject matter too! Now, nowadays we don't say things like "I did wake up this morning" or "I did cry out her name." But in the American black dialect of the blues, it is very common for a singer to say "I done woke up this morning" or "I done called her name." Maybe that mode of expression came straight from Tudor ancestry. And isn't there, by the way, something oddly Shakespearean about that phrase, "call her name"? Again, note the "Yea, verily" that creeps in. Just like "Yeah," isn't it? And when he calls his girlfriend his "lady," well, is it so very different is from "baby?" Listen! Here's three more verses from the same poem!'

Again, excitedly, the Professor reads from the old paper.

Lady, lady, lady, you have left a broken heart.
Oh yes, my lady, you have left a broken heart.
For it is not in this wise that I thought we should part.

I shall leave you, my lady, to ease the pain.
Yes, I shall leave you, dear lady, for to ease the pain.
Go down the station and take the next train.

I shall hie me to Chicago, that is my purpose now,
Let me get me to Chicago, I care not how.
For there are many ladies in that town, I trow.'

The Professor chuckles.

'I think that settles it,' he says. 'Over the years it developed into the traditional blues which we know as Going to Chicago. And we now know that it originated back in Tudor England!'

But surely, Professor, nobody in Britain knew about Chicago until the nineteenth century! There was no place called Chicago until the nine-teenth century! And there were no trains! It cannot possibly be a genuine Elizabethan lyric!

'I don't understand you,' says the Professor. 'This is a genuine manu-script. It must be genuine!'

He looks hurt.

I explain to him that there are such things as forgeries and hoaxes and practical jokes and student pranks ...

It slowly sinks in.

'Oh, my God,' he says. 'But I have already made a six-part TV series based on this! "Did Shakespeare Write The Blues?" It starts next Tuesday ... Oh, my God ...'

I creep away, leaving him to his pain and agony.

Independent, 2007

A WALK IN MARCH
WITH UNCLE GEOFFREY

It was a bright crisp sunny day in mid-March as Uncle Geoff and his brother's two children, Robert and Susie, set out along the Smuggler's Way which led from the village along the river to the old drove road.

'Splendid weather for bird-spotting, children!' said Uncle Geoff. 'Keep your eyes open for signs of birds pairing off and preparing to build nests!'

'And mate,' said Robert.

'And have sex,' said Susie.

'Shag,' said Robert.

'Robert!' said Uncle Geoffrey. 'Do they use words like that in your biology lesson?'

'Certainly,' said Robert. 'It's the name of that bird over there.'

'I think you'll find it's a cormorant, not a shag,' said Susie.

'I think you may be right,' said Robert. 'One point to you.'

Children today, thought Uncle Geoff sadly, were different from when he was a child. He might have had dirty thoughts back then but he kept them to himself. Just then, three ducks flew over.

'Look!' he said. 'Ducks looking for a good landing place. With any luck we'll see them land on the river. Have you ever noticed how they place their feet to act as brakes on the water?'

'I doubt they'll land this time round,' said Susie. 'That's two males after a female, and there won't be any landing till the libido has run out.'

'Female duck to traffic control,' said Robert. 'Seeking permisssion to land due to being rogered by following aircraft.'

Susie laughed.

'One point to you,' she said.

Uncle Geoffrey felt it was about time that he made a point as well, and stopped walking.

'Look, children,' he said. 'I don't mind a certain amount of playground talk, but I think enough's enough. There's nothing very clever about being smutty, is there?'

'On the contrary, Uncle Geoffrey,' said Robert. 'Without smut we die. The whole essence of nature is fornication, procreation and gestation. Nature = smut = nature. Fornico, ergo sum.'

'Oh – is fornicare really the Latin word for 'to make love'?' wondered Uncle Geoff, rather faintly.

'Just look at nature,' said Susie. 'It is endlessly driven by the urge to replicate itself. That's all it does. It is sex on a quite grand scale. YOU may say, 'oh, what sweet lambs' and 'look at the sticky buds' and 'see those birds pairing off,' but Robert and I can see only the heartless sexual drive involved. And believe me, it is a gloomy sight.'

At which the two of them burst into laughter.

'Of course reproduction is important,' said Uncle Geoffrey, thinking that the murder of young children was quite important as well, 'but it is a cynical teenage ploy to pretend that it is all that matters. Here we are, walking along this beautiful country lane . . .'

'Created by smugglers,' said Susie, 'for the sole purpose of cynical evasion of customs duty and amassing of money.'

'Coming soon,' said Robert, 'to the old drove road, created so that men could take animals to market and have them slaughtered for profit. And amass more money.'

'That is all that human life is about,' said Susie. 'Striving, accretion, accumulation.'

High overhead a plane excreted a vapour trail. They looked up at it.

'And war,' said Robert. 'Even now, that tiny plane may be carrying more bombs to Iraq.'

'And dropping them.'

'So that we can have oil.'

'To make our cars go.'

'To market, to buy cheap chickens.'

'Which were raised in Brazil, filled with chemicals, and flown here in another plane.'

Sure enough, high above them was a second plane going the other way. Uncle Geoff stared at it. He had never thought of planes like that before, as carrying dead birds halfway round the world. A nightmare version of bird migration. He became so wrapped up in his own thoughts that he didn't say another word on the walk, and when they got home he didn't hear Robert and Susie's mother ask them what they had learnt on the walk.

He didn't hear Robert say that Uncle Geoffrey had told them that the Latin word for 'to make love' was 'fornicare'.

He didn't see the very odd glance that their mother had given him. Which was just as well. For if he had, he might really have strangled them this time.

Independent, 2003

LADY AMABEL

I went to London and back one day in January, the day Irritable Parker Bowles Syndrome broke out, and the evening papers were suddenly full of Camilla Divorce stories.

When a story like the Camilla Divorce story breaks, you don't just get one report. You get it from all angles, especially in the *Standard*. You get Anthony Holden on the constitutional implications. You get Brian Sewell on the artistic overtones. You get photoessays on *that* relationship. You get a statement from the solicitor and/or the husband, including what I still think is the amazing statement that 'We have secretly been leading quite separate lives for several years' – a hard thing to do secretly, I would think. And I was reading the fourth or fifth piece on the Camilla Divorce scandal when suddenly my eyes opened wide. There, in front of me, was a picture of none other than Lady Amabel Lindsay, who apparently had once been one of Andrew Parker Bowles's old flames.

Who?

Well, that's what I would have said, had I not once lived in Notting Hill and shared a telephone number with Lady Amabel Lindsay, or very nearly. My phone number was 6606. Hers was 6006 on the same exchange. I know that, because I very often got phone calls for her.

'Hello, is Amabel there?' these aristocratic voices would bray.

I had never heard the name Amabel until I started getting these anonymous calls. It sounded like a misprint for Annabel. Well, I sympathised. Most people think that Kington is a mistake for Kingston. To begin with, I would say, *No*. Then I got curious. So many wrong numbers for the same name.

'Amabel who?' I said one day.

'Lady Amabel Lindsay,' they said. 'Is she there?'

She never was. After that I started asking what number they were trying to ring, and finally one of them, brighter than the rest, said it was 6006.

'Ah, but what you've dialled is 6606 . . .'

'Is it? Oh. How do you know?'

'Because that's my number and you've just dialled me.'

'Really? I say, that's awfully clever,' this upper-class caller said.

Armed with the right number, I could now put her friends right.

'Is say, is Amabel there?'

'No, this is 6606. The number you want is *her* number which is 6006. I'd try that if I were you . . .'

'I say, thanks most awfully.'

They never asked me how I knew her number. Perhaps they thought I was some sort of servant, or answering service. But then, all of Amabel Lindsay's friends who rang me seemed fairly stupid. Does that seem unfair? But surely you would have to be a bit thick, to get such a simple number wrong so often. Nor did any of them display the slightest curiosity as to who I was. Don't forget that whenever I answered the phone, even when giving my correct number, they always asked if Amabel was there. That meant that a) they never listened to what they were told and b) they saw nothing odd in having Amabel's phone answered by a complete stranger.

Did that mean that Lady Amabel quite often had strange men in the house with unfamiliar voices, manning her phone? Or did it mean that her friends never suspected anything wrong until it was pointed out to them?

As time wore on and the frequency of the calls did not decrease, I started to embroider my replies.

'I say, is Amabel there ?'

'No, I'm afraid the operation wasn't a success.'

'I *beg* your . . . Good Lord, what operation? What's gone wrong?'

Then I would put the phone down. Other answers I used included:

'She's helping the police with their inquiries at the moment . . .'

And:

'Well, she's never very coherent this time of day;'

And:

'I'm afraid she went off with a young man last night and she isn't back just yet.'

Then I left London and forgot all about her until suddenly there she was in the paper the other day. It said she had been a flame of Andrew Parker Bowles, but that they had never really got it together, for some reason. I suspect I know the reason. She got cross because he never phoned. He did phone actually. Quite often. But he always got me instead.

The Oldie, 1995

BLOOD BY HEINZ, NAMES
BY ORDNANCE SURVEY

Opposite *Punch*, where I used to go to work, or at least used to go, there was a large office building called Temple Chambers. I must have passed that building at least 500 times before it occurred to me that the name Temple Chambers was wasted on a set of offices. It was the ideal name for a fictional detective of the old school. He probably wore a waistcoat and a bow-tie, had insufficiently cleaned brogues and always solved his cases in a library in the last chapter. He played the violin on the side, like Holmes, but in the style of Stephane Grappelli.

Other signs have occasionally yielded good names for characters. Max Headroom is one I favour for an upbeat hero, though for a downbeat hero I would prefer Matt Finish. A Dutch hero with aristocratic over-tones could only be Hertz van Rental.

These names, though, have been hard to find over the years. Or at least they were till last year, when I was driving through the depths of the country dragging the double bass en route to some far-flung Instant Sunshine gig, and my companion cried out: 'Look! It's a tough American lawyer!'

Now, my companion is a sharp-eyed girl, but to spot an American lawyer in the English countryside, in pitch blackness, and to spot that he is a tough one, stretched the credulity. Yet she was right. Because we were passing through a village called Upton Scudamore, and if Upton Scudamore is not a tough American lawyer, I will eat my collected Raymond Chandler.

'Scudamore had hard eyes like diamonds, which he kept locked away behind bullet-proof spectacles. When his wife asked him if he had had a good day at the office, he probably charged her for the information. You get the feeling that if Upton Scudamore had been around in the Book of Genesis and offered his services to Adam and Eve, God would have ended up being evicted from the Garden of Eden, though all things considered, Upton would probably have preferred to act for the serpent . . . '

Yes, villages are the answer. What a wealth of fictional names lies there. Horsley Woodhouse, Haselbury Plucknett, Eccle Riggs, Morley Smithy, Hinton St George and Bubney Moor – all lying around on Ordnance Survey maps, just waiting for a passing Georgette Heyer Regency novel. I like the sound of Bushy Ruff, no doubt a moustachioed rascal with a heart of gold, good clean-living Christian Malford, affable lady-about-town Fenny Bridges and heart-stopping young beauty Honey Hill.

Don't imagine for a moment that all English village names make old-fashioned characters. There is a pair of villages near Shrewsbury called Wig Wig and Homer, who can only be villains out of Damon Runyon, and the same goes for Cutty Stubbs, Coole Pilate and Thick Withins. Thick Withins, I swear to you, is on the Buxton map, as are also Glutton Grange, Bumper Castle, Butchersick Farm and Dirty Gutter.

There is a village in Kent called Womenswold. Is this some kind of rural WI? I'm just off to the Womenswold – your supper is in the fridge. And is it related to another kind of gathering further north, the Nine Ladies Stone Circle? Which early jazz band did Bix Bottom play with? Did Auton Dolwells change his name when he came from Hungary? Why is there a village in Dorset called Barpark Corner and is it related to one in Sussex called The Mens? And will Lydiard Millicent ever get engaged to the village next door, Clyffe Pypard?

This morning I was passing a lingerie shop and cried out, pointing at a label: 'Look – it's an English village!' The label said 'Cotton Gussets'. My companion led me away, but only as far as next door, where I saw another village name: Lloyds Nightsafe.

'It's all right, dear,' she said. 'It's not a village name.' She's right. Lloyds Nightsafe is obviously a wild flower.

Moreover, Too, 1985

LET'S PARLER FRANGLAIS!

A L'AUCTION

Auctioneer: Allant une fois! Allant deux fois! Allé! (*Il donne un bang avec le gavel.*) Lot 52, *My Old Lady* par Whistler, sold au gentleman anonymeux avec le chèquebook. Maintenant, Lot 53. C'est un magnifique painting de Cannelloni (1567–1624), *Le Martyrdom de Saint Sébastien.* La propertie d'un country gentleman. La painting a été dans la famille depuis yonks, mais il est obligé de réaliser ses assets. Question de duties de mort. La vieille histoire. OK, qui va commencer? J'écoute £2m? (*Silence*) Messieurs? C'est un Cannelloni très rare. Une fois dans une lune bleue . . .

Bidder: Ce n'est pas un Cannelloni.

Auctioneer: Qui dit ça?

Bidder: Moi, je dis ça!

Chorus de Bidders: Nous disons tous ça!

Auctioneer: OK, OK. Assez fair. Vous avez peut-être raison. Je vais proposer une compromise. *Le Martyrdom de Saint Sébastien*, Ecole de Cannelloni (?1560–?1620). Maintenant, qui va offrir £1m? (*Silence*) Messieurs? C'est un painting, école de Cannelloni. Très bonne école. Quatre scholarships à Oxford chaque année, et excellent record de rugby.

Bidder: Ce n'est pas sixteenth century.

Auctioneer: Qui a dit ça?

Bidder: Moi encore.

2ème Bidder: Il a raison. C'est twentieth century.

3ème Bidder: C'est une fake.

Auctioneer: Ah. Maintenant que je regarde, je vois que vous êtes bang on. C'est une copie moderne. Mais, messieurs, quelle copie! Une masterpiece de la forgerie! Bon. Imitation en le style de Cannelloni (1900–?). Qui va offrir £500?

Bidder: Ce n'est pas une genuine fake.

Auctioneer: Je ne vous comprends pas.

Bidder: Ce n'est pas hand-made. C'est mass-produced.

Auctioneer: Oui, à être exact, ce n'est pas une copie originelle. C'est une page du *Sunday Times* Colourmag. Au revers, il y a un ad original pour Scotcade. Bon, une photo d'une painting en le style de Cannelloni. Qui va offrir 50p?

Gentleman: Un moment! Je viens de regarder *My Old Lady* par Whistler, pour laquelle j'ai payé £3m. C'est un postcard!

Auctioneer: OK. Pas £3m. 40p. Avec cette Cannelloni, thrown in gratuit. Maintenant, Lot 54, une page de notebook de Leonardo da Vinci. Absolument blank. Qui va offrir 80p?

Parlez-vous Franglais? 1981

ANOTHER FINE CASSEROLE
YOU'VE GOT ME IN

The burglars had been very careful. They had not taken anything. They had just contented themselves with opening the kitchen window and cooking a rabbit casserole, with mushrooms and red wine. I tried it. It was delicious. Then I sent for the police.

'Came in through the kitchen window, eh?' said Constable Mitcham. 'Then cooked a rabbit casserole? Well, I don't think we can really call them burglars at all, as they didn't take anything.'

'They took my rabbit from the fridge,' I said indignantly. 'That's theft. Not to mention my red wine.'

'And mushrooms,' mused the constable. 'They took your mushrooms as well.'

'Not true,' I conceded. 'There were no mushrooms on the premises. They must have brought those with them.'

There was a short silence as Constable Mitcham wrote laboriously in his notebook. (Why is it that policemen always write laboriously? Why does none of them ever write fluently, with an instinctive grasp of character interplay, as our leading novelists always do?) I looked over his shoulder as he wrote ...

'I shuddered as I glanced into the rabbit casserole,' I read. 'There, nearly hidden in the middle of the rich gallimaufry of redolent flesh, rendered fungi and rechauffé Fleurie, lay the unmistakable outline of a human hand! It looked well cooked. What horrible crime had led to this heartless ragout?'

Two things were immediately obvious to me. One was that I had been quite wrong about the constable's literary abilities and I owed him an apology.

'I'd like to apologize for thinking you wrote laboriously, officer.'

'That's all right, sir. At least you didn't think that I licked the end of my pencil before continuing my painfully slow scratching in my notebook. What about the human hand, then, sir?'

That was the other thing. Together we stared into the meaty recesses of the rabbit stew, and there, sure enough, was the unmistakable outline of a human hand. It was yellowish in hue, and one of the fingers was bent at an impossible angle.

'We have two crimes here,' said the constable. 'The theft of some mushrooms, and the murder of an unknown person. You, by your own admission, took the mushrooms. It seems logical to assume that you are also guilty of the murder.'

'It is not in the least logical.'

'No,' he admitted, 'but it saves a lot of time.'

He started writing in his notebook again and again I looked over his shoulder.

'Brian had now come to that stage in life where all men think of having one last fling,' I read, 'and start treating their wives better to compensate for it. Brian's wife, who knew everything that was going through his mind, was flattered by the attention, but secretly hoped he would have his little fling and get it over with . . . '

'What on earth is all that about?' I exclaimed.

'You mustn't believe that everything policemen write in their books is evidence,' he said. 'I myself am writing a novel during working hours. Other officers I know prefer poetry or military history. It's very personal.'

At that moment my wife arrived back home. She raised her eyebrows at the sight of the policeman.

'You didn't tell me you were bringing a friend home, George,' she said.

'No,' I said, 'actually . . . '

'What can you tell me about this rabbit casserole, madam?' interrupted the policeman.

'The casserole?' said my wife. 'Well, you soften some onions in butter, then you put in the bacon . . . '

'Do you mean to say that you cooked this?'

'Who else? Do you think that burglars burst in and cooked it?'

As the policeman and I looked at each other, she turned to the sink and found the pile of washing-up I had meant to do before she got back.

'George, you are hopeless. And where have you put the other washing-up glove?'

Before I could say anything, Constable Mitcham suddenly leant forward and pulled the yellow hand out of the rabbit stew. It was a washing-up glove.

'I think that clears up everything,' said Mitcham, licking his pencil and picking up his notebook. 'Except for the rabbit casserole recipe. It is my duty to warn you that anything you say will be taken down and given to a colleague who is compiling a cookery book.'

Welcome To Kington, 1989

CRISPS IN MY LAP: A
NEW MOTORWAY THRILLER

Introducing Hank Mogul, the detective who operates in the place we all know best, the motorway. But nobody knows the motorway like Hank Mogul . . .

Hank drew his battered Volvo Estate into the filling station at the Pork Scratchings Service Area, switched off the ignition, and walked into the little room where they take your money and hope you'll buy crisps and sweets while you're queuing.

'Fill her up,' said Hank to the cashier.

'It's self-service,' said the man, a spotty youth of about twenty whose main ambition in life was to go out and get drunk that evening. People don't have big ambitions like they used to. 'What happens is, you take your own petrol. You serve yourself and then you come in here and pay . . .'

Hank stared at him. The World Health Organisation has nearly eradicated smallpox, he thought. Why couldn't it do the same for acne?

'Fill her up,' he said again.

There was something about the way Hank looked at him, something about the way his eye glinted, something about the way Hank lifted him up by his bow-tie and shirt and banged his head on the ceiling, that impressed the spotty young man.

'I'll do it,' he said.

'Thank you,' said Hank.

Hank was going to need all the petrol he could get. He was going to need all the help he could get, come to that. The thing was, Hank was on the trail of an obscene telephone caller, and he didn't have much experience with obscene telephone callers.

In fact, he didn't have any experience with obscene telephone callers at all.

There are certain crimes which, in the nature of things, you don't encounter very often on motorways. Piracy is one. Cattle rustling is another. And Hank had thought that making obscene telephone calls was another. Until this bloke had turned up, this bloke who was making obscene phone calls using only the emergency phones at the side of the motorway.

The local car rescue firms were getting pretty fed up with it. Nobody knew who it was. The police didn't want to handle it. So they called in Hank Mogul to crack it, and so far he hadn't got anywhere either.

'Want me to wipe the windscreen and check the oil?' said the spotty young man sarcastically.

'Yes, please,' said Hank.

The man hesitated, then did it. When Hank came to pay, he tipped him a couple of quid.

'You've paid too much,' said the young man.

'It's called a gratuity,' said Hank. 'It goes back to the days before self-service. Ask your dad about it.'

'What do I do with it?' said the young man, fingering the two quid.

'Buy yourself a matching spotty bow-tie,' said Hank, and then he hit the road.

He settled into the slow lane, wondering as he did so why people called it the slow lane. Half the time it was more like the fast lane, as he knew you could safely do 80 or 90 mph between lorries. The police never stopped anyone for speeding in the slow lane. They probably never even noticed anyone in the slow lane. He settled gradually into the rhythm of the motorway again, the swish of passing vehicles, the bits of black tyre on the hard shoulder, the lorries flashing lights at each other, the children waving from the backs of coaches . . .

Hank found himself wondering just how this motorway phone pest worked. He probably took a risk, stopped right by the emergency phone, made his dirty phone call and sped off. Not like that poor bloke, thought

Hank, as he passed a man on the hard shoulder trudging along towards him. There was nothing like the misery of the motorist who one moment had been cocooned inside his safe little spaceship and the next was cast out into outer space.

Perhaps nobody except a motorway detective like Hank Mogul would have registered unease, but two or three miles further on he became worried. Why had he become worried? Because, he realised almost subconsciously, he had not passed a broken-down car. That man he had seen trudging along the motorway could only have been walking from a broken-down car. But there was no broken-down car. Therefore the man was just walking along the motorway. But nobody walks along motorways, unless . . . unless he is making anonymous obscene telephone calls.

Hank suddenly wanted badly to go back and talk to that man. But you can't go back along motorways. There are rules against it. One of the rules is that you have to wait for the next exit. However, the next exit was twelve miles on. On the other hand, there was another motorway service area coming up.

Hank came off the motorway, pulled up at the filling station and went to the cashiers.

'What pump number?' asked the attendant.

The man was about forty. He had bad acne. The WHO will have to get cracking before the problem gets out of hand, thought Hank.

'Listen to me *very* carefully,' said Hank. 'I am not buying petrol. I am buying information. Every motorway service area has two methods of access. One is from the motorway itself. The other is via a secret access road to some small local B road that only the employees know about it. I want to use it. Where is it?'

'We never tell people . . .'

Hank pushed across a £20 note.

'It's that little track in the woods over there.'

'Thanks.'

Hank drove out by the track, hit the B road and came back to the motorway again where he spotted, among some trees, just what he had hoped he would spot – an empty parked car, of a sort that might belong to a man trudging along a hard shoulder, who might just be an obscene telephone caller.

He stopped and went over to the car. It was locked. He unlocked it. (A motorway detective has to know how to unlock cars.) Then he looked inside. He registered the fact that the owner of the car possessed more Dire Straits tapes than it seemed possible for any one man to possess but he didn't have time to register any other fact before a voice behind him said: 'Stay right where you are!'

Like to know more? Stay tuned for the next episode of Crisps In My Lap! *Other Hank Mogul thrillers on sale include* Twiglets In My Turn-Ups, A Burning Cigarette Somewhere In My Lap *and* An Out-Of-Control Juggernaut In My Wing Mirror.

Motorway Madness, 1989

BRIBED TO FAIL

There is a very curious court case going on in London at the moment, in which attempted corruption is alleged to have taken place during a driving test. How can a driving test be corrupt? Well, let us join the trial with the cross-examination of the driving examiner, Mr Oscar Train, and find out.

Counsel: Mr Train, you have conducted many driving tests.

Train: I have indeed.

Counsel: Have you ever been offered a bribe?

Train: Yes, often.

Counsel: How does this happen?

Train: People offer me money.

Counsel: Yes, I know what a bribe is. What form does this take?

Train: Sterling, normally. I was once offered a cheque. I have also been offered Euros, but I don't take Euros.

Counsel: Do you take sterling?

Train: No. I take nothing.

Counsel: How do people try to bribe you?

Train: What normally happens is that when the pupil hands me his documents, I find a £20 note or two nestling in the pages.

Counsel: What do you do then?

Train: I hand the money back and cancel the test. It would be impossible for me to conduct a fair test, knowing that the person taking the test had offered me money to pass.

Counsel: But what if the examinee . . . is that the right word? What do driving examiners call those taking tests?

Train: Smarmy little bastards, generally.

Counsel: Officially, though?

Train: Officially they are candidates.

Counsel: Thank you. So, if a candidate takes the test, unaware that someone else had tried to bribe you, would you cancel the test then?

Train: It would depend . . .

Counsel: That brings us to the case of Queen v. Mrs Clandon, I think.

Train: I think it does.

Counsel: To the events of July 5th last, at 4 pm, when young Lionel Clandon was due to take his test. Will you tell us of your encounter with his mother?

Train: Certainly. Ten minutes before the test was due to start, the other examiners and I were in our office, when a woman who I now know to be Mrs Clandon entered and asked which of us was to test her son Lionel. I signalled that it was I. She then drew me aside in an agitated manner, and said that she had heard that many young men failed their first test. I said this was so, though many did not. She opened her handbag and said that what she was about to propose was very irregular. I told her that if she had any idea of bribing me to let her son pass, she should stop immediately. She said that nothing was further from her mind, and that she wanted to ensure that he failed.

Counsel: To FAIL? But that seems extraordinary . . .

Train: Quite so. I asked her why she wanted him to fail. She said that she had a dreadful presentiment that as soon as he was allowed to drive solo, he would come back home late, having drunk too much, crash and die. I asked her if he was that sort of youth. She burst into tears and said he was her only boy and her treasure and she did not want him to mix with the wrong sort, and then she dried her tears and took three £20 notes out of her handbag.

Counsel: What did you do then?

Train: I said I wished to have no further conversation with her and went out to give her son a test.

Counsel: Was it an uneventful test?

Train: No. The candidate often found himself in a difficult position when a car cut in front of him or pulled out without signalling, very dangerously.

Counsel: You make it sound as if it was always the same car.

Train: It was.

Counsel: Did you recognise the driver of this car?

Train: Yes. It was his mother. Luckily, young Mr Clandon handled the car superbly and there was no accident. Later, we nearly had a nasty moment when a pedestrian ran out on a zebra crossing in front of him.

Counsel: Did you identify the ...?

Train: It was his mother. Fortunately, due to the quick reactions of Mr Clandon ...

Counsel: Thank you.

The case continues. I am sure I speak for parents everywhere when I wish Mrs Clandon all the very best of luck.

Independent, 2006

NORMAL BUSINESS PRACTICES

Ah, Deborah. Come in. Yes, sit down. Well, I hope? That cold cleared up? Good, good. Don't want winter colds going round the office already.

Now, I'll come straight to the point. I am afraid I have to give you your notice. I am doing this very reluctantly and unwillingly, as I hate to lose anyone from the organisation especially at a time of unemployment, but I think you will agree that you simply aren't fitting in here. It's not just a question of personality, though that comes into it; it's the fact that you don't seem to be able to cope with the work and don't even seem to want to cope.

Certainly I will give you an example. I wanted to give you some letters to do on Friday at 4.30, but you had already left. Your contract specifies that you should be here till 5.30. Nor is this the first time . . .

That is not the point. I had had a long business lunch and the traffic was very thick, so I could not return before 4.30. As an executive I am sometimes forced to have long boring meetings over lunch, and afterwards I have to work as hard as possible to catch up.

Yes, sometimes I go straight on from Friday lunch to home. As you very well know, it takes ages to get to my place in Wiltshire and my wife and I like to leave well before the rush hour.

But this is not the point. As a secretary, your job is to be here during your working hours, ready to do work when called upon. Sometimes you complain of too little work, and sometimes too much. Surely doing a few letters at 4.30 cannot be called driving you round the bend with overwork?

No, I certainly do not remember any occasion on which I have come back stinking of garlic, giving off brandy fumes and attempting to force my loathsome advances on you. The whole thing is quite ludicrous. Why on earth should I want to? What scrap of evidence could you possibly have that such an unlikely event took place?

I did not know you had a tape recorder. The firm has not given you a tape recorder. You have your own tape recorder. I see. No, I would not be interested in hearing any of your tape recordings. It is quite beside the point. I am merely pointing out to you that I am very dissatisfied with your work and am disposing of your services.

Certainly I can give you another example. On Friday, at 4.30, in your absence when I was still here hard at work, I had occasion to look out a very important letter to a chairman of another company, as it was of somewhat confidential nature. I do not think much of your filing system, Deborah; that letter was nowhere to be seen. All you have to do is type and keep letters. You do not seem capable of doing either.

Why on earth would you want to keep that letter in your own home? It is of no conceivable interest to anyone but me. It is merely expressing interest in the activities of another company.

Yes, I suppose that I can imagine that our chairman might be upset to learn that I was looking for a better paid post elsewhere, but how could he possibly find out? By seeing the letter. Which you might have to send to him. I see.

This clumsy attempt at blackmail rather depresses me, Deborah. I haven't got where I am in business without having to deal with the odd spot of skullduggery and dirty practice, you know. You simply don't know me if you think I am going to succumb to blackmail.

Then what would you call it?

You would call it normal business practice.

I do not call it normal practice. I am not in the habit of going around blackmailing people into doing what I want them to do.

The Chambers deal. Yes, there may have been a small element of blackmail in the Chambers deal. Yes, there may have been a large element of blackmail in the Chambers deal. But that surely is going back before your time? How on earth could you know about the Chambers deal?

From Miss Whetstone.

With whom I had a close friendship.

Very close? It may have been. I cannot remember.

It may interest you to know, Deborah, that whatever may or may not have passed been Miss Whetstone and me is now at an end, and is a closed chapter.

Not to Miss Whetstone.

I see.

Yes, I vaguely remember writing letters to her. You will be disappointed to hear, Deborah, that she returned them all to me and I destroyed them.

But not before taking copies.

I did not know that.

Well, Deborah, I am a busy man and do not have time to go on with this petty argument, so let me just say that I am going to give you one last chance but that if your work does not improve I shall be forced to rethink my position. For the time being, you can get on with the letters left over from Friday, which I was forced to write out in long hand in your absence.

At a higher salary.

Yes, I think I could offer you another £200 a year.

Another £1,000. Yes, I think we could manage that.

Now I must go off to lunch. It may turn out to be a long one. No, don't bother. I'll do anything that has to be done when I get back.

Yes, I too am glad we've had this little talk.

Miles and Miles, 1982

MILES KINGTON INTERVIEWS
EMPRESS JOSEPHINE

Kington: Empress Josephine . . .

Josephine: Yes . . . ?

Kington: I'm sorry – it just seems strange for an Englishman to call anyone Empress. It isn't a title we've ever used.

Josephine: Well, it wasn't very common in France either, you know. Before me, there had been no emperors since . . . Charlemagne, perhaps? And Napoleon did love titles. It was a harmless weakness. To call yourself consul, then emperor – it made him feel in touch with the Roman Empire, and after all, nobody had ruled over so much of Europe as Napoleon, not since the Roman Empire. Noble titles he had no interest in – he had no desire to be a duke, or count, or baron. Those titles were for giving away to other people. The only titles he valued were those which involved power.

Kington: But why Emperor? Why not just King of France?

Josephine: I think because that would have put him on the same level as his brothers. You know he liked to reward his brothers by making them king of countries he had conquered? Joseph was King of Spain and Louis was King of Holland, and so on?

Kington: Yes.

Josephine: Well, for Napoleon to be just King of France would not have been enough.

Kington: And it might also have reminded him of the fate of the previous king?

Josephine: The guillotine, you mean? Oh, that would not have worried him. Don't forget that my predecessor was also guillotined . . .

Kington: Did that worry you ever?

Josephine: Oh, come now! I nearly was executed! I knew all about the terror! Don't forget that I was thrown into jail in the Revolution for my aristocratic connections, and so was my husband, and he was executed, so I knew what fear of the guillotine was all about . . .

Kington: That was your first husband . . .

Josephine: Yes, Alexandre de Beauharnais. The father of my two children.

Kington: Is that how you remember him? Just as the father of your children?

Josephine: It is not a part of my life I remember with much pleasure. He was constantly and steadily unfaithful to me. He behaved as if he were not married to me. And yet he accused me of having love affairs with other men, quite falsely. He even forced me to go and live in a convent for a while, as a sort of punishment. But I am glad he gave me the children. Not only were they lovely children, but it proved that I was fertile, so that later, when I could not give an heir to Napoleon, nobody could say it was my fault.

Kington: I think during your marriage you even went back home for two years.

Josephine: To Martinique, yes. I grew up in the West Indies, where it was warm and sunny and life was full of colour and music and gaiety . . . you cannot imagine what bliss it was to be young in the West Indies!

Kington: Unless you were a slave.

Josephine: I beg your pardon?

Kington: Most of the people then living in the West Indies were slaves.

Josephine: Not many of the people who I knew . . .

Kington: You didn't take much interest in politics, I take it?

Josephine: Never. It was the quickest way to getting your head cut off when I was a young woman.

Kington: But when you were married to Napoleon . . .

Josephine: The same. I left all politics and fighting and intrigue to him. Not that it would have got me very far – he found it hard to talk intellectually with women. But I wasn't an intellectual. That is one of the reasons he liked me. Even when I was Empress of France I could never get very interested in all those battles and alliances. He would send me letters from Italy to say he had just won a great battle against the Austrians, and I would be delighted for him, but I would also say to myself: Good Heavens – why do you have to go to Italy to fight the Austrians? Why not go to Austria? That was how little I knew.

Kington: So what part did you play in public life?

Josephine: I did all the things that Napoleon found hard. I smiled . . . I talked to people . . . I made guests feel at home . . . I tried to look nice . . . France was a party and I was the hostess. You know Napoleon had very little small talk. He hated chit-chat. He found it almost impossible to be trivial. I have known him go through an entire dinner and not speak. So I was needed as a counterbalance, I suppose, softness where he was hard, tolerance where he was irascible, a smile to his frown. And it was not just guests I tried to relax, but him as well – you know Napoleon was extremely tense most of the time, with so much going on in his brain. He was always planning . . .

Kington: Planning more battles?

Josephine: Oh, no! Much more than that! Conquering a place was only the beginning. After that he would plan a new constitution, new laws, new buildings, new roads . . . I have known him at dinner send for a secretary to dictate an idea for a new canal, of all things. And new laws! You know that he single-handedly brought in the civil laws that still rule France? The Code Napoleon?

Kington: Yes . . .

Josephine: He used to drive his brothers mad! He would make them a king of somewhere, and than bombard them with letters telling them how to run the place, and woe betide them if they didn't obey orders . . .

Kington: You didn't like his brothers, did you?

Josephine: I not like his brothers? You have it quite back to front! They hated me! His sisters, too. His mother, too – she could not stand me . . .

Kington: Why not?

Josephine: Because I was such a threat to them. Do not forget that the Bonapartes were a Corsican family – clannish, tight-knit, insular, suspicious. If one of them was successful, he had to share it with the others. They all wanted their snouts in the trough. Then I came along and married the successful one, so of course they saw me as receiving money and position and rewards that they should have had ... And they were so ambitious! They all wanted thrones, even the sisters! Perhaps that is why Napoleon had to conquer so many countries – to find thrones for all his brothers and sisters!

Kington: Were they all like that?

Josephine: Yes ... ! Well ... Lucien had his better moments. He married someone of whom Napoleon disapproved, and Napoleon said he could have a throne if he got rid of his wife, but to do him credit, Lucien refused.

Kington: So Napoleon tried to dictate his brother's wives, did he?

Josephine: Certainly. He had a younger brother called Jerome, you know, who went off to America and married an American girl called Patterson. Napoleon made him come back, forced him to annul the marriage, and married him off to some German princess and made him King of somewhere ... Westphalia, I think. Wherever that is.

Kington: Didn't Jerome object?

Josephine: Not at all. He loved it. He was the vainest young popinjay you can imagine.

Kington: What about his sisters? Did you get on with any of them?

Josephine: You obviously never met his sisters ... Caroline was the worst. She married Murat, you know, who was such a great cavalry leader ...

Kington: Yes, he sounds quite a character.

Josephine: Well, he certainly thought he was – all swagger, and moustaches, and bluster, and an eye for the ladies ... nowadays you would see him on a beach with suntan and medallion, you know? Napoleon made him King of Naples so that Caroline could have a title. But what she really wanted was to be Empress after me.

Kington: How could she be?

Josephine: Well, as long as Napoleon had no children, he had no heir, and there was great pressure on him to nominate an heir. A brother, or nephew perhaps. He never did. So after his death there was bound to be a fight among the rivals, and Murat was the most popular with the Army of all the candidates, so she reckoned that they would put him on the throne of France. At the same time, she never stopped telling Napoleon that I would never bear him a child, and I should be divorced as soon as possible.

Kington: But you had already had a child or two! You were obviously not infertile.

Josephine: Caroline tried to persuade him otherwise. She got him to prove that he could father a child . . .

Kington: But how . . .

Josephine: You probably won't believe this – I couldn't when I heard it – but she persuaded Napoleon to set up a mistress secretly in Paris, a mistress who was a virgin, and with whom only Napoleon would sleep. Then, if she became pregnant . . .

Kington: How awful! Weren't you jealous?

Josephine: Well . . . what was the point? If I were to become jealous of every woman with whom Napoleon had relations . . . They were always bringing him women, you know: actresses, singers, ladies of court . . . But they were all birds of passage. He was not in love with them. He was only in love with me.

Kington: Was he a great womaniser?

Josephine: He certainly chased and caught a great many women. Whether he left any of them satisfied with the encounter, I rather doubt. But I would rather not talk about . . .

Kington: May I just ask if the young lady became pregnant?

Josephine: Caroline's experiment? Yes, she did. Caroline was triumphant. She wrote to Napoleon, on whatever battlefield he was, crowing like a cockerel on a dung heap. Now you can divorce Josephine! That was the message. Mark you, many of us believed that the girl was not made pregnant by Napoleon at all, but by Caroline's husband.

Kington: Murat?

Josephine: Yes, he of the hairy chest and not much brain.

Kington: But he didn't divorce you?

Josephine: Not then. But after that I had an even harder time from the dreadful Bonaparte family. I feel sorry for your Lady Diana, you know. When I married into the Bonapartes, I united the whole family against me, so I know how she feels.

Kington: How did Napoleon treat your children?

Josephine: Admirably. He loved them as if they were his. Well, they were very lovable children. Eugene went into the army, you know, and the Emperor kept an eye on him, while Hortense, my beautiful Hortense, he married off to his brother Louis. I expect he thought he was doing the right thing.

Kington: And was he?

Josephine: He couldn't have made a worse choice. Louis was suspicious, insecure, moody, mean – a terrible husband. And to cap it all, Napoleon made him King of Holland! And my Hortense had to go off and live in that dreadful, cold, damp, low-lying place by the North Sea! Can you imagine what it would be like to grow up in the West Indies and then have to live in a land of frogs and rain?

Kington: I think so. Many people now living in London had to do it.

Josephine: Perhaps so. I wouldn't know.

Kington: You have talked somewhat about Napoleon's constant infidelity. Would you find it disrespectful if I mentioned that you, too, did once . . .

Josephine: I? *I what?*

Kington: Your liaison with Hippolyte Charles . . .

Josephine: With . . . ah . . . yes, that young man. Extremely good-looking. A lot of fun. I think the Emperor was away at the time.

Kington: I think he was away in Egypt shortly afterwards. That is where he found out . . .

Josephine: My God, how it all comes back! Thank you for reminding me of those dreadful times! That's right; it was while he was in Egypt, destroying every army sent against him and having his ships burnt by your Admiral Nelson. One of his generals presented him with proof that I was . . . emotionally involved with young Charles, and he went mad. Enraged. Like a bull. I have seen his tempers. I am glad I was not there. Anyway, he wrote to his brother Joseph ordering him to get a divorce worked out for me. My son Eugene, who was out in Egypt with him, also wrote me a letter to warn me that all this was going to happen and asking if I was really having an affair, and so on and the terrible thing was that the ship bearing both letters was captured by your blessed English navy.

Kington: Well, at least that meant that the letter never got to Joseph.

Josephine: It was worse than that. When the captured letters got back to London, the English published them! All over the public prints, his letter to Joseph talking about divorce, and Eugene's letter to me about my affair – for everyone to read! I don't know what the English press is like now, but then they had no qualms about printing confidential information of an intimate kind ... Of course, it was all over France the next day, and I was a laughing stock ... Mark you, there was a funny side to it ...

Kington: That seems hard to imagine.

Josephine: Well, in Egypt, Napoleon could not do anything about me, but he could at least show that he could take his revenge, so he took a mistress. One of his officer's wives. What was her name? I forget. Apparently he spilt wine over her dress at a party and took her upstairs to deal with it, and never came back ... Removed her dress rather than the wine ...

Kington: What about her husband?

Josephine: Oh, he had been sent up country on a mission. Just like David and Bathsheba. Meanwhile Napoleon and what's her name were going around together in public, her apparently dressed up like a general in a big jacket, and plumed hat, and tight white trousers ... Mark you, the Emperor was always a little attracted to girlish young men, so perhaps it was the same with mannish young girls ...

Kington: You can't have found all this very funny.

Josephine: We haven't come to the funny bit yet. The officer came back from his mission and was promptly sent off back to Paris with important dispatches. But his boat too was captured by the British, and the British sea captain realised who the French officer was: he was the young man whose wife was parading around with Napoleon back in Egypt. Well, never say that the English have no sense of humour, because the captain decided to take the officer back to Egypt and land him there as an embarrassment to Napoleon, which I am glad to say he did.

Kington: It's hard to imagine Napoleon being embarrassed.

Josephine: You are right. It was always the other way round. He embarrassed others. Especially women. It was quite dreadful the way he would have ladies presented to him at receptions and say openly: 'You're too fat' or 'What bony arms'. The only thing that embarrassed him was my extravagance ...

Kington: Were you extravagant?

Josephine: He thought so. Everyone else thought so. I didn't think so.

If you are an Empress, you have to keep up appearances. You have to be gracious, and beautiful, and calm, and well dressed ...

Kington: A new outfit every day?

Josephine: Certainly not! I changed my outfit three times a day. Nor would I even wear the same stockings twice.

Kington: Well, it saves washing.

Josephine: I wouldn't know. I have never washed a stocking.

Kington: But surely all your bills were paid by Napoleon?

Josephine: Life is never so simple. He made me an allowance. If I went over like that, the bills were not paid. Every now and then he would learn the truth and fly into a tremendous rage. And then pay the bills.

Kington: But did you live a life of great luxury?

Josephine: No, I think not. Of course Napoleon was used to camping with the soldiers, so he did not need luxury – in fact at Malmaison I had his room decorated with a great hanging drape so that he could imagine he was back inside his tent. And it was at Malmaison that I had my happiest times, just the two of us, in a simple house – not a palace but a homely house. The Emperor and Empress of France, at home, walking in the garden as the light fades – that is the happiest memory for me, not all the pomp and circumstance. We were happy, then ... *(Suspicion of a tear ...)*

Kington: You were famous for your tears. They never failed to have an effect on Napoleon, it is said.

Josephine: Monsieur, you are not very gallant.

Kington: That is not quite the truth. I am trying as hard as possible to avoid falling victim to your charm. Your legendary charm, which so many have written about, and which smoothed down so many feathers ruffled by your imperial husband.

Josephine: That is a little more gallant.

Kington: Did you love Napoleon?

Josephine: You are very blunt.

Kington: It is a question you must have asked yourself.

Josephine: To begin with, no. I did not love him. I needed him. I needed someone. I was a widow, 32 years old. I already had a 15-year-old daughter. I had to support myself and my two children. Here was this soldier, this

General Buonaparte, madly in love with me, determined to marry me. So I married him. But I did not love him. Not till later.

Kingston: When was that?

Josephine: We were married only five months after we met, you know. Even in those days, that was quick. And I will tell you a funny thing. When we went to my lawyer M. Raguideau, to get the marriage contract drawn up, Raguideau waited till Napoleon was out of the room then said to me urgently: 'Why are you marrying this young soldier? What if he is killed? You will have nothing! All he has is his cloak and his sword!' Well, what we did not know was that Napoleon was listening to him through the half-open door, and heard every word he said. He said nothing at the time, but eight years later on the day of his coronation he sent for Raguideau, the old lawyer, and said, 'Well, old man, better than a cloak and sword wouldn't you say?'

Kingston: So he had a sense of humour?

Josephine: Not a sense of humour, not exactly. A sense of timing. A sense of fun, perhaps. We French are too logical to have humour, I think.

Kingston: You thought of yourself as French?

Josephine: What else?

Kingston: Well, both you and he were born outside France. If he had been born a year or two earlier, he would have born Italian, for France had only just gained Corsica when he was born. In fact, Martinique, where you were born, had only just become French. A year or two earlier and you would have been English.

Josephine: This all sounds good, but none of it is true. Take Joseph for example.

Kingston: His brother?

Josephine: His *elder* brother. When Joseph was born, Corsica was still Italian. Was Joseph Italian?

Kingston: No . . .

Josephine: And nor would Napoleon have been. Of course, I know why you are saying all this. Deep down you would have liked Napoleon to be British.

Kingston: I don't quite understand what you're . . .

Josephine: The British have always rather admired Napoleon. They have written so many books about him. He seems rather heroic placed next to – well, placed next to your Duke of Wellington. Napoleon was sent to Elba, he came racing back, he gathered an army, he was beaten by the Duke of Wellington – but who had the more style, the more panache? Even in defeat Napoleon had more style than your dusty English aristocrat. Napoleon ruled France, and everyone remembers it. Wellington later ruled England, as Prime Minister. What does anyone remember about his premiership?

Kingston: Yes ... what were your feelings about the return from Elba and the Battle of Waterloo?

Josephine: I had none. I was, if you will pardon the expression, already dead at the time.

Kingston: Were you? I'm sorry.

Josephine: When Napoleon went to Elba, everyone thought that was the end of him. The victorious allies flooded into Paris. The place was full of Russians and British and Germans – quite awful. But the allied leaders were there as well, and some of them were well worth meeting. The Tsar of Russia, young Alexander, he was a very attractive man, you know. My husband also thought so. If Alexander had been a woman, he once said, I would have made him my mistress.

Kingston: A strange thing to say.

Josephine: Well, he was a strange man in many ways, or at least he liked to be thought strange. But in 1815, when Napoleon had fallen from power and was languishing in Elba, and I was living quietly in my house at Malmaison, the Tsar of all the Russias came to seek me out, and pay court to me. Of course he was curious to meet me, but he came back many days to see me, which made me feel like ... a true Empress, you know? To be sought out even after Napoleon's fall – that was quite something. We used to go driving ... I used to dress up for him. One day I went out in a dress which was far too thin for the weather ... I caught a bad chill ... it got worse ... I took to my bed and died. That was before Waterloo. So you see, I never lived to see the end.

Kingston: Or see the kings come back to the French throne.

Josephine: No.

Kingston: But you had seen Napoleon marry again?

Josephine: Yes, to the girl from Austria ... Mary Louise ...

Kingston: And have a baby by her?

Josephine: Yes, poor thing. He never really knew his father. How sad to grow up, son of the most famous man in Europe, and never to know him as a father. I am not surprised it was too much for him. He died at 20, I believe.

Kington: Yes. And all Napoleon's dynastic hopes went with him.

Josephine: And yet the extraordinary thing is that there was another Emperor Napoleon on the throne of France, but he was my descendant, not Napoleon's.

Kington: How so?

Josephine: You remember my daughter, Hortense? The one who married the dreadful Louis King of Holland?

Kington: Yes . . .

Josephine: They had several sons. One of them went into politics. He became president of France. He made himself Emperor in 1851.

Kington: He only lasted till 1870.

Josephine: That isn't bad for an emperor. It was longer than Napoleon. But this time the ending was different from Napoleon's. He fled the country when it was invaded by the Germans, and took exile in, not Elba, but England! Fancy a Napoleon going into exile in Chislehurst!

Kington: And his empress came too?

Josephine: Yes. She too had to live in Chislehurst. Poor thing. And what was worse, she had a son who like mine went into the Army, and died there, unlike mine. He joined the British Army, you know, and went to South Africa and was killed by the Zulus. What a fate. My great-grandson, killed by an African, wearing a British uniform!

Kington: Well, Empress Josephine . . .

Josephine: Fate is a funny thing, you know – who would ever have thought that I, a young Creole girl from the West Indies . . .

Kington: I'm afraid we don't have time for any more, your Highness.

Josephine: Nowadays Creole means mixed blood, but then it just meant, a French person living in the colonies . . .

Kington: I would like to talk more, but I'm afraid there is no more time.

Josephine: Must you go? I am so sorry. It has been very kind of you to call. You must come again some time. Goodbye. Thank you so much.

Kington: Er . . . goodbye . . .

Radio 4, 1993

CONVERSATION ON A TRAIN

'Have you ever tried helping an old lady across the road?' said a voice in my ear.

I was sitting in a train, which had just stopped at one of those stations called Something Parkway, a name that means it is right out in the open country and nowhere near the town of Something. The sort of station where you only get out to get into another train. On the opposite platform there was one single passenger waiting, an old lady, and there were no less than three railway employees clustered round her, trying to find out what she wanted and attempting to make she sure she got it.

I turned and saw that my companion was a distinguished-looking, rather elderly man reading a book.

'Me?' I said.

'You,' he said.

I tried to remember. There must have been some occasion on which I had been nice to an old person. But if there was, it had entirely slipped my mind.

'No,' I said.

'Well, you should try helping an old lady across the road,' said the man. 'It is an illuminating experience. It is one of the hardest things in the world to do.'

'Why is that?' I said. 'Because they resist being helped?'

'That's what I used to think,' he said. 'Very often old ladies won't set out from one pavement towards the other, and even when you've got them started, they may stop halfway. I remember once going across a road in Oxford with some old girl when she stopped in the middle of the road

229

and started chatting, and I could see this lorry bearing down on us – I had to drag her bodily across!'

Over on the far platform the three rail employees were now helping the old lady to look through her handbag for her ticket. I could see that they were getting rather frustrated with her though she, by contrast, seemed not at all displeased with the situation.

'Yes,' said the man, 'for a while I imagined that little old ladies whom you were trying to help across the street reacted with such lack of cooperation that you could almost base some scientific principle of inertia on them.'

'Perhaps even harness their resistance and convert it into energy?' I suggested.

'But then,' said the man, ignoring me, 'I realised that the old ladies weren't resisting at all. What they were doing was trying to prolong the process.'

'Prolong the process?'

'It is one of the great paradoxes of life that people with the most time behave as if it is running out, and people with very little time left behave as if they have got all the time in the world,' said the man. 'Young people are always in a rush – got to try this, got to go there, got to be off! Why? They've got all their life to do things. It's old people who should be in a hurry: they've got very little time left, so they should squeeze in as much as they can while they can. But do they?'

I glanced over at the far platform. The old lady was having things explained to her all over again, and enjoying every minute of it.

'No,' I said.

'No, they don't,' he said. 'It's the opposite, if anything. Have you noticed that when old ladies are in front of you at the cash till in a supermarket, they make a great performance out of paying, and they fiddle with their money, and they chat about the weather, and their ailments . . . ?'

'Yes,' I said. 'They're dithering.'

'No, they're not,' he said. 'They're looking for company. Old people don't get much company. They need contact, conversation, comfort. That's why they take so long to be helped across the road.'

'Is that why you're engaging me in conversation like this?' I asked, in what I hoped was an engagingly frank manner.

'Me?' He looked surprised. 'Oh, no. Nothing like that. I come from a different school of old people. I come from the school that believes that old age is the right time for a drastic gesture.'

'Pardon?'

'If a young man assassinates a tyrant, he might spend the rest of his life in prison. If an old man does it, he's nearly dead already, so it doesn't matter. I have always felt that that old people should use their last moments on earth to right some terrible wrong, or rub out some terrible person. Go out with a bang.'

'Right,' I said. There didn't seem much else to say. He went back to reading his book after that, but I couldn't help noticing that when he got up to get out at the next station and put his book in his brief case, there was unmistakably a small pistol lurking beneath it.

I have been studying the obituary columns with unusual interest ever since.

Independent, 2001

UNUSUAL JOBS

When Sam Kitteridge announces his job at parties, people tend to blink and ask him to repeat it. Did he say *sex* psychology?

'No, sock psychology,' he says. They then ask him if he studies the behaviour of people who *wear* socks. 'No, no,' he tells them. 'I study the behaviour of socks themselves.'

The study is based on Kitteridge's profound conviction that socks behave in a way quite different from anything else in nature.

'You yourself must have noticed that if you put five pairs of socks into a washing machine for an ordinary wash cycle, you will almost always get either eleven socks out or nine. Now, where does that extra sock come from? And where does that missing sock disappear to?'

Kitteridge also studies the way in which single socks with no matching sock build up in a household till there are as many as twenty or thirty unmatched socks, some of them not claimed by any member of the house. One of them is almost always a long red towelling sock.

He is also intrigued by the way in which a pair can increase to a trio of identical socks, as well as by the curious phenomenon of the unknown name-tape.

'This simply means the way in which socks, usually grey school socks, can turn up with names sewn on them which do not match any of the family's names. Very often, these names are of people totally unknown to the family.'

This sort of study may seem useless to people not familiar with academic research, but Kitteridge is convinced he is on the edge of an amazing discovery. He believes that socks contain the secret to some form of energy which is totally unknown to science.

'I know it sounds odd, but the only explanation for all these happenings is that socks move around in a way which we do not yet understand, and if only we could crack this form of movement we might be able to harness it to more useful ends.

'You yourself must have noticed that if you hang up a wash-load of socks on a washing-line, say over the bath, then the next time you come back some of the socks are lying in the bath. They may even fall on top of you as you take a bath. *There is no way known to science in which those socks could move.*'

At the moment he is working on a theory that socks somehow derive energy from the spinning of the washing machines in which they find themselves.

His early research was done in a Milton Keynes launderette, but he was banned from there for using too many machines, and he has now set up his research lab with six machines, four basins and a complicated system of washing lines.

So far he has isolated a pair of black dinner socks and a large woollen Scottish stocking which seem to have unusual hidden energy, but it is still too early in the day to draw any conclusions.

'I have at last established that this behaviour is limited to socks. After exhaustive washing and drying of ties, pants, vests and hankies, I am convinced that they show no urge to move around at all. This is a sock-limited phenomenon, as we would say.

'Only last week I stored a single green sock away in a sock drawer for further testing. It turned up three days later on my *feet*, matched to a grey sock. A female colleague of mine claims that ladies' knickers have the same powers of movement, especially if there is a teenage daughter around, but this is unknown territory to me.'

Does he *really* feel he is pursuing a useful end?

'Most certainly. At least, compared to my colleagues. One of them has devoted his life to comparing different books written about Milton's poetry. If he finds any hidden source of energy there, I will eat my hat.'

Moreover, Too, 1985

THE CLICHÉ MUSEUM

Every museum in the country is getting ready to attract crowds when the next Bank Holiday looms and the British Cliché Museum is no exception, already looking as bright as a button, and all ship-shape and Bristol fashion, to name only two of the thousands of clichés housed here.

This friendly little spot is not just a collection of all the objects connected with British clichés (on display you will find more bargepoles, doorposts, thick planks, new brooms, sick parrots etc than you could shake a stick at) but it is actively engaged in research and testing of clichés old and new.

'Oh, yes, there is hardly a cliché that we have not take a butcher's at,' says the new director of the British Cliché Museum, Jack Robinson. (All directors of the museum, as soon as they are appointed, are traditionally renamed Jack Robinson or Solomon Grundy.) 'You see, most people accept the working of the average cliché without thinking about it. Put the cart before the horse, they say, or take a horse to water, although none of them has ever handled a cart or a horse. Here is the one place in Britain they can come and see clichés demonstrated and tested, to destruction if necessary.'

If you do test a cliché to destruction, does that mean that people discard it?

'Good Lord, no!' says Jack Robinson. 'One of the first things we ever did here was to establish that leaving a sinking ship was a sensible thing to do, not a cowardly one, yet still to this day people are called rats for leaving a sinking ship. Clever old rats, I say. But no-one else does.'

He pauses as we pass an open office where a man sits at a desk, shuffling paper around.

'How're you feeling, doctor?' cries Robinson.

The doctor gives us a beatific smile. 'Great,' he says. 'Awesome. Marvellous ...'

'Good, good,' says Robinson, and adds to me, more softly, 'We're just seeing if he likes a taste of his own medicine. What we didn't know is that he prescribed people a lot of morphine and Viagra, so he's really enjoying himself. We'll have to do some more tests with doctors who dole out mostly cough medicine and flu jabs. Now here ...'

Here is an open bit of ground with some big bushes growing close together. They look quite tough.

'Cherie Blair was described the other day as looking as if she had been dragged through a hedge backwards. It's an old cliché. But is it true? On Bank Holiday Monday we've got a Cherie Blaire look-alike coming along who's agreed to be dragged through it backwards, and then forwards, to see if there's any difference.

'Mark you, the rate at which hedges are being grubbed up in this country, we will soon have to explain to people what a hedge is. Already we have to explain about taking coals to Newcastle, because people don't remember any more that Newcastle was in a coal-producing area. Some of them don't know what coal is. They associate the word with football because of all the footballers called Cole, like Ashley Cole and Joe Cole. A young boy said to me the other day, "Don't you mean taking Coles to Chelsea"?'

As I end my visit, I see a man preparing an enormous cheese on a table. What is he up to?

'Ah, he's mounting our cheese-paring demonstration. People talk about cheese-paring as if it is being stingy and mean, but in fact it's all about husbandry and economy. You get a lot more out of a cheese if you pare it properly. It's explained in our new recipe book.'

The British Cliché Museum has published a recipe book?

'It certainly has! It has such dishes in it as Humble Pie, A Pretty Kettle of Fish, Too Many Cooks Broth, Sauce for the Goose and Gander, Revenge ...'

Revenge? What kind of dish is Revenge?

'I'm not sure,' admits Jack Robinson. 'All I know is that it's best served cold ...'

The Independent, 2006

AIRPORT PAPERBACK

THE PASSION, THE POWER AND THE STORY

W hat is *Airport Paperback*?
      Airport Paperback is just about the hugest, most monstrous
success in publishing history, that's all!

It's sexy. It's outrageous. Yet it's also moving and emotional. Its action
sweeps continents and the ebb and flow of the generations, yet it also tells
of the quiet moments of the heart and the tender love of a woman for the
novel she is writing.

Airport Paperback tells the story of Emily, who was married to a man
she quite liked. Surely fate had destined her to do more in life than clean
up after someone, put his underwear in a washing-machine and make his
dentist's appointments? And so it was that in her kitchen, or at the
controls of her lonely two-action vacuum cleaner (it blows, it sucks), Emily
allowed herself to dream. Power, intrigue and passionate love, and the clash
of mighty business empires . . . these were the dreams that Emily had.

And one day a voice said: 'Write down your dreams. Tell the story of
your innermost desires, but make them happen to other people. Write
down this story in an exercise book. Take six years over it, in your quiet
moments, your rare time off, when everyone thinks you are at the controls
of your two-action vacuum cleaner.' Three-action, more like, thought
Emily: blow, suck and break down. 'Not a bad joke,' said the voice. 'Put
it in your – '

Airport Paperback! The story of how one woman fought against her
fate and rose from the humdrum ashes of her life to bring a blazing best-

seller into the world! Yes, for six long years Emily toiled away at her epic story and then she met Eric the publisher. 'It's not bad,' said Eric. 'Not bad at all.'

Emily blushed slightly at the condescending tone of this patronizing but handsome publisher, who had taken her out to eat in a posh London restaurant with big prices and tiny portions.

'I like the idea of writing a novel about the battle to control the world's airport bookshops. The idea that the world might be changed by the people who ordain what people shall read on holiday. I like it. We'll have to change a few things, of course. More sex. A few more jokes, perhaps — I liked the one about the vacuum cleaner.

'And then your novel will arise from this old exercise book like Cinderella going to the ball — it will appear in three lurid colours, with an embossed title, a caption reading 'The Great New Bestseller' and a tribute saying "You must read this – Jack Higgins".'

'Oh, really? Any other changes?' said Emily defiantly.

'Yes,' said Eric, leaning forward and very lightly touching her on the cheek. 'To you. We're going to take you out of those dowdy clothes, and give you a beautiful new face and a lovely new name and you're going to be a star, little Emily.'

That summer the publishing world could only talk of two things: the runaway, bush-fire success of Emily's novel, and the intense heat caused by her whirlwind romance with Eric the publisher, which withered two marriages as it crackled and burnt. Then she flew to Hollywood to discuss the screen transformation of the novel which one in every three airline passengers was reading, and met the man who was to break her heart.

'I'm Jack,' he said. 'I'm going to be producing your film.'

And giving you a child and leaving you cruelly, he might have added, if only he had known. Emily was to write many more runaway successes and make many more films, but she was never again to know a love like Jack's. She acquired glamour and money and power, yes, but after Jack she hid her softness and warmth behind a high security wall. Many men believed it was no longer there.

Only her child, Oscar, named after her first award, knew differently. (If a girl, she was to have been called Emmy. Their dog was called Pulitzer.)

For Oscar received all the love which she could no longer . . . etc. etc. When he grew up, he was to take revenge on Jack, the man she had never told him was his . . . etc. etc. But before that could happen, Oscar fell in love with . . . etc. etc.

Yes, it's all in *Airport Paperback!* It's the sizzling novel which strips the veneer from the glamorous world of airport fiction and shows you the seething jungle beneath! But is *Airport Paperback* the name of the book which Emily wrote? Or is it the book which tells the story of the book that Emily wrote? Or is it just the name of the book which Emily dreamt about writing but never did because she is still leaning on her two-action vacuum cleaner and weaving her fantasies?

Read *Airport Paperback* and find out!

Welcome to Kington, 1989

TRAIN CONVERSATION

There was a time when I used to talk to people on trains a lot, out of curiosity, mostly. You sit next to them or opposite them, for all that time, and you study what they are reading, or you listen to their phone conversations, and you wonder what makes them tick, and suddenly you think to yourself: 'If I talk to them, I can find out what makes them tick!' and so you do, and sometimes you regret it and sometimes you don't.

The most rewarding conversation I had on a train was some years ago, as I remember it was about the last time I ever took a bike on the train to London. (My wife forbade me to do it again, after being knocked off my bike in Grosvenor Square by a taxi driver who did not even stop. Thanks, mate.) There was one other cyclist loading his bike on the train, a small, wiry old bloke who came and sat opposite me and of course we got talking, first about bikes ('I wish I'd discovered biking in the country fifty years ago') then about physical violence. Why violence? Because his career had been as a stunt man, and a bodyguard, and a tough guy. He had worked for a while as a bodyguard to visiting film stars ('Paul Newman was not a bloke who liked chatting much') and also for one of the Krays ('Reggie Kray was a funny bloke. You never really knew what he was thinking. Know what I mean?' . . . No, but I nodded wisely . . .) and now he spent all his time either bicycling or keeping kids out of trouble in his local park. He had loads of stories to tell ('Remember the mysterious death of Freddie Mills, the famous boxer? I'll tell you what really happened . . .') and I was sorry when we got to London.

Alas, recently I have either become more shy or got more interesting books, because I seem to have kept myself more to myself and have no doubt missed some fascinating encounters, so in one way I am glad that the 12 o'clock train from Alnwick to Kings Cross broke down a few weeks back. I had been in Alnwick to do a talk at the finest second-hand bookshop known to man, Barter Books, and had been deposited on Alnwick Station with good time to spare, so that I stood in the bracing country breeze watching rooks collect twigs from the line for nest-building in a nearby copse before being startled by the stealthy arrival of the express from Edinburgh. Found a seat, got stuck into a book, and was only roused from it by the sudden cessation of the train just short of Newark.

'Sorry,' said the Customer Apology Specialist Announcer, 'but there seems to be a hold-up. As soon as we know what it is, we will bring you more information.'

(Have you noticed that everyone these days says they will bring you more information when you haven't had any yet at all? It's like ATMs that say, as soon as you have put your card in them, 'Please wait – we are dealing with your request,' although you haven't made a request, or people at the other end of the line who ask you to confirm your address, when they just want you to tell them your address and they haven't got anything to confirm at all . . .)

After we had sat for a long time in nowhere, staring out across a lake with bedraggled birds on it, we were told the train was well and truly broken down and another engine was sent for to push us into Newark, where we all got out, and piled into the next train, from Leeds. Gosh, how surprised those people from Leeds were to see so many hundreds of Newark citizens get on their train (which, it turned out, had already been delayed for an hour by our breakdown). I luckily found a seat at a table occupied by two other men, one old, one young, and cut myself off from them by putting on headphones and starting listening to some old radio programme I had taped previously.

It didn't work. At the first chance, the old man leant forward, tapped my tape player and asked me how good these machines were. Thing was, he said, he had an aged sister in Berwick on Tweed who needed amuse-ment, and this looked like the sort of thing . . .

Quite how we got on to it, I don't know, but ten minutes later he was telling me and the young man about his war experiences. He had been a professional train driver when the war started, joined the Engineers and found himself in the Middle East, driving trains in Iran.

'Why in Iran?' I asked him.

Because he was in charge of taking supplies up to the Russians. They were our allies, see. The line went all the way up to near the Russian border. Clothes, weapons, ammunition. Returned prisoners of war as well. It was hard work, because at one point the line went through some quite high mountains, up to 8,000 feet, and in winter it was perishing cold. One time he had said to his fireman, 'Come and help me with something.' Fireman had said, 'Sorry, I can't move.' Turned out he was frozen to the window, it was so cold. Later on he had gone to Italy and driven trains there as well. He once drove Mussolini's train. Really. The way it happened was this . . .

The young man and I sat entranced all the way to London as he told us his yarns. Not just train yarns. Sea-going yarns. The time he was court-martialled by a vindictive officer. The time he was ordered to provide a cabaret turn in mid-ocean and refused. The time . . .

'You should write all this down,' said the young man.

'That's what my son in Bristol keeps telling me,' said the old man. 'But I don't know . . .'

And so until King's Cross the young man and I sat, like the pair of boys in the *Raleigh's Childhood* painting, drinking it all in. Again, I was sorry to say goodbye to Jock, which had been his nickname in the war, as I felt he had lots more to tell. I drifted down to Kings Cross tube station, and as I stood looking at the indicator, trying to work out which was the next train to Paddington, a voice at my shoulder said, 'Is the next train for Paddington, do you know?' It was a middle-aged lady who turned to be heading for Stroud. We got on the right tube train together and travelled to Paddington, swapping life stories all the way. What was startling was that we were the only people in our coach talking. I had forgotten that people in London never talk to each other. It's only out in the country that total strangers still get on like a house on fire. Especially in the middle of nowhere near Newark.

Yes, I've started talking on trains again. After all, if 83-year-old Jock from Folkestone can do it, so can I.

The Oldie, 2006

LADY CHATTERLEY'S LOVER

L'AUTHENTIQUE VERSION

C'était dinner-time à Chatterley Hall.

Nothing posh. Un simple soûper pour deux.

Lady Constance Chatterley avait une salade. Elle était sur un diet.

Sir Clifford, dans son wheel-chair, avait une très petite salade. Il n'était pas sur un diet, mais dans un wheel-chair vous n'avez pas beaucoup d'exercice. C'est triste, really.

Mais les gens handicappés, ils ne demandent pas la pitié. La sympathie, oui. Un hand avec le wheel-chair, oui. La pitié, jamais.

La conversation était desultoire. Le traffic était mauvais dans le town . . . ? Encore un drop de mayonnaise . . . ? Cette sorte de chose.

Puis Sir Clifford parla.

'By the way, Connie, tu as rencontré Mellors aujourd'hui?'

'Le gamekeeper? Oui, pourquoi?'

'Tu sais. Ce sujet que nous avons discuté.'

'Quel sujet?'

'Mon sexual inadequacy.'

'Oh, Clifford! Really! Pas à meal-time!'

Je suis avec Lady Chatterley ici. Le sexual inadequacy, c'est un peu off-putting à meal-time. Avec le café et les liqueurs, peut-être, mais over la salade? Cela a un mauvais effect sur l'appétit.

Mais Sir Clifford insista. Il était comme ça, Cliff Chatterley.

'J'insiste, chérie. Il faut confronter les facts. Après mon wound en World War I, je ne suis pas un husband complet, et c'est très hard sur toi.

242

Donc, j'ai fait la suggestion d'un petit fling avec Mellors, qui est un grand, jeune bloke et un Lothario, I bet!'

'Clifford, c'est dégoûtant! Un gamekeeper!'

'Ne sois pas un snob, my dear. Une petite affaire avec lui serait très bonne pour toi. Pourquoi pas?'

'Parce que je ne trouve pas Mellors tres handsome et parce que je ne trouve pas sex très intéressant et parce que je suis heureuse comme je suis.'

Sir Clifford donna un shrug des shoulders.

Lady Constane fit signe au butler de rémouver les assiettes de salade.

Le butler alla à la cuisine, et répéta à la cook la conversation de Sir Clifford et Lady Constance.

La cook la répéta à la parlour maid.

La parlour maid répéta la conversation à son boyfriend.

Son boyfriend répéta la conversation a son ami, un Monsieur David Herbert Lawrence.

'Wow!' dit Lawrence. 'Un plot pour un novel là! Mais je suis sûr que vous avez la conversation le wrong way round.'

'How come?' dit l'ami.

'Well, je suis sûr que Lady Constance est engagée dans une affaire passionnée avec Mellors, et que sir Clifford est furieux.'

'Non, non, je ne crois pas . . .'

'Si, si! C'est la seule interpretation possible.'

Et David Herbert Lawrence commença son novel le next jour.

Moi, je n'ai pas l'intention de le lire.

Je trouve cette sorte de chose un peu naff.

Je suis avec Lady Chatterley là.

Vous pas?

Oui, j'en suis sûr.

The Franglais Lieutenant's Woman, 1986

HISTORY OF KING TONY

or *Labour's Lost, Love*

ACT IV

The scene is King Tony's council chamber, where King Tony is closeted with his ever trusty adviser, Sir Alastair Campbell.

Tony: That's settled then. We'll arm and take the field
Against the scurvy rebel leader Hague
Some time in May, when blossoms will be out!
And not just blossoms! Hague will be out too!
Out twice! First vanquished by our mighty troops
And then from power torn down by his own men,
The Spanish Don Portillo first among them!
Campbell: That is the plan. Nor can I see a way
In which our mighty purpose will be thwarted.
In three months time young Hague will be forgotten . . .

Enter a messenger.

Messenger: My Lord, I come from far Northumberland . . . !
Tony: How very nice! A lovely little spot!
I come from far-off Edinburgh myself.
Campbell: You do not have the vestige of a brogue.

Tony: And nor do you, brave Campbell, though your name
Doth promise Scottish ancestors galore!
Messenger: My lord! I did not come to talk of origins!
I bring you dreadful news from up the North!
Of new contracted foot and mouth disease!
The which, if it should spread, will paralyse
The daily traffic of this active nation!
Tony: Oh, merciful heavens! Not another plague
Sent down to torture my long-suffering folk!
First BSE, then Railtrack, now all this!
Campbell: And yet, if it is just Northumberland,
And nowhere else, we may still be all right . . .

Enter another messenger

2nd Mess: My Lord, I come hot-foot from nearby Essex . . .
A pleasant spot, despite the silly stories . . .
Tony: Forget the small talk and the urban myths!
Just tell us what the news is Brentwood way!
2nd Mess: The news is all of foot and mouth, my Lord,
Which like an unseen scourge flies through the air,
Alighting like a spider here and there
To weave its web of death and murderous deed . . .
Tony: Thank you. We'll let you know. Next, please!

Enter a third messenger.

3rd Mess: My lord, from Devon's hills I bring you news...
Tony: Of foot and mouth which has been spotted there?
3rd Mess: How did you know?
Tony: That's all we hear today.
But tell me, Campbell, if the land is cursed
By dead and dying cattle everywhere,
Must we postpone our battle with Lord Hague?
Is it better to show a calm resolve

By carrying out our forward battle plans
Or show ourselves aware of such grave things
By cancelling all our well-planned call to arms?
Campbell: There will be time enough to think of that,
But first we must take steps to crush the plague!
You must be strong! And also seen to be strong!

The scene is a square in London. After a fanfare of trumpets, the King's herald addresses the people.

Herald: Pay heed! Pay heed! A message from the king!
Pray silence for a royal proclamation!
1st Man: As if the traffic wasn't bad enough
Without this kind of stoppage in the streets!
2nd Man: Perhaps he will announce a policy
To modernise the Tube and Underground . . .
3rd Man: Oh, yes, he might! And pigs might fly as well!
Herald: Excuse me, gents! Can I just interrupt?
1st: Yes, yes, do carry on. We were just chatting . . .
Herald: Then be it known, by royal proclamation,
That as there is a plague abroad right now,
Which men call foot and mouth, throughout the land,
So we admonish you to stay away
From visits to the countryside this month.
Horse racing is OK. And so is sport. And golf.
And lots of other things in profit.
But otherwise we say, stay in the town!
So says the royal King! God save King Tony!

The Palace at Westminster. Enter King Tony, musing.

Tony: This foot and mouth seems like a curse on me.
Whate'er we do, we cannot cut it out!
Sir Nick, my trusty agriculturalist,
Doth huff and puff like some poor groaning steed

246

Who cannot bear the weight that's on his back,
Saying that all is hunky-dory, right as rain,
When quite the opposite is true, it's plain.
Like as a cow within the abbatoir
Doth sense the coming of his final hour,
So 'tis with Brown. I see there in his eyes
The coming of his imminent demise.
Well, well. He'll do a very useful job
When I need someone throwing to the mob . . .

Enter Sir Michael Meacher, hotfoot from the West Country.

Tony: What ho, Meacher! What news dost bring from Taunton,
The back of beyond, where nobody ever goes?
Meacher: That is the trouble, sire. There none do go
And all the pubs and hotels languish sore.
I do beseech you, sire, to tell the world
That now's the time to hit the country trail!
Tony: I did dispatch my herald yesterday,
At your command to bid them stay away!
Meacher: Well, now we ask the very opposite.
Tony: I shall, this time. Next time, make up your mind.

Meacher bows and leaves.

Tony: When reshuffling next becomes a feature,
I fear the axe might fall on Michael Meacher . . .

The scene changes back to that square in London, where again the royal herald calls for silence.

Herald: Hear ye, hear ye! By order of the king
I do command ye all to feel quite free
To go out to the countryside and there
Spend all the money ye can spare for it!

I know that I did say the opposite before
But that was wrong. This now is correct.
1st Man: He means, th'Americans have taken fright
And cancelled all their bookings, as they do.
2nd Man: And so the need for tourists falls on us!
3rd Man: Sod that for a lark! I'll stay right here!
The countryside's a place for us to fear!
What's there to fear right here in London town?
1st Man: Just muggers, thieves and houses falling down.
2nd Man: And traffic jams and men with ginger hair . . .
3rd Man: Ginger-haired men?
2nd Man: Indeed. Look over there . . .

He turns and sees, approaching severally, Sir Robin Cook and Sir Charles Kennedy. With a cry of fear, they all flee for the countryside.

Independent, 2003

A BUNCH OF KEYS

The other night I was in the underground Gents on Platform 1 at Paddington Station when I noticed a young man trying to get in who hadn't got the requisite 20p piece. (Spending a penny? Don't make me laugh.) So in a Samaritan spirit I sorted out the change in my pocket and found I had enough to change the 50p piece which was all he had, and let him in, to his blessed relief.

Ten minutes later, when my train was about to go, I found that my bunch of keys was missing. I ransacked all my pockets. Nothing. No sign of them. I must have taken the bunch of keys out when sorting my change for the young man and left it in the Gents. So much for doing people good turns. I raced back to the Gents. Another 20p to get in. No sign of the keys. The attendant hadn't the faintest idea what I was on about. Train going, so had to get on, minus keys ...

It had been years since I lost a wallet, or passport, or keys, or anything really vital, so I had forgotten that feeling of emptiness, that feeling of loss, deprivation, bereavement, call it what you will, that straightaway hits you when a vital part of your belongings goes missing. I am so used to the weight on my left thigh (I always keep my keys in my left hand trouser pocket, nowhere else) that without it I feel undressed, and rather odd. Well, I certainly felt oddly naked as I got on the 10:15pm home to Bath Spa, as if I would never be able to get into any lock ever again, be barred from my own house, my own car, my bicycle, my shed, my ...

Yes, what else was there? It suddenly occurred to me that I couldn't remember what half the keys were for. My wife has always complained that I keep far too many keys on my key-ring and that it wears holes in the left hand trouser pocket of all my trousers eventually, and I know she is right, but it seems wrong to discard keys so I never do, and now I had discarded all of them at once.

I decided to make a list of all the ones I could remember, and not having any paper on me, I turned to the end cover of the book I was reading. (*The Free Fishers* by John Buchan. Good yarn. Bad story. No, good story, but bad characters. And why was Buchan so scared of women . . .?)

Key to the front door and back door. Car key. Two bike keys. Suitcase key, though I never use it. And . . . that's it. That's all I can remember. Yet there were about a dozen keys on the bunch. And there isn't a single key that I can't get copied and replaced. So why am I feeling so bereaved? It's not as if I had lost my wallet. Credit cards are a nightmare, because they can be abused by naughty people, but if someone finds my keys in the Gents at Paddington, what use are they to them?

Oh, and the little tag given to me by a nun in Italy. I'd forgotten about that . . . Thing is, some years ago I found myself presenting a Channel 4 programme about Catholic relics. The director was obsessed with the presence in a church of Italy of what they thought was Christ's foreskin. As you all know, Jesus ascended whole and entire into Heaven, so anything bodily he left behind must have been something removed in his lifetime. Hair. Baby teeth. Fingernails. Beard. That sort of thing. And, him being a Jew and therefore circumcised, his foreskin. To cut a long story short, we never got to see his foreskin, but we did see some curious things (such as part of Thomas Beckett, and the Virgin Mary's own house at Loreto) and we visited Cascia to see the body of Saint Rita, patron saint of lost causes.

That was heartbreaking. Round her shrine were objects left by pilgrims seeking her help: photos of car crashes of which the victim was still in a coma, things belonging to people with incurable diseases, even pennants of football teams which hadn't won in two years. I was looking on with a cynical but sympathetic eye when a nun pressed a present in my hand. It was a metal key-ring tag. It had a picture of Santa Rita on it, and the prayer 'Santa Rita Proteggimi' – Saint Rita protect me. Superstitiously, I had worn it on my key ring ever since, and I think she has protected me all right. She just hasn't done a very good job on my key ring, that's all.

Well, it's a week later now, and I have replaced almost all the keys, and my bunch of keys is down to modest proportions now, and my trouser pockets are breathing a sigh of relief, so all in all it was a blessing in disguise, as if forced me to get rid of a lot of rubbish and keep the essentials. And it may well be that in the future, if all our keys are replaced by electronic devices, something like this will not be able to happen again. Already many hotel keys are no longer heavy objects with small planks attached to stop you taking them away by accident but small plastic wafers which can discarded. (There used to be a bar in Jersey Airport which collected passengers' accidentally retained hotel keys, which hung from the ceiling like Chinese wind chimes. All gone now . . .)

Indeed, perhaps I shouldn't have written about this personal loss in public. Still, if my place is burgled in the near future, or my bike is nicked, I am already able to give the police an accurate description of the culprit. It's a man. Who was in the Gents at Paddington on or shortly after June 1st, who reads the *Oldie*. And who has in his possession a small souvenir of Santa Rita of Cascia.

That should narrow it down.

The Oldie, 2006

NIGHT OF THE
MOLE HUNTERS

'I HAVE reason to believe that there is a mole in the Neighbourhood Watch,' said the Colonel strictly, looking round the meeting.

A mole! In the Neighbourhood Watch! The very idea! It was like saying that there was a Russian agent in the Royal Family. They all looked round suspiciously at each other.

'I'm afraid it's the only theory that makes sense,' continued the Colonel. 'Look, we all pool information about our movements so that we can keep an eye on each other's houses when we're out, and what happens? We've all been burgled!

'That suggests only one thing to me – that one of our number is a criminal who has joined the Neighbourhood Watch to get inside information.'

They knew it made sense. One of them must be the guilty party. They knew it must be so, because they had all read the kind of novel in which all the suspects were gathered together in the library. But who could it be?

They all looked so eminently respectable, from the vicar to Dr Peabody, from old Mrs Treadgold to Professor Brindle. The only one who might conceivably be capable of such a dastardly deed was . . .

'Simon Pullar!' said the Colonel.

'Yes?' said Simon, startled.

'You're the obvious suspect,' said the Colonel. 'You haven't got a job. You lounge around all day, and you only shave once a week. You smoke and drink too much and you wear the most dreadful ties.

'What clinches the matter, to my mind, is that you are the only one who hasn't been burgled.'

Now that the Colonel had pointed it out, it was obvious. Simon Pullar was an untrustworthy layabout, and the only reason he had been admitted to the scheme at all was that he had the remnants of a posh accent.

As the final chapters of Agatha Christie novels went, this was going to be a short one. They might as well take him out and lynch him now.

'Just a moment,' said Simon. 'I think you're all being a little premature. For a start, the reason I haven't been burgled is that I haven't been out of my house. I don't shave because I have a sensitive skin condition. I lounge around all day because my job keeps me at home.'

'What do you *do*?' said the vicar.

'I write detective stories,' said Simon. 'For this purpose I like to find out the personal details of my neighbours and use them as characters, and I must say I've found some *very* interesting things about you lot. For instance, would you be surprised to learn that the professor is not really a professor at all?'

'Nonsense,' said Brindle. 'I go to the university every day.'

'Yes, but your department was closed down last year. You daren't admit it, so you pretend to be employed.

'The doctor is a genuine doctor, but he has a drug addiction problem which is bankrupting him. The colonel is in trouble because he was discharged from the Army under dishonourable circumstances and gets no pension. The vicar . . . '

They all looked at each other furtively. This wasn't how the last chapter was meant to go. It turned out that they all had frightful secrets, nobody more so than Mrs Treadgold who had killed her sister to get her inheritance; all except Simon Pullar himself.

The comfy little middle-class village had turned out to be a diseased bed of bourgeois depravity.

'Are you trying to say that you are the only one who *isn't* a suspect?' said the Colonel defiantly.

'Not at all,' said Simon. 'For all you know, I might be such a bad detective story writer that I need the money badly enough to do some burgling.'

'Yes, tell us something you've written!' said the doctor, surreptitiously sniffing a little cocaine.

'Well, I've written this story for a start,' said Simon.

'If you're writing this story and we're all characters you've invented,' said the professor slowly, 'that can only mean two things. One, you have some terrible grudge against the middle classes. Two, you must know who the burglar really is.'

'I do,' said Simon. 'He is the man you've all forgotten about. The man who is not a member of the Neighbourhood Watch, but who comes to all our meetings. The man who said he would be along later this evening.'

As he spoke, the door opened and a latecomer entered.

'Sorry I couldn't make it earlier,' said Police Constable Wheelwright. 'Haven't missed anything important have I?'

Welcome To Kington, 1989

REFEREE'S LAMENT

'Been following the World Cup?' I said to the chap opposite, in a last desperate attempt to get a conversation going at a dinner party the other day.

'Yes,' he said. 'I've been following it.'

'Did you see the France v. New Zealand match? I said. (This was before Saturday's England v. France thriller.)

'Yes,' he said. 'Enjoy it?'

'Great,' I said. 'Very exciting. Not the greatest rugby in the world, but very exciting. Shame someone had to lose . . .'

This is how I always summarise any match I have seen. It never offends anyone.

'What was the name of the referee?' he said.

'Pardon?' I said.

'What was the name of the referee? You said it was a memorable match. So, can you remember the name of the referee?'

I tried. I had a vague memory of a silver-haired, young-old chap. But all referees are silver-haired, young-old chaps.

'I have no idea?' I said. 'Why?'

'Because,' he said, 'no-one ever remembers the referee. And yet if it wasn't for us . . .'

'Ah!' I said. 'You're a referee!'

He too was silver-haired, and old in a young sort of way, like all those ministers in New Labour cabinets.

'I am,' he said, 'and proud of it. Anyone who can get through eighty minutes in public dressed in black shirt and shorts, looking like a Nazi Boy Scout, must have something going for him.'

'Hold on,' I said. 'Rugby refs don't wear black. That's football refs. Rugby officials have gone all colourful and stylish recently.'

'Thank God someone noticed!' he said. 'Yes, we've made a drive for acceptance in this World Cup. It's going our way. We've won our battle to be allowed to wear casual dress. We've been allowed to have radio mikes so that the crowd can hear what we're saying, even if the players can't, and we can show off our language skills to 80,000 at a time. Do you want to know what "Crouch . . . Touch . . . Engage!" is in Spanish?'

'No,' I said.

'We're allowed to make signs so that even the players can understand us. And we nearly, nearly, nearly got our pre-match dance allowed.'

'Pardon?'

'The New Zealand All Blacks have got their haka, haven't they? Samoa and Tonga have got native dances as well, to frighten the opposition with, before the game starts. The English have got God Save the Queen, which they try to stupefy the opposition with. But what have the ref and line judges got?'

'Nothing,' I said. 'You're right. The least the three of you could do is have a little routine worked out . . .'

'We did have a routine worked out,' said the ref, dully. 'A war-like flag dance. Got a choreographer in to do it for us. After the two sides had had their anthems and all that, it was our turn to line up threateningly against both sides. The touch judges had their flags, and the ref had his red cards, and for half a minute we did this beautifully rehearsed routine, backwards and forwards, a bit like three matadors, blowing our whistles, chanting and stabbing with our flags. Ending up with a blood-curdling cry of "Off! Off! Off!" . . . and pointing to the sin bin.'

'Sounds great,' I said. 'Why haven't I seen it happening?'

'We gave it a try out in one of the pre-qualifying matches,' said my friend. 'The crowd loved it. We got an encore, would you believe? We were cheered throughout the rest of the match. Every time we gave a penalty, they chanted our war slogan: "What are we? Fair! Fair Fair!" But the authorities gave it the thumbs down and banned us from doing it again. Said it brought the game into disrepute. Disrepute! If they could see the half of what goes on inside a maul, they wouldn't talk about disrepute . . .'

And my friend sank into a disillusioned silence for the rest of the meal, and didn't say another word, but ever since then my mind has been a jungle of images of refs and touch judges strutting their stuff through a threatening, thrusting kind of tango, while seventeen-stone men in beards cower away in terror from their advancing flag tips.

Independent, 2007

AN AUTUMNAL WALK
WITH UNCLE GEOFFREY

Although there had been one or two slight frosts in October, most of the leaves were still on the trees, waiting for the big fall. Uncle Geoffrey paused under a walnut tree, looking up past the curling green leaves into the branches, seeking signs of a nut harvest.

'There don't seem to have been many nuts this year,' he said. 'It's odd how some years are so much better than others.'

'If you ask me,' said Robert, 'the walnut trees have already been stripped bare by scavenging hordes of Women's Institute members, pickling everything in their path and turning it into chutney and preserves.'

'Like locusts they move across the landscape,' said Susie, 'stripping all fruit, cooking it and turning it into jars for sale as Christmas presents. And when they run out of home-grown fruit, they ship it in from far-off Seville and turn it into marmalade.'

'I didn't know that locusts made chutney, Susie,' said Robert.

'You know what I mean,' said Susie.

'Yes, I know what you mean,' said Robert. 'But does Uncle Geoffrey know what you mean?'

They turned their innocent eyes on Uncle Geoffrey. Uncle Geoffrey blinked at them, thinking how much he would like to have them turned into some undrinkable juice or unsaleable mixture, and quietly disposed of. But what he said was:

'Look at the blackberry briars, children. I always think that even when the fruit has gone, the colour of the leaves is one of the glories of autumn, don't you?'

Robert looked closely at the brambles, ignoring the leaves.

'I don't think the avaricious ladies of the W.I. have done a very good job, you know. On every bramble there are dozens of wizened blackberries, dried and wasted. No bird ate them. No Mrs Barnaby-Scott plucked them. There they are, surplus to requirements, doomed to be useless.'

'But this is the eternal story of nature,' said Susie. 'Nature is incredibly wasteful and spendthrift. Does it take 10,000 seeds to get another syca-more tree going? Then nature cares not for the 9,999 that do not make it. Will most of the baby eels setting out across the sea perish? Nature does not care as long as enough get through.'

'Nature has the same attitude to life as Russian generals do to their man-power,' said Robert. 'I remember once reading about an American general and a Russian general who met after World War II and got round to discussing the best way of clearing a minefield. *What we always do*, said the American, *is send out specialists with the most modern equipment. Do you*? said the Russian. *Oh, we send out a squad of infantrymen surplus to requirements and make them walk across the minefield. You'd be surprised how quickly it clears the mines.*

'That is abominable,' said Uncle Geoffrey, who had been listening aghast.

'But nature would approve of it,' said Susan. 'Just as it would approve of those restaurants which throw away so much good food and those supermarkets which chuck out everything past the sell-by date, though there is nothing wrong with it.'

'The Tesco theory of natural survival!' said Robert. 'Brilliant, Susie!'

'Look!' said Uncle Robert, desperate to change the subject. 'Little wild plums! I bet they're sweet and juicy after the recent lovely sunny weather! Let's try one.'

'They're not plums,' said Robert. 'They're sloes. They're bitter. They're horrible. I wouldn't try one if I were you … Oh. Too late.'

The spectacle of Uncle Geoffrey bent over, doubled up with agony, seemed to support his theory.

'We could always make sloe gin, I suppose,' said Susie.

'Waste of time,' said Robert briskly. 'Gin already tastes delightfully of juniper berries. Why adulterate it with piles of tooth-rotting sugar and palate-curdling sloes?'

'You're right,' said Susie. 'Come on, Uncle Geoffrey – keep up!'

And as the children turned purposefully for home, Uncle Geoffrey, still creased up with the horror of the mouth-puckering sloe in his mouth, followed them slowly, with comforting thoughts of child-poisoning bubbling in his heart.

Independent, 2003

FORTY RULES FOR BLACKBERRYING

Have you been blackberry picking yet?

You should have been, because now is the season for the only great British hunting ritual left to us that Tony Blair has not threatened to ban.

You don't know how to pick blackberries? Rubbish! Picking blackberries is the easiest thing in the world, as long as you know the forty basic rules.

Oh, yes. Even blackberry picking has its own basic rules. Would you like me to tell you what they are? Or would you rather that I turned my thoughts today to the fate of Mo Mowlam?

I thought so. Here are the forty basic rules of blackberry picking:

1. The blackberry is the fruit of the vicious bramble or briar, a fruit so aggressive that it was given star billing in David Attenborough's series: *Great Fighting Plants Of The World.*

2. The annual harvesting period starts on the day when you say: 'I don't think they're ready yet', and ends on the day when you say: 'I think they've all gone over now.' This lasts about three days.

3. The blackberry goes through various stages of ripeness, which can be distinguished by the colour.

4. These colours are, in order, green, red, purple and mouldy purple.

5. Blackberries should not be picked when they are green or red (unripe) or mouldy purple (over-ripe).

6. Nor should they be picked when they are purple, if they do not come off the stem readily.

7. The normal approach is to approach a cluster of purple blackberries, select the one which looks ripest and attempt to pull it off.

8. It will not come off.

9. It will resist all attempts to pull it off.

10. But it will impart a vibration to the other berries which knocks off the ripe ones which you should have gone to first.

11. These ripe ones will fall to the ground.

12. And disappear.

13. It's no use looking for them.

14. They have disappeared into the undergrowth or grass or hedgerow, where they will use their considerable cunning to stay hidden.

15. You won't find them.

16. Don't even bother trying.

17. All right, you may find one or two of them.

18. But while trying to pick them up your fingers will mash them into a jelly.

19. So don't bother trying.

20. While picking blackberries, you will find your fingers being stained red.

21. With your own blood.

22. This is because (see No 1) the blackberry has two fighting weapons which you cannot defeat.

23. The cruel thorn which gashes you.

24. And the tiny prickle which sticks in your finger and which you can feel but cannot see and is agony.

25. The juiciest blackberries are the biggest purple ones.

26. That is why they have attract so many wasps, flies, etc, which tend to be already squatting on the blackberries you want, either sucking from them or apparently sticking their backside into them, and doing something worse.

27. So what you do is go to another unoccupied ripe blackberry, thinking to yourself: 'This one has probably already been abused by an insect . . .'

28. But don't think about that.

29. You will be tempted to eat many of the better blackberries when you pick them, instead of putting them in the basket.

30. But you will resist.

31. Saying to yourself, 'No, the more I take back home the better pleased people will be!'

32. When you look in the basket to see how you are doing, you will be amazed how many you have got.

33. You will also spot one blackberry with a worm crawling out of it.

34. While attempting to remove this, you lose sight of it.

35. You will take back your basket of blackberries, conscious that there are lots of little things in there.

36. But you don't mention that to the person who is going to deal with them.

37. The person then takes the fruit and puts it in a pan with sugar and reduces it to a black sludgy mess, not tasting a lot of anything.

38. At which point you wish you had eaten all those blackberries instead of putting them dutifully in the basket.

39. Later, you find lots of unsuspected wounds all over your body, and inexplicable purple stains all over your clothes.

40. The blackberries have won again.

Independent, 2000

MORE FROM MILLS & BANG

The response to the creation of our new publishing house, Mills & Bang, was remarkable – all titles were sold out within days of hitting the bookstalls, and Yomping into Passion *appeared briefly on the Cross-Channel best-seller list.*

Now we are is proud to announce a further selection of Mills & Bang novels – the novels that are as tough as old boots yet as soft as a first kiss!

Cavalry Tulle, by Yolanda Dubbin

Debbie felt the wind streaming through her hair as she kicked Marmaduke into a gallop. How good it felt to be on her favourite horse once more, the soft turf of the downs beneath his hooves and the English Channel twinkling in the sun, way, way in the distance. Her memories of Oscar seemed just a bad dream.

Suddenly she became aware that another rider was closing in to meet her. Crossly, she reined in and waited for him to arrive.

'I'm sorry,' said the newcomer affably, 'but this is private property. Restricted, you know.'

'To whom, may I ask?'

'Members of the regiment. Captain Bruce Derwent at your service.'

'And I,' said Debbie coolly, 'am Major Deborah Merryweather, newly joined to the regiment.'

Derwent's face changed. But before he could bring himself to salute her, a shot rang out and whistled past them. Quick as a flash he had leapt from his horse, bundled her from hers and rolled them both into a safe position in the grass.

'Who's trying to kill us?' she gasped, thrilling strangely to the touch of his uniformed arm.

'Nobody. It's an army firing range. They could kill anybody. By the way,' he said, his mouth not six inches from her perfect ear, 'I believe you know my best friend, Oscar Threadgold. Major,' he added reluctantly.

Oscar! His dark handsome face came before her, with its twisted smile. Then she looked at Bruce's sandy open features. How were their destinies to be intertwined?

'Perhaps you could put me down now, Captain,' she said icily.

A Man's Girl, by **Grenada Pinn**

'Sorry to bother you, sir,' said the sergeant, 'but I'd like to have a word about Private Simple.'

'What's the trouble?' said the captain.

'Fact is,' said the sergeant, 'I think Private Simple's a woman.'

The captain drummed his pencil on the desk.

'Extraordinary thing to say, sergeant. What makes you think so?'

'Difficult to pin down, sir. The way he walks. The extra large battle tunic. The tendency to use lipstick and shave his legs.'

'Does he pull his weight otherwise?'

'Absolutely. Best soldier in the platoon.'

'Then I wouldn't worry too much, sergeant. We need all the good men we can get, even if they are women.'

Damn, thought the captain. They're on to Yvonne's and my little scheme. It was only as the door closed that the captain realised there was something odd about the sergeant. He was wearing high-heeled shoes. Were their destinies to be intermingled in some strange way?

Free Fall Love, by **Alberta Smithwick**

Rowena, flushing, went hot and cold. She felt limp. There was a roaring in her ears. Not surprising, as she was half-way through her first-ever parachute jump.

'I say!' said a voice. She looked round. There was a man in the air near her. 'I say, I'd open your parachute if I were you!'

How stupid of her. She pulled the ring and the huge white canopy opened above her. The man smiled and put his thumb up as he floated away. She hated him instantly, and yet there was something about his warm crinkly eyes that told her their destinies would, given half a chance, be on the same downward path together.

Other titles coming soon: One Girl's Resistance, *by Jean Hackett*, NATO Nancy, *by Marcia Hastings*; Passion in the Pay Corps, *by Briony Hanrahan.*

Moreover, Too, 1985

MORE ALBANIAN PROVERBS

Those delicate flowers of wisdom which are so beautiful out of the corner of the eye, but which tend to wilt and droop when looked at straight on.

Three things that nobody likes but everybody uses: barbed wire, aftershave and national anthems.

We all think we are about to fart soundlessly.

A fart is the perfect joke. It is unexpected, it is brief, and it sums up what we all feel about the government.

A warm handshake leaves no fingerprints.

You are never more than ten days away from forgetting someone's birthday.

Three unpleasant personal habits: sniffing, humming inaudibly and using torture as an instrument of repression.

Out of the frying pan on to the floor, and back into the frying pan again before someone sees.

Do you wish to make friends with strangers? Put up balloons on your gate.

A pessimist is one who thinks a glass is half empty. An optimist is one who drains it and asks for a refill.

God only knows. That's it. That's all he does. He does nothing else. God only knows.

Independent, 2006

HOWARD'S END

UN INSPECTOR E.M. FORSTER MYSTERY

Howard était stone dead.

Il n'y avait pas room pour doute.

Howard était mort, all right.

Mort comme un plank de bois.

Et la cause de death n'était pas visible.

Blimey, pensa Inspector E.M. Forster. Encore un baffling murder case. Exactement ce que le docteur a ordonné.

'J'ai trouvé le corps ici,' dit l'estate agent, sweating. 'Il était sur le floor. Dead. Comme ça.'

Ils étaient dans un empty house. Totalement vide. C'était TO LET. Pas un stick de furniture, pas un item de food, pas rien.

L'estate agent avait passé that way, et, seulement pour checker le wood-worm ou regarder le gas meter ou something, il est entré.

Et il a trouvé Howard. Mort. Dans un locked room.

Seulement l'estate agent avait le bunch of keys.

'Mais comment il avait pu entrer par la porte?' dit l'estate agent. 'C'est impossible.'

C'était la 7ème fois qu'il l'avait dit.

'Oui,' dit Forster. 'Mais il n'est pas entré par la porte. Ce n'est pas la seule mode d'entrée.'

Forster traversa le bare plancher jusqu'à la fenêtre. Il regarda par la window-pane.

'Ah, le room with a view,' dit l'estate agent.

'Le quoi?'

'C'est une phrase employée par les estate agents. Si l'interior d'un room n'est pas attractif, nous directons l'attention du client à l'exterieur. Room with a view, means, room with no other attraction.'

Forster n'écoutait pas. Il regarda le view. C'était magnifique. Sussex et les Brighton Downs.

'Pouvez-vous identifier le smell?'

'Quoi?' dit l'estate agent, startled.

'Il y a un smell dans la chambre. Faint, mais défini. Dans mon opinion, c'est un smell de curry.'

L'estate agent faisait un sniff. Oui. Curieux. Un smell de curry.

'Une autre question. Avez-vous remarqué la porte secrète?'

Inspector Forster traversa la chambre jusqu'au panelling et faisait tap-tap-tap avec son doigt. Il était hollow. Il tirait le panelling qui, avec un petit bruit, venait dans la chambre. C'était une porte secrète.

'Mais quoi . . . ?'

Forster beckona avec la main.

'Ne posez pas des questions. Venez voir.'

Derrière la panelling il y avait un opening, et dans l'opening il y avait beaucoup de darkness, et un corridor qui commençait dans le panelling and continua dans le darkness. Il semblait être un endless corridor.

Très indistinctement, dans le corridor, on pouvait entendre le bruit distant d'un autre continent; très, très loin il y avait le shouting de people et les cris des animaux. Et il y avait ce vague mais défini smell de curry.

'Qu'est-ce que c'est?' dit l'estate agent.

'C'est un passage à India,' dit Inspector E.M. Forster, simplement. Quelque part, un long way off, il crut entendre un éléphant.

'Et par ce passage à India, Howard est entré, dans le room avec un view. Pour recontrer son end.'

L'estate agent réfléchit.

'Et qui l'a tué?'

'Ah!' dit l'Inspector. 'Ça, c'est un job pour l'Indian Police. Ne trouvez-vous pas?'

So saying, il ramassa Howard, le mit dans le corridor et ferma la porte secrète.

The Franglais Lieutenant's Woman, 1986

MILES KINGTON INTERVIEWS
MATA HARI

Kington: So you are Mata Hari, the beautiful spy . . .

Mata Hari: That is what I am called now. It was not what I was called then.

Kington: What were you called then?

Mata Hari: Oh, many things. For a time I called myself Lady Mcleod, you know . . .

Kington: Really? Why?

Mata Hari: Oh, for many reasons. It is a long time ago . . . But Mata Hari, the beautiful spy . . . It sounds good! But it is not really true, is it?

Kington: Why not?

Mata Hari: Well, after all, Mata Hari was not my real name. Beautiful? (*Laughs*) And I was never, never a spy. But apart from all that, you are quite right.

Kington: It is nearly a hundred years since you died, and yet you are still famous as Mata Hari the beautiful spy.

Mata Hari: I am very flattered.

Kington: But that is all that people know about you. That you were a spy, that you seduced secrets out of people by your beauty, and that you were called Mata Hari. Otherwise, nobody remembers anything about you, Not your nationality, not your real name, nothing.

Mata Hari: Extraordinary.

Kington: And now you tell me that what little we do know about you is wrong?

Mata Hari: Absolutely. I seem to have preserved my cover better after my death than I did before.

Kington: Despite which you have achieved fame.

Mata Hari: Extraordinary.

Kington: Were you famous in your lifetime?

Mata Hari: As what? As a dancer?

Kington: Well, no – as a spy.

Mata Hari: I was not a spy. I thought I had explained.

Kington: Well, you were shot as a spy.

Mata Hari: That is true. These little mistakes happen.

Kington: How did it happen?

Mata Hari: Oh, the French were shooting a lot of people at the time.

Kington: You mean, shooting Germans?

Mata Hari: Not just Germans. The French were shooting a lot of their own side too. This was 1917 and the War was going badly, and the fighting had gone on too long, and many French soldiers were sick of the mud and the blood, and sick of their officers and sick of the whole thing, and so a lot of the soldiers mutinied and they were shot by the firing squad, and there was so much shooting of their own soldiers that maybe they thought for a change they would shoot a foreign woman to cheer everyone up, and I was available . . .

Kington: You sound very matter-of-fact about it.

Mata Hari: I've had time to get over it.

Kington: Perhaps we ought to go back to the beginning.

Mata Hari: If you wish. It is not a very interesting beginning but what do you want to know?

Kington: Your real name . . .

Mata Hari: Gertie.

Kington: . . . Gertie?

Mata Hari: Have I shocked you?

Kington: Well . . .

Mata Hari: It's always nice to shock people. I don't often get the chance . . . Anyway, my husband called me Gertie. My full name was Gertrude Margarete Zelle, and I was born in Holland in 1876, on August 7th.

Kington: So you were Dutch?

Mata Hari: Yes. Extraordinary, isn't it? That a nation of dull, boring people like the Dutch should produce a famous, beautiful spy with an exotic name... If I challenged you to name another Dutch spy, or another beautiful Dutchwoman, or even another Dutch dancer...

Kington: I... don't think I could.

Mata Hari: Really extraordinary, isn't it? All those tulips and windmills and clogs, and then – little me!

Kington: Well, the Dutch haven't always been safe and boring. They fought wars... they had an empire...

Mata Hari: Don't I know it! The Dutch East Indies! I spent the most boring years of my life out there... Aagh!

Kington: What took you out there?

Mata Hari: Who took me out there... A man called Mcleod.

Kington: A Scotsman?

Mata Hari: No, a Dutchman. With Scottish forefathers. God, how he used to go on about his forefathers. Do all the Scots go on about their ancestors?

Kington: They do, quite a lot. Not if they've got Dutch ancestors, of course. They'd keep quiet about that.

Mata Hari: Quite so. Anyway, this... man... married me and took me out to the Dutch East Indies to make a fortune, and it didn't work out, and we didn't get on, and so...

Kington: You left him?

Mata Hari: Not so easy to leave a man when you're 5,000 miles from home and nowhere to go. No, I just got bored. I had nothing to do. Lots of women started drinking out there, you know, just from boredom but I was lucky – I met someone who took me to one of the temples in Java, and I fell in love with the way they danced, and I decided to learn how to do it. It was so... sensuous, and exotic, and liberating... Then finally – oh, it's a long story, but I managed to get rid of the husband and came back to Europe and suddenly found I had to earn my living. Not an easy thing for a lone woman to do. But one day I was showing some people at a party what I had learnt in the temples of Java, and a man came to me afterwards and said that he ran a music club and he would love to present me as a performer, of course he would pay me... I didn't realise then exactly what kind of club he had in mind. I thought he was maybe a serious artist.

Kington: He wasn't?

Mata Hari: No. He was a serious businessman. He knew that people . . . men . . . would pay good money to see exotic dancing, if it was sufficiently . . .

Kington: Sexy?

Mata Hari: We didn't use the word sexy then. It was far too blatant. Let us say . . . artistic . . . exotic . . . advanced . . .

Kington: And so you performed Javanese temple dances in a Dutch night club . . . Was that not a bit irreverent?

Mata Hari: Well, it might have been if there had been any Javanese in the audience to offend, but there weren't. So I stopped being a colonial settler's wife and became an exotic dancer.

Kington: It's a bit like a Somerset Maugham story in a way.

Mata Hari: It's better than a Somerset Maugham story! It actually happened, for a start . . . Anyway, when I became an artistic dancer I took on the name of Mata Hari . . .

Kington: Why?

Mata Hari: Because I don't think an exotic dancer would get very far under the name of Gertie McLeod . . .

Kington: No, I mean, what is the significance of the name Mata Hari?

Mata Hari: It is Javanese for 'Eye of the Morning' . . . Not only did I change my name, I rapidly adapted my dance to Western tastes, or at least to the tastes of those present.

Kington: What sort of people were they?

Mata Hari: Have you ever been to a strip club?

Kington: Me? *(Nervous Laugh)* Well, maybe once a long time ago . . . out of curiosity . . . you know . . .

Mata Hari: Yes, I know. Well, that's the kind of person who wanted to see me dance . . . Ordinary men, like you . . . Big men in their profession . . . Important men at work . . . Little boys when out on their own . . .

Kington: And you did a strip tease?

Mata hari: No! Well, yes. But it was very artistic . . . The way I removed the last veil was said to be very . . . cathartic. Soon I got a reputation for being *extremely* artistic and I moved out of the clubs and started doing private performances.

Kington: You mean, private parties, with wild goings on . . .

Mata Hari: Some. Maybe. I don't remember. What I do remember is making some very influential friends. In the Army.

Kington: In the German Army?

Mata Hari: Some . . . some also in the French army. When you are a lone woman, you need all the protection you can get.

Kington: In what form did the protection come?

Mata Hari: Jewels . . . fur coats . . . money . . .

Kington: Military secrets?

Mata Hari: I was mixing with army officers . . . army officers talk about military matters . . . I would have had to be deaf not to pick up military information.

Kington: Did you sell it?

Mata Hari: Maybe. Maybe not. I can't remember.

Kington: Oh, surely you must be able to remember!

Mata Hari: Things don't work like that. It's not that easy. Look, let's say I have a friendship with a German army officer . . .

Kington: Major von Kelle, perhaps . . .

Mata Hari: Ah, you know about my friend, the German military attache in Madrid.

Kington: Yes.

Mata Hari: My, we *have* done our research well, haven't we? Yes, Major von Kelle, the top German officer in Madrid and, I may say, a very nice man. So we are friends. So he gives me a place to live. So we go out together to the opera. So we spend the night together sometimes. And sometimes he gives me presents. *Does this mean that I am selling my body?*

Kington: Those are not the terms I'd use . . .

Mata Hari: Well, if I was not selling my body, I was not selling military information either. Sometimes I heard things. I told other people these things. Later these people gave me presents. That's all.

Kington: It sound like spying to me . . .

Mata Hari: Maybe now it would be called spying. But things were different then. You must remember that we had no professional spies – or at least, no country had an organised spy service. All spies were free-lance. They were not on anyone's side. They worked for themselves, not for a cause. They stole a secret, and then looked for the highest bidder, a bit like being an art auctioneer ... Do you read Sherlock Holmes?

Kington: Sometimes. Why?

Mata Hari: There was a story called 'The Second Stain'. In it, the Prime Minister of England comes to Sherlock Holmes and says that a very important letter has been stolen, a letter from a foreign leader, a letter which is so inflammatory and so tactless that if it were known about, it would mean a European War. By the way, it is quite obvious from what is said that the foreign leader Mr Conan Doyle is talking about is the Kaiser, though he is not named. Now, do you remember how Sherlock Holmes starts to look for the letter?

Kington: I'm not sure I ...

Mata Hari: He says to Dr Watson that there are three intelligence agents in London clever enough to have stolen the letter and that even now whichever of them has stolen it must be looking for a buyer. You see? He doesn't say that it must be a *German* agent or a *French* spy, but a freelance agent! Just what Mrs Thatcher would approve of! Do you think your Mrs Thatcher would have liked such a market approach? Her government spies selling her government secrets to the best tender?

Kington: No, I don't think so. But I don't see where all this is leading us.

Mata Hari: Then I will explain. You asked me right at the beginning if I was the beautiful spy. I said, *No,* I wasn't a spy. Because we didn't have spies in the sense that you are meaning! Today there are millions of spies trained professionally by their countries who go out with their radios and codes and disguises and dropping-off points and contacts and God knows what, and you have thousands of spy novels written about dreary little men who work out of offices and double-cross each other and they have dwarfs' names ...

Kington: Dwarfs' names?

Mata Hari: You know, the seven dwarfs? Like Sneezy or Happy or Jolly or Smiley ...

Kington: Oh, you mean Smiley! George Smiley! John le Carré's spy character.

Mata Hari: Yes ... that boring little man ... Well, all your spies are like that now, men with professions, bureaucrats, time-servers ...

Kington: I see what you mean.

Mata Hari: I wasn't like that. I heard a few interesting things from some friends. I passed them on to other friends. That's all . . .

Kington: But surely all that must have changed when the Great War started. I mean, the major nations must have put their intelligence-gathering on a proper footing . . .

Mata Hari: They tried. They had already tried. I remember reading that the English sent two naval officers over to Germany in 1910 to spy out the coastline and the German naval defences. This was four years before the War, remember. The Germans spotted the two men spying and arrested them and tried them and . . .

Kington: . . . And shot them?

Mata Hari: No, no . . . Just put them in prison for a while. They didn't start shooting people seriously till the War. But you see, it was all very amateur then: just send a couple of officers over to have a look round. The British must have got the shock of their lives when they were actually arrested.

Kington: Did the British kick up a fuss?

Mata Hari: Absolutely not! They disclaimed all knowledge of them. 'We don't know what they are doing in Germany – must have been a private trip . . . We take no responsibility for them . . .' That, at least, was up with modern thinking. Leave your agent to carry the bucket.

Kington: Carry the can.

Mata Hari: Yes. And then when the War did break out, there was spy mania all over the place. *Everyone* was suspected of being a spy. You only had to have a German name, or an English name in Germany of course. Even Beethoven was suspected of being a spy.

Kington: What? Beethoven? But he had been dead for a hundred years!

Mata Hari: Then why did the English ban his music from their concert halls? So stupid . . . But I was going to tell you the story of the lady's maid who was caught leaving Germany after the war started, which will give you some idea of how advanced spying was in those days. They suspected her of carrying secrets, I can't remember now why she seemed suspicious, so they had her searched by a policewoman: strip-searched, I mean. And you'll never guess what they found . . .

Kington: No, I won't.

Mata Hari: Writing on her bottom! On her bottom, quite clearly, lines and lines of writing! I am not making this up. So they had her bottom photographed . . .

Kington: The Germans had a lady's maid's bottom photographed in case it was carrying secrets?

Mata Hari: This is the truth. And they found that what had happened was that she had been travelling on the train in Germany and had worried about the hygiene in the toilet, and had spread out a newspaper to sit on, on the toilet seat, and the writing had come off the paper and gone on to her bottom!

Kington: I don't believe it!

Mata Hari: True! It was the headlines from that morning's Frankfurt paper that she was smuggling out of the country! But people go a bit mad in wartime, you know.

Kington: Of course, this was the first European war there had ever been . . .

Mata Hari: Well, that's not true. I think Europe was much more embroiled in Napoleon's time than it ever was in the Great War. There were many countries in Europe not even involved.

Kington: Like Switzerland, you mean?

Mata Hari: Oh, Switzerland is never involved in anything. I was thinking of Spain. It's always strange being in a neutral country during a war, because you can mix with the enemy . . .

Kington: You did a lot of mixing with the enemy . . .

Mata Hari: Now, hold on! I didn't have an enemy! I was Dutch! I was neutral . . . I lived with Major von Kelle in Madrid, yes, but why not? He was head of German intelligence out there, yes, but that's not why I lived with him . . . Not like Madame Richer . . .

Kington: Who?

Mata Hari: Yes, people have forgotten about her . . . Though she was famous in her day as L'Alouette . . . You know what an 'alouette' is?

Kington: It's a skylark.

Mata Hari: That's right. She was a Frenchwoman, and she became famous as 'The Skylark' . . .

Kington: She sang?

Mata Hari: No, she flew.

Kington: Flew?

Mata Hari: She was one of the first aviators: one of the very first woman aviators. Her husband was an officer in the French army, and he was killed quite early in the war, so she was recruited by one of her late husband's friends to do a bit of spying, and she was sent to Madrid to infiltrate the German intelligence network. She seduced the German naval attache and set up house with him – a man called Baron von Krohn.

Kington: So you were living with the German military attache and she was living with the naval attache?

Mata Hari: Yes. Actually, the old Baron was mad about her, which helped, because she got a lot of secrets out of him and sent them back to Paris. She was a mine of information about submarines and things. But after the war . . .

Kington: So she survived the War?

Mata Hari: Oh, yes. We didn't all get shot. After the War she came back expecting a heroine's welcome, but her employers gave her the cold shoulder. They apparently thought it was wrong of her to have enjoyed seducing the Baron so much. Strange people the French. You can sleep with the enemy for duty, but not for fun. Perhaps that's why they shot me. I was having too much fun . . .

Kington: I'm not sure quite what . . .

Mata Hari: No, my point is that the Alouette was a genuine spy. She was good. She was lucky. She retired. Actually, she retired to England and married an Englishman called Crompton. Can you imagine if her neighbours had known! 'So, Mrs Crompton, what did you do in the war?' . . . 'Well, actually I slept with the German naval attache in Madrid and did a lot of spying . . .' She got the Legion of Honour in 1933. I was shot in 1917. Not really fair, is it?

Kington: And you are famous and she . . .

Mata Hari: Well, there is that, of course.

Kington: What I still haven't worked out is whether you actually did any spying at all.

Mata Hari: No, of course not. I aided the flow of ideas a little, that's all. I mean, as I said to the French when they arrested me, how could I be a German spy if I was living with the German military attache? The only secrets I could get from him would be known to the Germans already.

Kington: Yes, but there was some story of you being sent to Amsterdam by the French, and they gave you a list of six agents to contact, and within a week, the Germans had picked up and shot one of those agents . . .

Mata Hari: Meaning, that I betrayed him?

Kington: Yes.

Mata Hari: So many questions. I am tired of so many questions! It's like being questioned by the French all over again. Please, no more questions.

Kington: Just one.

Mata Hari: What is it?

Kington: What's it like to be shot?

Mata Hari: Why?

Kington: I have never met anyone who had been shot before.

Mata Hari: It's not nice. They offered me a blindfold. I said no. I wanted to have my last bit of daylight. They tied my hands behind my back. Why do they do that? Do they think I will try to escape? I remember thinking – this is stupid! I am a Dutchwoman! They cannot shoot a neutral! Especially as I have done nothing wrong! Then – bang!

Kington: And you are dead?

Mata Hari: Not quite. Six men with big guns, and they couldn't kill an unarmed woman. They didn't deserve to win the war. Then the officer leant over me with his revolver and pouf! An innocent woman dies.

Kington: And becomes famous.

Mata Hari: Oh, thank you very much! That kind of fame I can do without! I would much rather have lived to a ripe old age and taught my grandchildren how to do a little Javanese dancing . . .

Kington: But maybe you died at the right time. Whom the gods love . . .

Mata Hari: . . . die young. Quit while you're ahead. Leave them wanting more. Oh yes, I know all that. And yet at the time one doesn't say that. One says: I am young . . . !

Kington: You were 41 when you died.

Mata Hari: You are not gallant, monsieur. I am not sure how hard I would have tried to get military secrets out of *you* . . .

Kington: Ah! So you do admit you were getting military secrets out of people!

Mata Hari: I admit nothing. I have never admitted anything. I will never admit anything.

Kington: Gertrude Margarete Zelle . . . Lady Mcleod . . . Mata Hari . . . Thank you very much.

Mata Hari: You are welcome.

Radio 4, 1993

A COUNTRY WALK IN SPRING
WITH UNCLE GEOFFREY

'I sometimes think this is the best time of year for flowers,' remarked Uncle Geoffrey, as they looked at a bank of primroses. 'Hardly are the daffodils and the primroses beginning to fade than the bluebells are upon us, with the great white starry flowerheads of the wild garlic hard upon their heels. And all the time we have had the wood anemones, and the celandines, and the loveliness of the violets.'

'The loveliness of the violets, Uncle Geoffrey?' said Susan. 'That's a bit judgemental, isn't it? Scientifically speaking, a violet is either white or purple but not lovely.'

'She's right, Uncle Geoffrey,' said Robert. 'Calling flowers lovely lays you open to two charges. One, that you are describing nature subjectively, not botanically. Two, that you are suggesting that if violets are lovely, there may be other flowers which are not lovely. Or do you think that all flowers are lovely?'

Why did conversation with the children always contrive to take the wind out of his sails, wondered Uncle Geoffrey?

'No,' he admitted, 'no, I suppose there are some flowers I do not find particularly attractive. The dock, perhaps. The celandine I always think is a little vulgar compared to the buttercup. The dandelion is pretty ordinary...'

'How can you say that!' shrieked Susan. 'Look at that meadow there!'

And it so chanced they were passing a meadow wherein a large carpet of brilliant dandelions covered fully half the field, turning it a yellow as deep as any yolk.

'What a great display,' said Robert. 'Oh, Uncle, how can you justify your heartless attack on the dandelion?'

'When it is not only decorative but useful,' said Susan,' for as you know it is prized among the health food people for its diuretic qualities – hence its vulgar French name – its curative powers for the liver, and its use as a coffee substitute when you roast and grind the root. Coffee substitute? Perhaps even an improvement on coffee, as it has none of the damaging effects on the nervous system produced by caffeine!'

'In Derbyshire, the application of the milky sap or latex derived from the dandelion is said to cure warts,' said Robert.

'Though whether this is also believed in neighbouring Lancashire and Cheshire is doubtful,' added Susan.

'Maybe folk are just naturally wartier in Derbyshire,' mused Robert. 'Bumpier in Buxton . . . molier in Matlock . . .'

Poor Uncle Geoffrey! Little did he realise that, as was their wont, they had looked up one flower on the Internet before coming out, and determined to steer the conversation round to that flower and then to blind him with science, or at least to stun him with swotting, for the expression to 'blind with science' gives quite the wrong impression of what science does, does it not, children?

'To a farmer, a dandelion is a weed,' said Robert. 'But the people who grow dandelions for heath food purposes must think of it as a crop.'

'And if wheat is found growing in it, then the wheat will be a weed!' said Susan.

There was a pause. Uncle Geoffrey wondered why things seemed so complicated to them, and so simple to him. Then, without thinking, he asked: 'And what is the vulgar French name of the dandelion?'

'Piss-en-lit,' said Robert promptly. 'They think it causes bedwetting, if you eat it. As they do in France. As a salad leaf.'

'I wonder if there is a lot of bedwetting in Derbyshire?' said Susan. 'You know, caused by application of dandelion juice as a wart cure. What do you think, Uncle Geoffrey?'

What Uncle Geoffrey thought was that he would willingly strangle his nephew and niece, but what he said was, 'Ah! I think I hear a skylark! Can anyone with sharp eyes see it?'

Independent, 2006

PEDANTRY D.I.Y. TEST

None of us like to think that we are guilty of pedantry, yet we are all, in varying degrees, likely to find it aggravating when friends and relations commit tiny trivial errors. Often we insist on correcting those errors, and although we think that thereby we are building a reputation for wisdom and knowledge, in fact we are just getting a name as a clever clogs and a pain in the backside.

People never own up to this, so I have devised a D-I-Y test which will tell readers just how much of a pedant they really are.

Here are some of the more common symptoms of pedantry. Just tick the ones which apply to you, and find your rating at the end of the mini-quiz.

1. When you started this article, you automatically thought to yourself: 'Hold on – grammatically speaking, shouldn't that be "None of us LIKES to think"?'

2. You also frowned when you came to the word 'aggravating', and you said to yourself: 'He seems to think that "aggravate" means to "irritate", whereas it just means "to make worse".'

3. When people say: 'Sorry, could you repeat that again?' you find yourself saying: 'Well, not really. I have only said it once and I haven't repeated it at all yet, so I can't exactly repeat it again. I could however repeat it for the first time, if you like.'

4. You are irritated by the use of the phrase 'steam train.' It wasn't the train that was steam-driven. It was the engine. So people should say 'steam engine.' Even better, 'steam locomotive.'

5. You hate it when peop
le mix up 'fewer' and 'less.'

6. When we came to the end of the twentieth century, you agreed totally with those who could see quite clearly that 2000 AD was the last year of the old millennium, and not the first of the next, so you celebrated the date a year later than everyone else.

7. When the conversation gets round to red and grey squirrels, you find it very hard to resist saying that a grey squirrel isn't really a squirrel, but a kind of rat.

8. And that a spider is not strictly speaking an insect.

9. And that a slow worm is not a snake at all, but a kind of legless lizard.

10. You get very cross when people insist on pronouncing 'macho' as 'macko' and 'machismo' as 'mackismo.' It's pronounced as written for heaven's sake! The Spanish 'ch' is exactly the same as our 'ch.' They wouldn't have a dance called the 'cha cha cha' otherwise, would they? And he wasn't pronounced Kay Guevara, was he? Well, then.

11. You get just as cross when people say that they are 'disinterested' in something they find dull. No, they're not, they're 'uninterested.' 'Disinterested' is a very useful word for 'impartial.'

12. You hate it when people seem to think that Frankenstein was a monster. Frankenstein *built* the monster. That's why we say 'Frankenstein's monster.'

13. When people say 'tomorrow to fresh fields, and pastures new,' you find it hard to resist pointing out that Milton actually wrote: 'Tomorrow to fresh *woods,* and pastures new.'

14. People sometimes talk about 'reaching a crescendo.' But a 'crescendo' is a process of growing louder, so you can't reach it. All you can reach is a climax. Right? Right

15. You find it intensely irritating when people talk about 'the hoi polloi.' 'Hoi polloi' is Greek for 'the many.' So when you say 'the hoi polloi,' you are actually saying 'the the many.'

Right: now add up your score.

If you got 12 or more out of 15, you are an exhibitionist and a pain in the neck. You love 'University Challenge' and are probably in a pub quiz team. No wonder people shun you.

If you scored between 4 and 11, you are still an exhibitionist and a pain in the neck, but you prefer 'The Weakest Link' to 'University Challenge.'

If you only scored 1-3, you are either highly tolerant or pathetically underinformed.

If you didn't bother to do the test, you are completely normal. Well done!

Independent, 2005

THE DAY THE A LEVEL
RESULTS CAME THROUGH

The day that Sidney Delamere's A Level results came through, he almost didn't open them. He was late for work and had decided to leave his post till the evening. But his wife reminded him of the last time he had done that, and how he had nearly missed a very important invitation, and so he reluctantly decided to stay an extra five minutes and open the morning mail.

One of the packages contained his A Level results.

'Good God,' he said.

'What is it, dear?' said his wife.

'It seems to be my A Level results,' he said.

'I didn't know you had been doing any A Levels,' she said.

'I haven't,' said Sidney. 'Not recently. Not since I left school. These are the results of my A Levels at school.'

Sidney Delamere was in his mid-fifties. He was the accounts manager of a large firm of undertakers. He wasn't interested in A Levels. He was interested in money and pension rights and tax schemes, which is not the sort of thing they award A Levels for, even in these enlightened days.

'Well, surely you got the results of your A Levels when you were at school,' said his wife. 'Why are they sending them to you now?'

'I don't know,' said Sidney.

'What A Levels did you get?' said his wife.

'Three.' said Sidney proudly. 'French, Maths and Art. I . . . Hold on! What's this?'

He screwed up his eyes and stared at the paper.

'I don't believe it! It says that I failed Maths and Art! They're sorry, but I got only one A Level, in French . . .'

Moments later Sidney was on the phone to his father.

'Dad, I know this is going back a long way, but can you remember what happened when I got my A Level results back in the early 1960s?'

Sidney's father could remember. Sidney had been away doing a holiday job on the continent, and all Sidney's friends had got their results, and Sidney's hadn't come, so his parents, assuming the news would be good for Sidney as well, had told a white lie down the phone and said he had got three A Levels. Sidney had gone through life assuming this was so. But now his results had finally got through to him, forty years late. And he had failed two of his A Levels!

'Don't worry, son,' said his father. 'You've done very well without.'

That wasn't the point, thought Sidney. The point was that he had always thought he was a success at school. And now he had discovered he was a fraud. It was tragic. Mark you, he could see the comic side of it as well, as he told his colleagues at work.

Mid-morning, his boss sent for him.

'Sidney, what's this I hear about you failing A Levels?'

'True, I'm afraid,' said Sidney.

'If this is so,' said his boss, 'I'm afraid we're going to have to rethink your position.'

'I'm afraid I don't . . .'

'When you first joined us nearly forty years ago, it said on your CV that you had three A Levels. If this was not so, you joined us on false pretences. In which case I have no choice but to let you go. We can't employ cheats at Withergill and Follow, *The Undertakers to Die For*.'

'But I did have three A Levels then! At least . . .'

The upshot was that Sidney had to apply to the examiners, asking them to regrade his results. The examiners wrote back saying that it was impossible, as appeals could only be lodged within a month of the results being received. Sidney wrote back saying that this was the case and he had only received the results ten days previously.

After a short silence, they wrote back to him to say that all the examiners who had examined him were now dead, and he would have to resit the exams. Sidney said he was quite happy to do that, as after forty years he would have no problem. But when he came to resit the exams he had not done any serious revision and he failed all three. He therefore became the first pupil in British history to have an A Level stripped from him forty years after he had been awarded it. He also, sad to say, was given the boot by Withergill & Follow, *Undertakers To Die For*.

Moral: Having an A Level doesn't tell people how clever we are. It tells them how clever we used to be.

Independent, 2000

SPARE CHANGE

The other day I was visiting London for reasons which must have seemed good at the time, and as I was walking along the street a man sitting on the pavement in very raggedy clothes looked up at me and said: 'Got any spare change?'

Well, it's always nice to be talked to by anyone in London, I suppose, but it did seem a strange question. (A bit like those weird questions you see on cards in phone boxes in London, such as 'Do you want to be punished?' or 'Have you been a bad boy?' Honestly, I worry about Londoners sometimes.)

I felt the rattle of coins in my pocket and said, 'Yes, thanks.'

(I was somewhat relieved, actually. Like many men, I keep far too much in my pockets, because I haven't got a handbag, and occasionally this wears a hole in one of them. If it's a jacket pocket, the objects in my pocket start to drop deep into the lining. If the hole appears in a trouser pocket, the first sign is usually a slither of coins down my right leg, inside the trouser, leading to a small cascade of money from ankle level most of which goes on the floor but a little of which usually ends up in my sock or shoe. It is almost always highly embarrassing though on the other hand I have sometimes been very relieved to find a bit of money in my shoe.)

The man sitting on the pavement looked quite pleased to learn that I had some spare cash. He thought about it for a moment.

'Can I have it?' he asked.

I thought about this for a moment.

'No,' I said.

'Why not?'

'Because I need it.'

'Then it's not spare change, is it?' said the man. 'I asked you if you had any spare change, and you said you had. Now you're telling me that it's not spare after all. If you need it, it's not spare. You've changed your story. You've shifted the goal posts.'

'You've got a point,' I conceded.

'Then can I have it?'

'No.'

'Why not?'

I thought rapidly for a good reason.

'Because I might need it. I am a stranger to London and I have heard that people get mugged pretty often, and muggers get very angry if the victim has no money on them, and beat them up. So I might need this money.'

'Have you got a wallet?'

'Yes.'

'The muggers will take your wallet. They won't worry with your change. Let me look after it for you . . .'

I decided to try another tack.

'I am following the government directive which has asked us not to give to beggars but to donate directly to a charity.'

'I know about this directive,' said the man on the pavement. 'And since you heard about it, have you given to a charity instead of to a beggar?'

'No,' I admitted.

'Then I think I can help you,' said the beggar. 'For I have listened to that very same government directive and I have become an agent for half a dozen leading national charities. You may donate directly to me and I will handle the donation for you.'

'Can you handle donations to Shelter?' I said.

'One of my favourites,' he said.

I got out my cheque book and pen.

'Not cheques,' he said.

'Not cheques?' I said.

'We prefer cash,' he said.

'We?' I said.

'Me and Shelter,' he said. 'In-house study by me and Shelter has shown that cheques lead to too much bureaucracy, and paperwork. Cash can be activated immediately.'

'You mean, you'll spend it straightaway?'

'We prefer to say "put the cash to work," rather than "spend it," but yes, that's the idea.'

I put my hand in my pocket. All I could find was a bunch of keys jammed in the opening of a small, new hole in my pocket. Any change I had must have fallen through it. I became aware of a cold sensation against my foot.

'Just a moment,' I said, and took my shoe off. Inside there was a pound coin and a 50p coin. I offered them to him. He hesitated.

'It won't smell,' I said. 'Socks fresh on this week.'

'It's not that I'm worried about,' he said. 'It's just that anyone who has to keep his cash in his shoe must be worse off than I am in. Look, take this . . .'

And he handed back the 50p coin, keeping the £1 for himself.

Independent, 2000

FORTY WINKS AT ST MARTIN'S

When I lived in Ladbroke Grove, several of my neighbours used to disappear on Friday afternoon in their enormous wagons to go down to Wiltshire to their second homes for the weekend. I never envied them much. Oh, I envied the idea that they were off to the country, at least in the abstract, but when I saw them packing the wagon with dogs and clothes and food and children and furniture and rolls of kitchen paper and all the other things they should have been buying in Devizes from local shops, and thought of the frantic hours of driving which would precede and follow their country idyll, I gave thanks for the delights of Notting Hill.

My perspective is slightly different now.

I live in the depths of Wiltshire and go to London only on the odd occasion.

And they do seem to be odd occasions.

For instance, I was asked to do an after-dinner speech in January for a gathering of building surveyors, an offer which I accepted unhesitatingly because money was going to change hands, and because it was in the unlikely but interesting surroundings of the crypt of St Martins In The Fields, the elegant church which dominates one corner of Trafalgar Square.

I got to London early to have lunch with an old friend and then found myself with a whole afternoon and early evening to get through before the big event. It was cold, and I felt tired, and what I wanted more than anything was forty winks, but without a home in London I didn't know where I could have a quick siesta. I don't think I had ever encountered the problem before, and I thought nostalgically of the late Paul Jennings's half-joking invention of the 'Zizzomat', a sleeping space rather like an enlarged left luggage locker into which the tired businessman or traveller could insert himself for a quick zizz after having inserted some coins in the lock . . .

Well, I did what visitors to London are meant to do and went to an exhibition in the National Gallery ('Painting Very Quickly in France In The Nineteenth Century' or some such; a nice selection of Impressionist paintings) and emerged, as I always do from dutiful culture, feeling even more tired and pallid than before. It occurred to me that I could just get on a Circle Line train and fall asleep till I got round to my original station, which would give me somewhere warm and dry to snooze, but some second sense told me that the train would probably break down miles from home, and then some third sense told me: Why not go into St Martin's church itself and adopt a praying position? Nobody will disturb you there unless you snore . . .

And so I did. The last time I had entered the church it had been crammed full of people come to share in Ronnie Scott's memorial service. This time there was nobody except a couple of musicians doing some rehearsing who serenaded me for a while and then packed up and went; a couple of old chaps in homeless beards; a lady or two genuinely praying; and me, trying to find the best position in which I could a) look as if I was being devout b) go to sleep c) not attract any attention. It's usually the other way round for me in church. Thanks to a non-stop Christian upbringing I am now not much of a believer, so when I find myself at weddings or funerals I think it is hypocritical of me to kneel and pray, and I tend to lean forward in a sitting position instead with chin on my hands, looking like Rodin's *The Man Pretending to Pray*. Here in St Martin's I wanted very much to look as if I were praying, so that I wouldn't be thrown out for dozing.

It was rather odd to be in a large space in central London with life teeming outside the windows and nothing much going on here, but it was very restful, and I slept well. The only thing that awoke me was an announcement that the church would now be closed for afternoon service, and would people *please* stop wandering round. For a fleeting moment I felt I should leave, but then realised that if I didn't wander round, I was quite safe, and indeed I think the people who arrived to celebrate afternoon service, which took place quite close to me, assumed that I was a fellow participant, if over-devout.

It must be several decades since I last sat through an ordinary church service, and it hasn't changed much, I think. Though as there were only a dozen or so celebrants, the clergyman didn't trust them much to sing, and insisited on saying the psalms. There was a prayer for the Prince of Wales, and one for the Queen Mother's health, and there was a prayer for 'Clare to get her job back', which I think must have been a special request from someone in the congregation, and in and out of all this I slept and dreamt, while the light faded outside the church, and the night grew crispier and frostier. An enchanting experience . . .

I awoke in time for the dinner downstairs, which I joined, much refreshed. The building surveyors turned out be a jovial and stimulating lot, and when I finally got the last train home, I was never in the slightest danger of sleeping through Bath and finding myself in Weston-super-Mare. Years ago John Wain wrote a short story about a man who approached sleep as other people approach sex – as a voluptuous experience to be enjoyed in as many different ways as possible, from sleeping in dry leaves to snoozing in a crowded hall – which, for some odd reason, I have always remembered when I can never remember anything else he wrote, and I think I would unhesitatingly add sleeping in church to that.

Just so long as you don't get locked in by a zealous vicar. Now, that would be even worse than sleeping on till Weston-super-Mare.

The Oldie, 2001

A GHOST STORY

I didn't see him at first. I had got into the train at London and sat down in a seat which faced the sunshine so, semi-blinded, I did not realise there was someone sitting opposite me. But when the train drew out, there he was, a man in a dark suit, reading a hardback book of very serious aspect. Are you like me? I always long to know what other people are reading on trains. I will twist and crane my neck to get a good look at the spine. If necessary, I will wait till the reader goes to the toilet or the buffet, then quickly pick up their book and have a good look at it. Once, and once only, I started reading the book, and was still reading it when they came back. Most embarrassing.

In this case, it was very easy to read the name of the book. He was reading *The National Trust Handbook.* It seemed an odd choice of leisure reading. In fact, as soon as I got a chance, I said so. I can't remember now what the pretext was for two English people who had never been introduced to talk to each other, but when we did get talking I said it was a most unusual way to relax, reading lists of ancient properties.

'Oh, it's work,' he said. 'I work for the National Trust.'

'What do you do there?' I said.

'I look after the supernatural,' he said.

'Pardon?' I said. 'I thought for a moment you said you looked after the supernatural.'

He smiled.

'People always look surprised when I tell them,' he said. 'But you have to remember that the National Trust owns and looks after a lot of very ancient buildings, and some of them are haunted, and someone has to be in charge of that kind of thing. You wouldn't be surprised if I said I

296

was in charge of weathervanes, or stabling. But ghosts are just as much a feature of old houses as weathervanes and stables. So someone has to look after it.'

'What happens if a house isn't haunted? Or doesn't seem to be? Do you have to check them all out?'

'Checking a house for ghosts is not a science, you know,' he said. 'We have to depend on tradition and old stories and eye witness accounts. The odd thing is that some houses are totally free of any supernatural presence at all, while others have more than their fair share of ghosts. I know of one house in Yorkshire where at least five different ghosts have been sighted. It would be rather nice if you could share these ghosts out, and give one or two to a house to that hasn't got any, but that isn't the way that ghosts work.'

'So how DO ghosts work?'

'Have you ever seen a ghost?' he said.

'No.'

'Most people haven't,' he said. 'At least, they think they haven't. I once spotted a gardener at a hall in Dorset wearing the most peculiar old-fashioned clothes, with leggings, and watched him for a while sharpening a scythe with a whetstone. Turned out later there hadn't been a regular gardener there for years. Last one had committed suicide. Cut his throat with a scythe. So maybe I saw his ghost . . .'

As the man droned on, I found it hard to concentrate on his words in the hot sun, and actually closed my eyes and dozed off. I don't know how long I was asleep for, but when I woke up he had gone, and so had his *National Trust Handbook*, which suggested that he had got off while I was asleep. One wouldn't take a book to the buffet or toilet, after all . . .

'Tickets, please,' said the ticket collector. I showed him mine.

'Anyone else sitting at this table?' he said.

'There was someone,' I said, 'but I think he got off at the last station.'

'What last station?' said the ticket collector.

'Well, I don't know,' I said, 'but wherever we last stopped.'

'We haven't stopped anywhere yet,' he said. 'We haven't stopped since London.'

'That means he must be on the train somewhere,' I said. 'But that's odd . . .'

'Maybe you were seeing things,' said the ticket collector.

'Seeing things? But people don't see things on trains!'

'You'd be surprised,' said the ticket collector. 'I've seen things. Things that weren't there. And people. In this very carriage, actually. At this table. I sometimes wonder if this coach isn't haunted . . .'

He moved on to the next coach. I was alone at my table now, but there was a friendly-looking woman at the table across the way, with a small dog in a basket, and when I got talking to her, I asked her if she had heard what the ticket collector had said.

'What ticket collector?' she said.

'The one who came through ten minutes ago.'

'I didn't see any ticket collector,' she said. 'Are you sure? I'm sure there wasn't one. I should know. I've been keeping my eye open for him, because I don't know if the dog has to have a ticket or not. So I would have seen him if there had been.'

I opened my mouth and was about to describe him when I suddenly realised that there had been something odd about him. He was wearing a uniform I hadn't seen on a train for years. It was almost as if . . . I remembered what the National Trust man had said about the old gardener. I felt a sudden surge of horror and fear. I suddenly hated this train. And just then, as if answering my prayers, the train drew to a halt at a station, and I impulsively got to my feet and jumped out. I can always get the next train, I thought.

The first thing I noticed about the station was that it seemed disused. There was grass growing between some of the paving stones, and the benches were very dirty. Only one of them was occupied, by a young man holding some notebooks, pens and a camera. I know a train-spotter when I see one. I strolled over to him and said hello.

He said hello.

This is normally as far as you get in a conversation with a train-spotter, but I persevered.

'Did you get the number of the train I just got off?' I said, jovially.

'What train?'

'The one I just got off?'

'I didn't see any train stop here,' he said. 'Trains don't stop here any more. This station was closed two years ago.'

'Look,' I said, 'I just got off a train which stopped here. Do you think I am making it up?'

'I have been here for four hours,' he said, 'taking engine numbers, and I think I would know if a train had stopped here. I like this station for the very reason that nothing ever stops here.'

I felt that reality was starting to float away from me, and that if I didn't keep very close to this train-spotter, I would be told in a moment that the station had been closed ever since a horrific accident to a young train-spotter two years ago ...

That is as far as Miles Kington's story goes. It was found in this state in his computer. Nothing has been seen or heard of him since then. Unless he returns before the next issue, we shall replace him with a rather more reliable writer. – Ed.

The Oldie, 2007

LET'S PARLER FRANGLAIS!

DANS LE HEALTH-FOOD SHOP

Client: Bonjour. Je cherche un plain strong white flour.

Assistant: Ne cherchez pas ici, monsieur. White flour est toxique et deadly. Nous sommes un magasin sérieux.

Client: Oh. Quelle sorte de farine vous avez?

Assistant: Nous avons wholemeal, wheatmeal, mealwhole, 110% full-wheat, 120% wheat-of-the-loom ou 150% millstone grit.

Client: Et la différence?

Assistant: Nulle. Elles sont toutes organically grown avec real dung et hand ground dans notre mill à Buckminster Fuller. Elles sont transportées ici dans un organically built farm wagon

Client: Et les sacs sont rangés sur les shelves ici par ruddy-cheeked yokels dans smocks traditionnels?

Assistant: Of course.

Client: Hmm. Je prends un 1lb sac de 200% stonewheat.

Assistant: Ça fait £4.80.

Client: C'est cher.

Assistant: Health food est toujours cher. C'est le wholepoint. Nous ne voulons pas avoir chaque Tom, Dick and Harry dans le shop.

Client: Hmm. Et je veux acheter un carrier bag.

Assistant: Quelle sorte de carrier?

Client: Il y a différentes sortes?

Assistant: Oui, bien sûr. Wholeweave, brownbag recycle, Third Worldweave, Arty Dartington ou Jethrotwill.

Client: On peut les manger?

Assistant: Non. On peut manger les Chinese rice paper bags, mais ils ne sont pas très forts.

Client: OK. Un sac de stonewheat et un Chinese paper bag.

Assistant: Un moment, je vais calculer sur mon abacus. £4.80 + 60p, c'est ... c'est ...

Client: £5.40.

Assistant: £5.80.

Client: Votre abacus est sur le blink.

Assistant: Un abacus ne va jamais sur le blink. J'ai simplement ajouté 40p pour le Save the Honeybee Appeal.

Client: Le honeybee est en danger?

Assistant: Non. Pas encore. Mais il faut anticiper. Sauvons le honeybee maintenant.

Let's Parler Franglais Again! 1980

MAN DELIVERING AN EEL
TO THE WRONG ADDRESS

Think you could make a good clergyman? Have you got what it takes to organise a fête, love thy neighbour and understand the Bishop of Durham? Then try this little quiz and seen how you do.

1.   A man comes to your door and tries to give you an eel which you don't remember ordering. What do you say?
     a) I'm afraid we've already got all the eels we can manage.
     b) Please come back at Harvest Festival Time and not a moment sooner.
     c) If you're the bloke that already delivered the pigeon and the overgrown poodle, get them out of here before I call the police.

2.   If he says, 'Ere, Reverend, watch me change this eel into a white dove. Look!' which is the right answer?
     a) A bit more practice, and you're on for the church fête.
     b) I paid you to work in the garden, Capstick, not show me silly little tricks.
     c) That's nothing. Watch me juggle these seven invisible balls.

3.   If, instead, he says, 'I am the Bishop of Durham and I feel a song coming on,' what should you say?
     a) And I am the Queen of Sheba.
     b) Make it the Song of Solomon, and beat it out in E Flat.
     c) Good heavens, I believe I feel rain coming on. Some other time, perhaps.

4. If the eel should say, 'I can show you a tree with the most amazing apples on,' what should you do?

The correct response in all cases is to pretend they have come to the wrong address and direct them to the next clergyman down the road. If you got it right, why not write to "*Tell Me More About Becoming a Clergyman*", Canterbury, Kent?

Vicarage Allsorts, 1985

COMPOSERS AND DEATH

About a month ago, when I was in hospital, I began to entertain a notion that the creation of classical music was likely to have a severe effect on you, both moral and physical, and probably mental as well, not to say fatal.

This may have just been a morbid fancy brought on by hospitalisation, but when you hear the facts, you may think differently.

I had to retire to hospital for tests on a genetic condition called heamachromatosis, which involves a lot of sitting around waiting for results and more tests, so I was not too ill to write pieces for the *Independent*. One of the pieces I wrote was based on a cutting I had taken in with me, quoting Norman Rosenthal of the Royal Academy as saying: 'I don't watch any television, as I prefer to go to the opera.'

I thought it might be fun to write a fictional diary by Rosenthal in which he learnt all he knew about current affairs from going to the opera. You know the sort of thing; he goes to Aida and says in his diary: 'More trouble in the Middle East, it seems . . .'

The trouble was that as I have no taste for opera, I was ignorant of most of the famous plots, so I asked my wife to bring in a few reference books. One of them was *The Guinness Guide to Classical Composers*, dating from a time about twenty years ago when editor Keith Shadwick had put together a stimulating bundle of brief biographies, and although I didn't learn much about opera, when I had dealt with Norman Rosenthal, I started browsing through the great lives.

I was appalled. I simply had no idea how many great composers had gone to an early grave or suffered their way to a later one.

We all know about Mozart's wretched life, of course, and how his magic creative impulse was constantly thwarted by bad luck, ill-health, financial agony and the wrong guys getting his jobs and commissions, until he pegged out in misery at thirty-six. We comfort ourselves with the thought that it wasn't like that for the rest of them, and we are right – it was often worse.

Schubert, for instance, had none of Mozart's success in his lifetime. Not only did he not get his orchestral works played, he did not even *hear* them played. At the age of twenty-five he learned he had syphilis; it took only another six years to kill him. Syphilis also did for Delius, turning him into a tottering shadow; nor was he the only one: 'The rest of Donizetti's life was lived under the shadow of increasing physical and mental stress brought on about by the advent of tertiary syphilis.' He was forty-six at the time. 'Final visits to Austria and Italy left him drained and he sank into an irreversible state ...'

You can imagine my jolly frame of mind in hospital as I jotted down details like this. Chopin learnt at twenty-seven that he had consumption and would never grow old. Weber knew the same in his early thirties. Paganini nearly died at thirty-five. But Bellini takes the cake. Here he is in Paris in 1835 ...

'The world was at his feet, and with Rosini in retirement and Danizetti his only real rival, Bellini could look forward to a glittering future. Alas, it was not to be; complications from a further bout of gastro-enteritis led to a fatal inflammation of the bowel and liver. Bellini died in Paris at the age of thirty-three.'

Thirty-three! Older than Schubert, at least, but still a baby. Plenty of composers never reached forty – Mozart, Mendelssohn, Weber, Chopin, Gershwin ...

With writers it is different. It is very rare to find a writer who is struck down in his prime – they all plug on to a useless old age. Nor can I think – apart from Maupassant – of any writer who was cut short by syphilis. But the appalling death rate among young composers makes you think that they were dispatched, not into music, but over the top into no man's land.

Now, I have clearly loaded the dice in favour of my theory by gently omitting all those composers who lived to a ripe old age, such as Bach, Verdi, Beethoven, Liszt and so on. (Ripe? Not quite. Beethoven went deaf. Bach went blind.) I still think it's an area of actuarial disaster, and if a young composer came to me looking for life insurance, I'd send him down the road to someone else.

Or recommend Rossini to him as an example. At the age of thirty-seven, in 1829, Rossini announced that he had written enough operas and made enough money, and would never compose another one. And he didn't, and he lived another thirty-nine years in Paris cooking, entertaining, and writing a few piano pieces, before expiring in 1868 at seventy-six, never knowing that the Prussians were about to invade France. If any composer had exquisite timing, it was Rossini. And if anyone cheered me up in hospital, it was him.

The Oldie, 2007

METAMORPHOSIS

PAR FRANZ KAFKA

First thing au matin, quand K s'éveilla, il trouva qu'il avait été transformé en un giant cockroach.

Voilà une fine thing! Un moment, un bloke, le next moment, un cockroach.

Il pouvait anticiper l'attitude de sa famille. L'apathie... le boredom... le neglect... le lack total d'intérêt.

En quoi, il était terriblement wrong. Car, après breakfast, ils sont allés au shop pour acheter un giant economy pack de cockroach poison.

Et, par lunch-time, c'était all over.

The Franglais Lieutenant's Woman, 1986

HISTORY OF KING TONY

or *Labour's Lost, Love*

ACT V

The mighty battle of June 9, which will decide the fate of Britain, has broken out all over the country. Enter the rebel leader, Earl Hague, with Don Portillo, his friend and successor.

Hague: Forward with Hague, though backward still from Europe!
Forget the Euro! Let us keep the pound!
Attack King Tony, till he falls defeated!
We shall reduce your taxes, then spend more!
Also hospitals, and schools, and railway trains . . .

He reels, exhausted. Don Portillo catches him.

Portillo: Alas, his mighty mind is near its end.
No longer do the words make sense, I fear.
He drives himself too hard to win this fight,
As if he knew that all is up for him.
This day upon the field will be his last,
His hour as leader now is ebbing fast . . .

Earl Hague revives.

Hague: Attack! Advance! Let's charge towards the foe!
That's the way to do it! Go, man, go!

He charges off madly in all directions. Portillo follows, shaking his head.
The scene changes to the command headquarters of King Tony, where Tony
is surrounded by his advisers (Sir Alastair Campbell, etc), his photogra-
phers, his minstrels, his hairdressers etc.

Tony: All over Britain now the war doth rage
Between our forces and the men of Hague.
From daybreak on, from Torbay to Carlisle,
Great bands of fighting men at arms come forth
To rally to our banner and our cause.
We cannot lose! The victory is ours!
Campbell: Why, this is true. The victory is ours.
But not the rest. These armies are a myth.
Of all the men and women who could march
To fire a loyal shot in your defence
Not one in four has left his home to fight!
Tony: Not one in four! Then where are all the rest?
And why have they not rallied to our cause?
Campbell: What cause is that? Where is your rallying cry?
Tony: You know it well! To all the world I say,
We have commenced, now let us carry on!
Campbell: O that is hardly fresh or new, my liege!
For did not old Sir Magnus Magnusson,
Th'exemplar of the learned questioner,
Say just the same: I've started, so I'll finish?
And you have fought a national campaign
With slogans borrowed from an old quiz show!
Tony: I shall ignore your supercilious barb,
For I have work to do on victory day.
That is to say, I must draw up my plans
To chop and change my ministers of state.
I have a mind to discard Sir Nick Brown,
But who instead shall I make head of farms?
Campbell: May I suggest Sir Peter Mandelson?

A farmyard job would suit him very well.
Not for the first time, he'd be in the shit!
Tony: I sometimes sense a vulgar streak in you.
Not suited to the highest in the land.
You too can be reshuffled, as you know!
Campbell: My Lord, I stand rebuked. I am at fault.
Tony: Then watch it. That is all I have to say.

Exit King Tony.

Campbell: O, I do hate him when he's in this mood,
Drunken with modesty, and humble to a fault
– A monster of humility, no less!

The scene changes to another part of British battlefield, where Sir Charles Kennedy, Scottish freedom fighter, gallops in.

Kennedy: Those who like not Tony, nor Hague much more,
I offer you a cause worth fighting for!
Come, disaffected all, come follow me!
And sooner or late, we'll find an enemy!

He gallops off, followed by many men with ginger hair, specs and sandals. Enter Earl Hague with Lady Ffion.

Hague: And so at last our dreams are ended here!
For four long years we both have set our hearts
Upon the throne, and it was not to be.
I care not for myself, but you, my dear,
Will never now be queen, which grieves me hard.

He looks at her. Lady Ffion says nothing.

Hague: Right to the end, thou'rt silent as the grave.
For someone Welsh, you know how to behave . . .

Defeat doth mean I'll never wear a crown
And I must now resign.
Ffion: No! Not 'resign'! 'Step down'!
You are too grand for mere resignation!
Stepping down's a better designation!
Hague: You're right! I will step down! That sounds much better!
A letter of resignation? No! A stepping down letter!
And now it's time to sleep. Let's hit the pillow.
And later work out how to thwart Portillo.

The scene changes to King Tony's HQ. To King Tony, enter the man in the white suit, Sir Martin Bell.

Bell: King Tony, farewell! I come to say goodbye.
No longer will I haunt you with my look
Betokening disapproval of your deeds.
I thought that Brentwood might become my base,
But no-one there did seem to like my face.

Tony: I shall not miss you, though your suit's resplendent.
Life's better with no watchful independent.

Enter Dr Richard Taylor, victor of Wyre Forest, in a white coat.

Taylor: Then know, King Tony, that there's one still here!
Your actions will be my study – have no fear!

Tony: The battle may be won, but all in vain –
For here come my old troubles once again!

Independent, 2001

PUB CONVERSATION: MURDER

'Have you ever noticed?' said the man with the dog.

Then he ordered a pint.

Then he took it back to his seat.

Then he sat down.

We looked at him expectantly.

He noticed us looking at him expectantly.

It's a great way of getting people's attention.

'What was I saying?' he said.

'You were asking,' said the lady with the brown hairdo, nursing her small, matching Tia Maria, 'if we had ever noticed.'

'Oh, right,' said the man with the dog. 'Have you ever noticed that when people come on television, pleading with their runaway loved ones to come back home, it quite often transpires that they are not missing at all but they have actually murdered them?'

'That's true, actually,' said the resident Welshman. 'And when a girl say that unidentified assailants attacked her and a boyfriend in a car, and killed the boyfriend, but mysteriously left her alone, it often turns out that she killed him.'

'I take your point,' said the Major, 'but it must get counter-productive after a while. I mean, if it becomes obvious even to the police that people who burst into tears on TV tend to be cruel murderers, then it would be a foolish murderer who went on TV and burst into tears, asking for the loved one to come back.'

'And what are the non-murderers going to do instead?' said the resident Welshman. 'If you don't get emotional, what CAN you do? Let's say, for instance, that my wife had run away ...'

'You haven't got a wife,' said someone.

'No, she ran away,' said someone else. Everyone laughed. But the Welshman is made of too stern stuff to fall for cheap jibes.

'Let's say I have a wife and she runs away and I am desperately afraid for her safety, and someone asks me to go on TV and plead with her to return, and I think to myself: hold on, if I do that, people will naturally assume I have murdered her ... Then what do I do? What do I do INSTEAD to convince people that I love her and haven't killed her?'

'Well,' said the brown-haired lady, 'instead of going on telly and bursting into tears, which makes everyone suspicious apparently, you'll have to go on telly and say: come back home, you bitch! The housework needs doing and I haven't had a decent meal since you left! Also, it says in the diary, in your writing, that we are going to have dinner with the Caddises on Friday. Who the hell are they? And incidentally, where did you put the bloody corkscrew? ... Wouldn't that convince people you weren't a murderer?'

There was a silence.

'And that you missed her a bit?'

There was another silence.

'I don't think you have got it QUITE right,' said the Major.

'Trouble is,' said the Welshman, 'that everyone has to find their own way on this one. There is no right way to be a murderer. There is no training. There is no tradition. Even if you are a paedophile, then you can apparently link up with like-minded people on the Internet and learn what to do, but there is nothing like that for murderers. There is no murder community, as there is a gay community, or paedophile community.'

There was an uneasy pause.

'Well, there's a reason for that, isn't there?' said the man with the dog. 'Once you're gay or a paedophile, you're stuck with it. It's your lifestyle. But a murderer isn't a murderer by conviction, or vocation, not unless he's a serial murderer. There's no murdering lifestyle. He's just someone who very badly wants to get rid of someone. He gets rid of them. Then he stops murdering. It's as simple as that.'

'Are you saying,' said the Major, 'that murderers shouldn't be put in prison, because they are so unlikely to reoffend?'

The man with the dog debated inwardly whether to nail his colours to the mast so obviously.

'Yes,' he said. 'I think that is what I am saying.'

'I think I agree,' said the Major.

It isn't often you get a pub conversation about murder which doesn't end in a call for capital punishment.

Quite the opposite, in fact.

A moment to treasure.

Independent, 2003

THE UNITED DEITIES

1. The Chairgod proposed a vote of thanks to Quetzalcoatl for his gift of chocolate to keep their spirits from flagging during the session. Whatever mankind had thought of the gift of chocolate, he, the Chairgod, said he had found it very refreshing.

2. A Hindu Goddess with an unusual amount of limbs said that chocolate, like all gifts to humanity, had proved a double-edged sword. It might have been refreshing, cheering and nourishing, but it was also addictive, fattening and left horrible stains when it melted, which wasn't much fun when it went down all your six sleeves.

3. Like fire, said the Chairgod.

4. What did he mean, *like fire*? said the Hindu Goddess, waving several of her arms impatiently.

5. The Chairgod said he meant that all gifts to humanity were a double-edged sword, and that given half a chance, humanity would muck up the gift. Like alcohol, for example. Or sex. But especially fire. When the human race had originally been given fire, many years ago, there had been a long and heated discussion at the United Deities as to whether it should in fact be a gift at all.

6. An old Norse Sea God said he had not been present at that debate, or if he had, he had no memory of it, which was quite possible as he had had quite a bad mead problem for a long time round about then. What had been the objection to humans being given fire? Surely it was just a harmless aid to cooking? His Viking worshippers had always enjoyed putting places to fire and sword. It wasn't quite the same just putting them to the sword.

7. The Chairgod said that before any decision about fire had been made, they had done some research into its uses, and it rapidly became obvious that, once given fire, humanity would use it for many things beside cooking. They would discover how to make things of metal, they would make metal weapons, they would discover gunpowder, they would make guns, then bombs, then nuclear arms . . .

8. The Norse Sea God asked if they had really deduced all that in advance?

9. Oh, yes, said the Chairgod. We may not be omniscient, but between us we know pretty well all there is to know. We knew perfectly well that if we gave man fire for cooking and drying, it would lead inevitably to international wars on a huge scale.

10. Then why the blazes did you decide to give it to him? the Norse Sea God wanted to know.

11. They had NOT decided to give it to him, said the Chairgod. They had decided against. But the Greek person Prometheus had come along and breached security, and fled with the secrets of fire, and given them to mankind – and, well, it was a long story and he didn't want to go into it again.

12. Had a full inquiry and everything, did they? chortled the old Norse Sea God. Had a lot of buck-passing and blame-shifting, and heads-must-roll stuff, did they? And at the end of the day, were there any Gods for the chop? No, he didn't expect there was. Old Gods' network at work again.

13. That was not the way they did things, said the Chairgod reprovingly. Blame-culture was for humans. All that Gods were interested in was divine justice and divine fairness.

14. The Norse Sea God said they should tell that one to the mermaids. From his experience of seeing Gods at work, they were just as cack-handed as humans, and caused a lot more damage. He had known Gods who were so inefficient that they couldn't organise a piss-up in an ambrosia factory.

15. The Chairgod ruled this out of order, and said that if the Norse Sea God could not behave properly, he should not say anything at all.

16. A minor Assyrian God said he had never spoken at one of these meetings before, but he was very much looking forward to the American war

against Iraq, as it was being fought on his old home ground, where he had seen some great battles in the old days. He wondered if anyone knew the definite starting date for the War, as he didn't want to miss it.

17. The Chairgod said that the starting date for the War was known to the committee, but they were not circulating it, for fear that some unscrupulous Gods should try to influence the outcome.

18. The old Norse Sea God said a plague on the lot of them and stormed out of the meeting, which was then adjourned.

Independent, 2003

THE SWALLOW AND
THE MIDGE: A FABLE

O nce upon a time there was a midge in the Highlands of Scotland
that spent its summer happily biting people who had come from
across the Border for their holidays.

High overhead there also wheeled a swallow who had come to Britain
to get away from the arid heat of her African homeland. But when the
summer began to fade, she announced that she would soon be off home
again to the Sudan.

'Can I come with you?' said the midge. 'I would like to see those far off
countries you keep telling us about.'

'It is a long way,' said the swallow, 'and I do not think a midge has ever
flown that far.'

'Maybe that is because a midge has never tried,' said the midge. 'I would
like to expand the horizons of midgedom! I will become the first trans-
continental midge!'

'Then you had better start practising,' said the swallow doubtfully.

The next day the swallow felt a small chill in the wind and knew it was
time to start packing for home. She went out to get a last rich dinner
from the insects of the air and, by mistake, swallowed the midge who was
out for a flying lesson. Several days later the midge did arrive in Africa,
but, alas, dead inside the swallow.

Moral: travelling by air? Make sure you get your travel insurance sorted
out in advance.

Independent, 2001

FIVE COMPLETE PLAYS
PAR OSCAR WILDE

LADY WINDERMERE'S FAN

La résidence de Lady Windermere. Il y a un knock à la porte. Lady Windermere ouvre la porte. Il y a un bloke là.

Bloke: Vous êtes Lady Windermere?

Lady W: Oui.

Bloke: Ah, Lady Windermere, je crois que vous êtes très spéciale. Non, mais vous êtes vraiment wonderful, une superlady. Non, mais honnête-ment je suis votre plus grand fan. Non, mais really . . .

Lady W: Not today, merci.

Slamming de la porte.

Curtain

UNE FEMME DE NO IMPORTANCE

La résidence de Lady Windermere. Il y a un knock à la porte. Lady Windermere ouvre la porte.

Lady W: Pour la dernière fois, j'ai dit – Not today, merci!

Femme: Pardon?

Lady W: Oops – ma mistake. Et qui êtes-vous, madame?

Femme: Oh, nobody spécial. Je fais un peu de canvassing pour le SDP.

Lady W: In which case, vous pouvez aller à la tradesmen's entrance. Je ne discute *jamais* la politique avec total strangers.

Femme: Merci, I'm sure.

Slamming de la porte.

Curtain

UN IDEAL HUSBAND

Un autre knock à la porte. Entrent Lord et Lady Windermere.

Lady W: Je suis fed up avec le constant knocking sur la porte. Les rues sont pleines de total strangers nowadays. Dans mon youth, everybody connaissait everybody.

Lord W: Yes, dear.

Lady W: Il y avait une femme à la porte just now, qui voulait me parler de la politique. La politique n'est pas un topic pour une lady. Mon père était le Prime Minister pendant un fortnight, vous savez, mais je ne savais jamais de quel party il était un membre.

Lord W: Yes, dear.

Knocking sur la porte.

Lady W: Eveiller Duncan avec ton knocking! Ah, si c'était seulement possible! . . . C'est une allusion Shakespearienne, vous savez. Une éducation n'est pas très lady-like, je sais, mais une single line de Shakespeare n'est pas excessif.

Lord W: Yes, dear.

Lady W: Vous êtes un ideal husband, je sais bien, mais l'exchange de witticisms et epigrams avec vous est quelquefois hard going.

Lord W: Yes, dear.

Elle ouvre la porte. Nobody là. Slamming de la porte.

Curtain

SALOME

La résidence de Lord et Lady Windermere. Un knock à la porte.

Lady W: Ce knocking à la porte est endless!

Lord W: Peut-être c'est death watch beetle, dearest.

Lady W: Je ne crois pas. Généralement, le death watch beetle entre without knocking.

Un autre knock à la porte.

Lord W: Come in!

La porte s'ouvre. Entre un crowd de Jews, Nazarenes, soldats Romains, Syrians, dancing-girls, Pharisees, publicans, sinners, etc.

Lady W: Good Lord. Ils sont vos amis, Freddy?

Lord W: Non, my dear.

Lady W: Ladies et gentilhommes! La stately maison n'est pas ouvert au public aujourd'hui! Thursday, 10–5.30!

Crowd: Madame, nous cherchons les Samaritans. Nous sommes dans un mood de mass depression.

Lady W: Les Samaritans? Dans un upper-class drawing-room in Knightsbridge? Pas très likely, je crois. Essayez Samaria.

Crowd: Samaria! Good thinking, votre ladyship! Sorry pour la disturbance.

Exit crowd. Entre Salomé, avec la tête de Jean le Baptiste sur un platter.

Salomé: Bonjour. Je fais une porte-à-porte collection pour une good cause – Le Decapitated Prophets Distress Fund.

Lord W: Voilà un guinea.

Tête de Jean le Baptiste: Merci, guv.

Curtain

L'IMPORTANCE D'ETRE ERNEST

Le drawing-room de Lord et Lady Windermere. Lord Windermere est upright, auprès de la mantlepiece. Lady Windermere s'occupe avec le tea trolley. Salomé joue avec les spaniels. Jean le Baptiste (head only) est sur le silver salver, humming softly.

Lady W: Un cup de thé, my dear?

Salomé: Vous n'avez pas un beaker de riche et rare Tyrrhenian wine, plein de le golden sunshine de la Mer Méditerranéenne, redolent de clusters de grapes et de l'antiquité classique?

Lady W: Non. Seulement Earl Grey.

Salomé: Super.

Lady W: Je suis si fond d'un bon cuppa. Un monde without tea, c'est unthinkable. Vous savez que pendant les Middle Ages le tea était absolument unknown? No wonder que les Middle Ages étaient si dreary.

Salomé: C'est un peu après ma période. Je suis AD 0, ou thereabouts.

Lady W: Fascinant. Vous avez rencontré Jésus Christ, peut-être? A un cocktail party ou une réception?

Salomé: Non.

Lady W: Je ne suis pas surprisé. Il ne mouvait pas dans les best circles. Il avait un distressing penchant pour les publicans et les sinners. Les sinners, je peux pardonner cela, mais les *publicans* . . . !

Tête de Jean le Baptiste: Coming soon! Coming soon! Jésus Christ, le saviour!

Lady W: Je ne crois pas que vous m'avez presentée à votre petit ami.

Salomé: Un oversight unforgivable. Lady Windermere, je vous presente à Jokanaan, mon fiancé, a.k.a. St Jean le Baptiste.

Tête de Jean le Baptiste: Répentissez! Répentissez! Jésus Christ sera dans votre neighbourhood bientôt.

Salomé: Jokanaan! *Please*! Où sont vos manners? Parler de la moralité à un tea party, c'est très infra dig.

Lord W: Votre fiancé voyage toujours sur un silver tray?

Salome: Oui. Il a perdu son corps dans un petit accident, and maintenant je le porte everywhere.

Lord W: Comme un handbag, by Jove.

Lady Windermere est sur le point de dire 'Un handbag?' mais il y a un knocking à la porte. Elle ouvre la porte. Le bloke est là, le bloke de Lady Windermere's Fan (see 2 pages back).

Fan: Ah, Lady Windermere, vous êtes plus spéciale que jamais! Non, mais je vous adore.

Lord W: Qui est ce jeune homme?

Fan: Je suis Lady Windermere's fan.

Lady W: Il vient tous les jours, avec un bunch de fleurs, et il demande mon autograph.

Lord W: Il est strangely familiar. Jeune homme, avez-vous par quelque chance extraordinaire, un acorn-shaped birthmark sur votre left shoulder?

Fan: Oui, mais . . . ?

Lord W: Mon fils! Vous êtes mon long-lost son et heir, Ernest.

Fan: Alors . . . Lady Windermere, vous êtes ma mère!

Lady W: Non, je ne crois pas. Je n'ai jamais été pregnant. C'est si vulgaire.

Fan: Alors, qui est ma mère?

Tête de Jean le Baptiste: Sa mère est Mary, mais son père est God Almighty!

Salomé: Jokanaan – keep quiet!

Lord W: Alas, j'ignore les whereabout de votre mère. Quand j'étais un wild young bachelor, j'ai eu une affaire passionnée avec votre mère, Dorothy, mais après votre birth elle émigra. Elle voulait faire des 'good missionary works'. C'est 20 years ago. Mais où est-elle maintenant?

Un knock à la porte! Lady Windermere ouvre la porte. C'est la femme de no importance (see 2 pages back encore une fois).

Femme: Bonjour. Je suis une canvasseuse pour le SDP.

Lord W: Dorothy!

Fan: Mother!

Femme: Pardon?

Lady W: C'est un peu compliqué, mais va expliquer après le final curtain, quand il y aura more time. Meanwhile, je crois que nous avons maintenant un happy ending. C'est thirsty work, les happy endings. Anyone pour un sherry?

Toute le monde: Oui. *(Ils laissent le drawing-room et disparaissent off-stage, tout except le tête de Jean le Baptiste.)*

Tête de Jean le Baptiste: Eh, Salomé! Quelque chose pour moi, eh? Un mug de honey, peut-être? Et a few locusts sur un stick? Salomé? SALOMÉ?

Curtain

The Franglais Lieutenant's Woman, 1986

THE DOG AND
THE SHEEP: A FABLE

One day a dog approached a sheep, and at the sight of him the sheep backed off.

'Get away from me, O dog!' he said. 'All dogs are wicked and they have evil in their hearts!'

'Not at all,' said the dog. 'Why should I mean you harm?'

'Because you will chase me and kill me and eat me up!' said the sheep.

'What rubbish!' said the dog. 'My master gives me lovely bones to eat. Why should I bother with an ugly, scrawny, maggoty, lanolin-flavoured creature like you?'

'I am not ugly!' said the sheep. 'I am made in the image of the Almighty, the Supreme Sheep, who has created everything.'

'I have news for you,' said the dog. 'There is no Supreme Sheep. We owe everything to the Divine Dog, in whose image I am made, and who has given me the teeth and the speed to destroy you if I wish.'

'If that is true,' said the sheep,' then not only is my belief system flawed, but I am in even worse physical danger than I thought. Oh dear . . .'

Moral: there is more than one way for a dog to worry a sheep.

Independent, 2001

HERE WE GO AGAIN

CHAPTER ONE

'Will you be needing a cheese grater at university, dear?' said my mother.

She was holding one up, presumably in case I didn't know what a cheese grater looked like.

'For heaven's sake, woman!' said my father crossly, 'how on earth does he know if he's going to need a cheese grater? Don't you think there are more important things right now to worry about? He's just about to go off to university for three years, and the sort of things he's going to need are perseverance, and a work ethic, and a nice set of friends, and driving ambition, and . . . and . . . resourcefulness, and maybe a bicycle, and all you want to know is whether he wants a cheese grater!'

He paused for a moment and then, as he often did in his absurdly logical way, began to consider the other side of the question.

'Still, that's all part of the broader picture, and I suppose we have to leave those sorts of thing up to him. We can't provide him with friends or application, much as we would like to. No, all we can do is make sure he has the creature comforts on which he can base his career, and I suppose that does presuppose that he will have to do a lot of his own cooking. So, yes, lad, do you think you'll be needing a cheese grater?'

They both looked at me expectantly.

I was going to miss them.

It was the day before I was due to start university and I had been very careful to finish my packing three days previously, so that everything I needed would be ready to go before they started fussing about what I should really take.

'I had thought of taking my bicycle, father,' I said, 'but it's quite a good one and I am afraid it will be stolen at university. I think it would be better to wait till I get there and buy a cheap second-hand one. I bet there's a brisk trade in cheap bikes at university.'

'Or you could steal one, of course,' he said.

'Father!' said my mother.

'Well, that's what students did in my day,' he said. 'We didn't call it stealing. We called it borrowing. If you needed a bike and there was one handy, you just took it, and then left it for the next person.'

'Anyway,' I said, 'we wouldn't be able to get it into the car.'

'It's not a very large cheese grater,' said my mother.

'Mother!' I said. 'I'm talking about the bicycle!'

'You could always send it PLA by train,' said my father.

PLA? Well, I should explain that in the period I am talking about, which is the early 1960s, our railways were much more advanced than they are today, and you could send anything anywhere by train, without having to accompany it. Passenger's Luggage in Advance, it was called, or PLA. Most guard's vans on most long distance trains were stacked high with bicycles and racing pigeons in baskets and musical instruments and heaven know what...

Guard's vans? Look, we really don't have time right now to explain all this period detail. Later, perhaps.

'What am I going to need a cheese grater for?' I said. 'And please don't say, for grating cheese.'

'For grating cheese on to the potatoes,' said my mother.

'What potatoes?' I said.

'Could you get them for me, father?' said my mother.

My father went into the larder and came back dragging a large sack.

'What on earth...?' I said.

'Potatoes,' said my mother. 'It's a sack of potatoes. I racked my brains what to get for you to take with you, and it suddenly occurred to me that students eat a lot of potatoes, and it's about time you learnt how to cook, and what better to learn on than potatoes?'

My head reeled.

'How on earth am I going to cope with . . . ?'

'We thought of that,' said my father. 'And this is my present to you.'

So saying, he handed me a book. It was called *The Potato Cookery Book*. More than a hundred recipes for . . .

I read no further.

'Mother, I can't begin life at university with a sack of potatoes and a hundred recipes.'

'Of course you can, dear. You will quickly get a reputation as a cook, and girls will fall over themselves to get invited round.'

'Failing which, you can always sell the potatoes,' said my father. 'In the last days of the War, they were used as a form of currency in Poland. Or was it as a form of ammunition? One of the two.'

'Father, mother!' I said. 'This is a very highly strung moment for me! Tomorrow I am off on the biggest adventure of my life so far. I am going to be surrounded by the cleverest and most competitive young people in the country. It's like waiting to go into no man's land and charge towards an unknown enemy. No – it's like preparing to go into the jungle and not knowing how to survive or what to survive. It's like going to a country where you don't know the language or the customs and being expected to prosper! It's like . . .'

'Accumulating useless similes is all very well in English exams, but it's not much help in real life,' said my father. 'In any case, we have all had to face situations of which we had no prior experience. In my case, it was joining the army.'

'In my case it was being married to your father,' said my mother. 'And having children.'

'And in your case it is going to be cooking,' said my father. 'Worry about cooking, and you will forget your worries about university. Worry about the small things, and the big worries will sort themselves out by themselves.'

'Do you really believe that?' I said.

'No,' he conceded, deftly swapping sides in an argument again. 'It sounded good when I said it, but now that I have listened to what I said, I have to disagree with myself.'

'This is what your first year at university is going to be like,' said my mother.

'Endlessly debating the truth?' said my father.

'Going round and round in fatuous circles, more like,' said my mother. 'I don't see the point of going to university when you could create exactly the same effect by staying here at home, sitting up late with your father drinking coffee, and talking rubbish.'

'I thought you wanted me to go to university,' I said.

'Oh, we do, we do,' said my mother. 'Having got Ralph off to drama college last year, the place quietened down considerably, and as soon as you have gone ...'

'Did you give Ralph a sack of potatoes?' I said.

'Of course.'

'How did he get on?'

'We never had any complaints,' she said.

'I hope they have got chips in here,' I said, picking up the potato recipe book.

'You don't need a recipe for <u>chips</u>!' said my father. 'Chips isn't a recipe! It's like baked potatoes! You just put it in and later you take it out! You don't need a book to tell you how to do that!'

'Put it in ... take ... it ... out ...' I said, pretending to write all this down.

'Ralph made gnocchi,' said my mother.

'Did he?' said my father.

'What are they?' I said.

'Sort of dumplings made with a bit of flour mixed with mashed potatoes, and then boiled in a big pan of water. The Italians love them.'

'Typical,' I said. 'It's so typical of Ralph to pick on something poncey to impress his actors friends with. I'll stick with chips.'

'Chips are something you buy,' said my father. 'There are certain dishes you never make at home. They are too easy to buy. Nobody ever makes fish and chips at home. It would be like making your own potato crisps.'

'Look,' said my mother, 'this is getting us nowhere. The boy's going to university tomorrow. We must start packing.'

'Ah,' I said, relishing the moment to spring my big surprise, 'but I finished my packing three days ago. I'm all ready to go!'

'I know, dear,' said my mother. 'I wasn't talking about you. I was talking about your father and me. We have decided to take advantage of your absence to go for a short motoring trip up north. We have never been to Yorkshire.'

'Yorkshire!' I said. 'You're going to Yorkshire without me!'

'You've never shown the slightest desire to go there,' said my father.

'Yes, but . . . When are you going?'

'Tomorrow. After we have seen you off at the station, we're going to lock the house and go away for the week.'

'Tomorrow! You couldn't even wait for a day or so!'

'My dear boy,' said my mother. 'We've waited eighteen years. Isn't that long enough?'

'I suppose so,' I said.

I felt a bit ashamed.

'I'm sorry,' I said.

'That's all right,' said my mother, and kissed me.

There was an emotional pause.

A rather precious moment.

Then my father lifted something in the air.

'So, are you taking the cheese grater or not?'

Here We Go Again (unfinished sequel to *Someone like Me*), 2006